DO I GET MY ALLOWANCE BEFORE OR AFTER I'M GROUNDED?

Sara Gray

VANESSA VAN PETTEN is a youthologist and the founder of RadicalParenting.com, a blog written by Vanessa and one hundred teen contributors that won the Mom's Choice Award in 2009. In addition to writing for her site, Vanessa pens columns online for CNN, Partnership for a Drug-Free America, Brazen Careerist, and Mom Logic. Named one of the Top 100 Women Bloggers to Watch by *Women's Business Week*, Vanessa has appeared on *The Doctors*, CNN, CBS News, and ABC News Now, as well as in the *Washington Post*, the *Wall Street Journal*, *Good Housekeeping*, *Teen Vogue*, and *Businessweek*.

Praise for
Do I Get My Allowance Before or After I'm Grounded?

"Not yet a parent, not far out of her teens, Vanessa Van Petten offers simple, commonsense advice with a healthy dose of respect for both ends of the generation gap: Here's a girl who knows that

parenting isn't about friending your kids on Facebook . . . it's about guiding them with some old-school face *time*."

—Philip Van Munching, author of *Boys Will Put You on a Pedestal (So They Can Look Up Your Skirt): A Dad's Advice for Daughters*

"[Van Petten] parents a candid view of the contemporary teen's world in this eye-opening text. Like a crafty spy, Van Petten comfortably segues from parent to teen perspective, and while noting that each adolescent is unique, she skillfully opens doors to the collective teen psyche." —*Publishers Weekly*

"Vanessa has been called many things, from a parenting expert to a youthologist, which all fit the bill. But more important, her writing feels like a friend over your shoulder filled with helpful advice and actual action steps. Highly recommended."

—David Siteman Garland, creator/host of the number-one Internet talk show *The Rise to the Top*

"Vanessa's unique approach blasts the bejeepers out of the misperceptions, off-base judgments, and unnecessary fears that undermine parent-teen relationships. Parents *and* teens need to read this—again and again."

—Sue Blaney, author of *Please Stop the Rollercoaster! How Parents of Teenagers Can Smooth Out the Ride*

Praise for Vanessa Van Petten

"She's young, hip, and knows what's going on."

—Lynne Curtin, *Real Housewives of Orange County*

Do I Get My Allowance *Before* or *After* I'm Grounded?

Stop Fighting, Start Talking, and Get to Know Your Teen

Vanessa Van Petten

A PLUME BOOK

PLUME
Published by Penguin Group
Penguin Group (USA) Inc., 375 Hudson Street, New York, New York 10014, U.S.A. •
Penguin Group (Canada), 90 Eglinton Avenue East, Suite 700, Toronto, Ontario, Canada
M4P 2Y3 (a division of Pearson Penguin Canada Inc.) • Penguin Books Ltd., 80 Strand,
London WC2R 0RL, England • Penguin Ireland, 25 St. Stephen's Green, Dublin 2, Ireland
(a division of Penguin Books Ltd.) • Penguin Group (Australia), 250 Camberwell Road,
Camberwell, Victoria 3124, Australia (a division of Pearson Australia Group Pty. Ltd.) •
Penguin Books India Pvt. Ltd., 11 Community Centre, Panchsheel Park, New Delhi – 110
017, India • Penguin Group (NZ), 67 Apollo Drive, Rosedale, Auckland 0632, New Zealand
(a division of Pearson New Zealand Ltd.) • Penguin Books (South Africa) (Pty.) Ltd., 24
Sturdee Avenue, Rosebank, Johannesburg 2196, South Africa

Penguin Books Ltd., Registered Offices: 80 Strand, London WC2R 0RL, England

First published by Plume, a member of Penguin Group (USA) Inc.

First Printing, September 2011
10   9   8   7   6   5   4   3   2   1

 REGISTERED TRADEMARK—MARCA REGISTRADA

LIBRARY OF CONGRESS CATALOGING-IN-PUBLICATION DATA
Van Petten, Vanessa.
   Do I get my allowance before or after I'm grounded? : stop fighting, start talking, and
get to know your teen / Vanessa Van Petten.
      p. cm.
   Includes bibliographical references and index.
   ISBN 978-0-452-29741-8
1. Parent and teenager. 2. Teenagers. 3. Parenting. I. Title.
   HQ799.15.V34 2011
   306.874—dc22

                                                         2011015708

Printed in the United States of America
Set in Janson Text • Designed by Eve L. Kirch

This book is dedicated to Scott Edwards.
You encourage me, you love me, and you inspire me.

Contents

Introduction

I'm a teenage accomplice, fighting to balance both sides of the parent and teen struggle. I can tell you what happens to teens' faces when they lie to their parents: their eyes widen, their brows pinch together, and the sides of their mouths turn downward. I can also tell teens how to know whether their parent is making rules out of love or out of fear.

But as often as I catch and decipher hidden emotions, I also help both sides get what they want—at home, at school, and in life. I have negotiated for teens to get more allowance, bargained for more freedom, and convinced a parent or two to back off. At the same time, I also help parents get what they want: honesty, connection, communication, and household calm. I have commandeered pantry cleanouts, dissected arguments, and searched sock drawers.

I am not a therapist, a doctor, or a counselor. I am not a parent or a fellow judgmental teen, but I am young enough to get kids to open up and old enough to be a translator for parents— conveying and deciphering the true intent behind harsh words or actions. These are often hidden in micro facial expressions, gestures, and tones. I expose parents to a different, perhaps more vulnerable side of their child, so they can see the emotional intent behind a curse or verbal assault and then find the answer to address it. The confessions in this book range from scandalous to inspirational to funny, and they come in the form of parent worries, teen diary entries, kids' bucket lists, scientific research studies, and e-mail rants.

That's not to say that I don't often have to convince teenagers I am not picking sides when I translate their emotions for parents. One particularly angry seventeen-year-old boy shouted, "You are ratting us out!" after one of my events. I had just shown four hundred parents how kids sneak around parental control software. He was mad—until I showed him the slide entitled "Why You Should Give Your Kid a Later Curfew."

About Me and My Work

When I was a teenager, alcohol made me sleepy, sex made me nervous, and smoking pot scared me. Therefore I decided the best way to rebel against my parents was to write a book exposing them. Unfortunately (or maybe fortunately), as I started interviewing other teens about their own parents, I realized mine were not so terrible after all. In fact, I began to recognize my parents were pretty decent; they were just severely misinformed. I saw them reading parenting books that told them to say and do the exact things that drove me crazy—and pushed me further away from having a strong relationship with them.

Soon I realized that there were thousands of resources for parents written by and for adults, but none from the teen perspective! From a cramped desk at Emory University and using a lot of babysitting money, I decided to launch the first teen-written parenting resource, RadicalParenting.com. The blog exploded—mostly because parents were dying to read the teen confessions, interview transcripts, and secrets I had gathered from teens all over the world. After graduating from college, I dedicated all my time to answering the hundreds of e-mails, instant messages, and video chats I received daily from distressed teens and parents.

My blog, e-mail in-box, and answering machine became a collective mecca for troubled, distressed, and lonely families, and I learned to pick up on the emotional cues of teenagers. I started speaking around the country and hired teenage writers to write their own parenting advice—as anonymous "exposers" of the teen world. Since I am no longer a teen, I have no problem giving away secrets—like vodka eye shots or teen biting trends—because I know that in opening the lines of communication, teens stay safe and will have better relationships with their parents in the long run. Yet I still listen to the same music, play FarmVille on Facebook, and shop in the same stores, so I can relate and connect with teens on the issues they are dealing with—because they are my issues, too! I am also not a parent, and I believe this lets me take a step back and see problems and patterns from a different viewpoint.

Why This Book Is *Super* Different

Some of the advice you read in this book you may not like. Parents might find the advice I give both atypical and counterintuitive, but it is useful and current. Today's teens are dealing with the same life issues as previous generations—flirting, homework, and careers—in completely different ways, from Facebook e-flirting to wiki study guides. My goal is not only to highlight current teen trends and the most cutting-edge research on youth, but also to point out patterns and vicious circles I am sure you experience every day but haven't quite figured out how to fix.

I am not afraid to talk about fears and failures—and then resolve them. When I walk into a speaking engagement, whether with teens or parents, the room feels like it is holding its breath.

Everyone is worried. Teens are worried about their popularity, that they won't do well enough in school to get into a top university, or that their parents aren't proud of them or their accomplishments. Parents are freaked out that their kids might do drugs, stop loving them, or make unsafe choices. Both parents and teens have many nagging doubts about their own familial roles and their individual drives for success. Many parents feel alone. Virtually every mother and every father I've worked with feels as if they are losing their relationship with their teen.

Parent Confession

"I'm drowning every day. I dread picking her up from school because I have no idea what kind of mood she will be in and how I should react. School seems to be so stressful these days, and I don't know how to help her—I don't even understand her homework!"

—Chellie, mother of two

I will be using real quotes, interviews, e-mails, and advice from actual teens I have worked with and readers of my blog. This book addresses the current needs, questions, and advice parents crave and delves into subjects that teens, mature tweens, and late-blooming twenty-somethings all struggle with.

This book is not about being a perfect parent. Believe me, there is no such thing as either a flawless parent or a perfect teenager. I think when I first started this journey, I was looking for the ideal family. Though I did not find the "perfect parent" to model my own behavior on, I think I did discover the most important concept of all for parents, the one I will implement when I feel it is the right time to have my own family: you are your own best parenting expert. The central premise of this book is to teach you how to be exactly that.

What to Expect

In this book I will give you a new way of interacting with your children and help you make sense of some of the new youth behaviors and trends emerging in the last few years. I have broken the book up into three parts: building a relationship, learning about their life, and seeing why you don't need to worry too much, all based on understanding the mentality and attitude of today's teens. Each chapter begins with a true story. I will dissect the trends, characteristics, and issues that the story exemplifies and offer resolutions to the specific problems it raises. Then I'll conclude with points for you to remember (you can flip back to these points after reading the whole book, as needed) as well as challenges for you to do, either individually or as a family, to improve the relationship between you and your teen.

Part 1 examines the most fundamental aspects of constructing a solid relationship with your child and the common communication traps parents fall into when trying to connect with teenagers. Chapter 1 focuses on how both parents and teenagers are emotionally programmed to have false expectations about each other, and how to overcome related setbacks. Chapter 2 delves into the differences between communication and arguments. This is where I show parents both how to avoid friction with their teen in the home and how to stop and solve it once a fight is already under way.

Part 2 covers the major areas of a teen's social life: peer relationships, technology, and risky behavior. Friendships among teenagers are the focus of chapter 3. Here I talk about everything from longtime friends to bad peers and show what parents need to do to ensure that their children have a strong social support network amid an increasingly socially illiterate generation. Chapter 4 is an in-depth look at how the Internet, social networking, and mobile devices have changed the way teenagers interact with each other as well as with their parents, and how we can leverage the benefits and avoid the negative consequences of online activity for teens. In chapter 5 I talk about the new bully. Cyberbullying and meanness are, unfortunately, a huge part of life for many teens today. Although this is an old issue, in the digital age many aspects of bullying and being a victim have changed. Chapter 6 is an overview of what motivates teenagers to put themselves in dangerous situations, what those circumstances are, and how parents can minimize risk without limiting their teenager's independence.

Part 3 covers today's teen attitudes about lifestyle, school, and their futures. Chapter 7 reviews the academic lives of teenagers today. Whether you have a slacker or a unicorn—a student who always feels the need to be perfect—the tips and stories in this chapter will help you help your teenager do well in school, without adding more pressure. In chapter 8 I share how this generation of young people is more motivated, entrepreneurial, and creative than any previous generation and how parents can encourage these streaks for good.

Some of the advice you read will be absolutely familiar and will make you think, "Yes! That totally happens to me, I love it and live it." Other solutions you might find interesting or intriguing. Finally you will read some sections that you think are outside your comfort zone or not relevant to your family. These are the sections I hope you will give the most attention to. As I have learned with teenagers, you never know what to expect. What is an issue now might be gone tomorrow, and problems you never thought you would be dealing with could come up for your family next week. I always want the parents I help to feel prepared. In addition, what brings us out of our comfort zone also ignites the most change. When we leave what is familiar and safe, we have more opportunity to reset bad habits and cycles. So, when you read something that sounds a little different or untraditional, all I ask is that you keep an open mind and see if it has the potential to transform an area of your family life that you have grown too comfortable with. There are many pieces of advice in this book. Don't think you must tackle every area at the same time. Pick the issues you think are most important and implement them slowly; trying all the techniques at once might scare your teen and overwhelm you.

You are welcome to read this book passively, laugh at the funny stories, pick up a few interesting tidbits, and move on to the next book on your shelf. Yet I want to offer the idea that, as with everything in life, the more positive energy you put in, the more you'll get back.

PART I

. . . .

Build the Relationship

Change How You Talk

"The trouble with the world is not that people know too little, but that they know so many things that ain't so."

—Mark Twain

In many families, we are programmed to view and interact with each other based on false expectations, media stereotypes, and "lensing." Often, three types of what I call emotional programming can block our ability to clearly see and connect with our children in a genuine way—and respond authentically.

Last month I was called to work with a wonderful family. At the first meeting, the mother, Daphne, a very intelligent and savvy woman, began to explain their situation to me. "My son Derek is great—very smart and all that—but something is happening. I know it might seem small to you, but there has been a change in him that I think is indicative of larger things, and I want to figure it out before it gets too late." I looked at Daphne's worried face, pinched eyes, and pursed lips. Her voice tone was tight and I could literally see her fear. I could already tell that emotional programming was tainting their relationship.

I patted her hand reassuringly. "You know what? Your taking note of the problem already puts us a step ahead. Too many people come to me when it is too late. So, what is the change in Derek?"

She fiddled with her cup of tea and I braced myself for the worst. "He stopped playing piano."

I narrowed my eyes, unsure if I heard correctly. "He . . . stopped playing piano?"

"Yes, he used to play all the time. I really thought he would be a professional pianist someday. He is so talented and he loved it. He begged us to play after dinner. I knew when he became a teenager everything would change."

"And so is that what happened?" I asked.

"Oh, I was so worried he would change as soon as he became a teenager, and it happened." She touched her forehead with her hand—a telltale sign of shame and guilt. *If she truly believed she was right, why would she feel guilty?* I wondered and made a mental note. She continued. "A few months after he turned thirteen, we started arguing. He needed to practice to get into jazz band, but he pushed back. Now he won't play at all. It has been three weeks since he touched that piano." She pointed to a large Steinway in the living room. I shook my head, wondering why he would have stopped playing and why she felt guilty about being right. I ran through the options in my head: *Did he lose interest? No*, I thought, *no one switches off that fast. Does he think it's uncool? Has it become a chore?*

The anxious mother continued, "I love hearing him play, but mostly I'm upset because you talk on your blog all the time about the importance of passions. If kids have passion they are less likely to succumb to peer pressure, they have better college applications, and they are more well-rounded. This was his passion and now it is gone." Daphne fully buried her head in her hands. "I knew it. I knew this would happen." I calmed her down and set up a time to talk to her son.

A few days later, I came to the house and met Derek—a very tall, brown-haired thirteen-year-old. We made small talk about the music posters on his wall and figured out that we had been to the same concert a while back. Settling into his desk, I started casually, "So, Derek, tell me, what are your hobbies?"

"Clearly, I love eighties rock. I'm also an aspiring pianist. I hope to have my own band one day, maybe pick up guitar." My heart skipped a beat at his easy mention of the piano. I always try to let the teen bring up the touchy subjects so they do not feel that I am prying.

"An aspiring pianist, wow, that's amazing. Do you play a lot?" I asked, hoping to talk about his temporary sabbatical.

"All the time. Every day. I'm working on a new piece right now, actually," he said, shaking his head. This threw me off. *Every day? Working on a new piece?* Derek did not strike me as a liar, nor did his body language or facial expressions suggest he was trying to deceive me. I have had a lot of practice picking up on teen lies and none of my typical alarm bells were going off. I decided to dig a little deeper.

"Do you usually practice at school or at home? You must need to practice a lot of hours."

"Oh, yeah, I practice both at school and at home—well." He interrupted himself and waved his hand in the air as if dismissing a thought. "I practice a lot." I picked up on his nerves and what human lie detectors call "self-interruption."

"What was that all about?" I mimicked his hand gesture.

He rolled his eyes. "I usually practice at home, but recently, well, things have been a little tense, so I have been, uh . . ."

"Yeah?" I waited.

"I've been practicing at our neighbors'," he finished with a touch of embarrassment. I was shocked at the revelation, but was happy to hear the embarrassment. It meant he had not made his mind up yet.

"The neighbors'? I saw your beautiful Steinway and your mom mentioned you love to play, but that you have been taking a break recently. Have you been hiding your piano playing?" I asked. I work with a lot of teens who hide things from their parents—drugs, girlfriends, pregnancies—but never did I expect that playing piano would be a cause for secrecy.

Derek crossed his arms over his chest, and I suspected he might be recalling some family battles. "It's my mom's fault. Before I started high school, piano was just one of my hobbies. I played and liked it. Then all of a sudden, I get into high school and she starts nagging me to play. I take one night off and she freaks out, telling me I need to have a passion and that it's for my college applications. She turned it into a chore like everything else." His chin jutted out in anger, but I did not see any facial signs of contempt, which meant we could still make progress. I have found when kids begin to flash contempt, rather than anger, while talking about their parents, I have a much harder time getting them to compromise and be empathetic to their parents' side. But then he said something that I think turns all parental blood cold: "So I stopped playing just to spite her."

What happened in this family occurs all the time. What children like to do, parents often hate; and what parents like their kids to do, children often grow to hate. Daphne and Derek aren't alone; this happens over and over again. Their interaction exemplifies all three types of programming: emotional expectations, media stereotyping, and lensing.

Let's first review the power of expectations. In my conversation with Daphne, she kept mentioning that she "knew this would happen" when Derek became a teenager. She had the false expectation that all teens act erratically, become lazy, and discard previous positive activities for more dangerous amusements. With these expectations, the moment Derek turned thirteen she began to nag him about playing, hoping her "encouragement" would prevent the inevitable turn from piano.

This, I realized later, was why she showed a flash of guilt when talking about how she had been right. Subconsciously she had an inkling that she was driving him to hate playing. Daphne admitted later that part of her could feel his disgust when she began to nag him. Yet, she explained to me, "I couldn't help it. I couldn't help but try to push him because I was so scared he would stop playing." This plays into something else I've learned, which is that our own fears make us more susceptible to programmed responses and expectations because they are easier than dealing with the worry.

So Daphne's actions actually achieved the opposite of what she had hoped. Her emotional programming caused her to push Derek to play more. Yet the nagging drove Derek to dread piano and fed into his own expectations and programming about strict, overachieving, annoying parents. That explains, in turn, why Derek wanted to punish his mom for her nagging by not playing, even if it meant not being able to pursue his passion at home.

· · · · · · · · ·

A fascinating study from the 1980s demonstrates the power of parental expectations on children. Harvard researcher Katherine Nelson closely followed a family in New Haven, Connecticut, with a baby daughter named Emily. Emily's parents noticed that she talked to herself before bed every night. Wanting to know what their daughter's nightly babblings meant, they began to record them with a small tape recorder. Shocked, they realized that Emily's conversations with herself were far more advanced than her conversations with her parents during waking hours.

Katherine Nelson and her team looked through the 122 transcripts of Emily's private discussions and were surprised to see that she used rich vocabulary and advanced grammar and created narratives about her day, her parents, and the activities she usually participated in. Here is an excerpt from one of her night talks:

> Carl and Emily are both going down to the car with
> somebody, and we're going to ride to nursery school,
> and then when we get there, we're all going to get out
> of the car, go into nursery school, and Daddy's going
> to give us kisses, then go, and then say, and then we
> will say good-bye, then he's going to work and we're
> going to play at nursery school. Won't that be funny?
> Because sometimes I go to nursery school 'cause it's a
> nursery school day.

The researchers were fascinated and eager to understand why Emily's speech was so much more advanced when she was alone than when she spoke with her parents. After looking at different types of children and their parents, experts theorized that when parents speak to their children in baby talk, the toddlers and babies "dumb down" their speaking and respond in baby talk, thinking that the adults can only speak to them that way.

This is an amazing example of how our expectations are realized. Parents are programmed to think their babies can only speak and understand baby talk, so that is exactly how the children respond. I read this study and began to see it replicated in my teen and parent relationships. Daphne expected Derek to act out, so she treated him as though he would, and then he responded by doing exactly what she expected.

My experience with a mom named Sarah and her daughter Blythe is another example of how our programming causes us to set up negative expectations that are often realized.

> Subject: Help with my teen!
>
> Dear Vanessa,
>
> I was hoping you could help me with my teenage
> daughter Blythe. She is so awful at this age! I try to

talk to her and use the tips from your blog, but she is so surly and mean. She rolls her eyes and barely listens to a word anyone says. I was hoping we could do a video session (we are in Wyoming) and you could talk to her and see what I mean so we can come up with some compromises.

Please do not get offended by her rudeness, she does it to everyone and I apologize ahead of time for her awful behavior. I must be a terrible mother for raising a daughter like this. I hope it is not too late for us to make some progress.

Thanks,

Sarah

I read this e-mail and held in my breath thinking about a session with Blythe. I have dealt with angry and rude teens, but it is never easy. We set up a Skype appointment for later in the week, and at the designated time, a wisp of a girl flashed on the screen.

"Blythe?" I asked. I looked at this tiny girl through my video camera with surprise. Somehow I had been expecting a giant, red-faced monster of a teen, foaming at the mouth. Blythe could not have been taller than five feet and had freckles and pale features.

"Hi!" she chirped.

"How are ya?" I asked.

"Super! This is so cool that we are on video chat. I feel like this will be the therapy of the future."

I laughed. "Pretty futuristic, but I'm not a therapist. Did your mom explain what I do?"

"Oh, yeah, I know you are not a therapist; that is why I agreed to talk to you. I watched your YouTube videos—which are so funny!"

"Thanks," I said.

Before I could continue she gushed, "Have you seen the new Fred video? It's *hy-ster-i-cal*. I bet I could file-share with you if you wanted." Who was this girl? I was expecting a mean, uncommunicative teenager. We talked for a few more minutes about YouTube videos. I asked to see her favorites to get an idea of what her personality was like. She seemed bubbly and optimistic, and she expressed a desire to have a better relationship with her mom. I was perplexed, but asked her to call her mom into the room so we could talk together.

Sarah walked in and took a seat next to her daughter. "See what I mean, Vanessa?" Instantly Blythe's face dropped. Her eyes went dull and she crossed her arms in front of her chest, preparing to be defensive. Like Emily's parents, Blythe's mother expected her to communicate a certain way with her—and she does.

The second type of programming is media stereotyping. TV shows, movies, and Web shows are becoming more and more like real life—and we often confuse the two. Take this example:

Dan escorted a brooding teen boy into the back of a car and slammed the door behind him. Wearily, he turned back toward the house to see his fuming teen daughter bound down the stairs after her exiled boyfriend. Her fight was futile, because Dan had already decided that her boyfriend would not be joining their family for the holidays. Slowly the car pulled away and Cara screamed after it, placing her warm hand on the cold window, mouthing words of longing to her boyfriend. The car drove out of sight and Cara spun on her heels and glared at her father.

"You are a murderer of love!" she screamed.

If you are like me, you watched this scene from the movie *Dan in Real Life* and laughed heartily. *Oh, that's such a perfect representation of a love-struck teen and a strict dad*, I thought to myself. But a few days later, I heard the exact same line used toward a real dad from his very real daughter, and it suddenly wasn't so funny. Melissa's tear-stained cheeks, wild eyes, and piercing scream startled both her parents and me to our cores. "You are a murderer of love!" she yelled.

The real-life dad, Robert, turned to me and asked, "Is having an extra half hour at the dance really that serious?" Judging by Melissa's extreme—or as we often call it, drama queen—reaction, yes, it was that serious. I took her aside later. When I asked Melissa why that was so important, she shrugged and calmly explained that the last few songs at a dance are always the best, and that she had wanted to stay.

"Do you think it was really necessary to call your dad a murderer of love, though? I mean, just for a few extra songs?" I asked. She laughed and replied, "It was just a joke." But I noticed her hollow laugh and that her eyes lacked the necessary wrinkles of a genuine smile. I looked at her face more closely.

I shook my head lightly. "You don't really think it's a joke, do you? You looked mad. Your eyes were narrowed and your teeth were bared a little, too." I should explain that I had spent the last few sessions with Melissa reviewing microexpressions—the small facial gestures people make that flash their true emotion. I was helping her build the skills to help her read the facial emotions of the girls who were teasing her. I also showed her how she could use them to communicate more clearly with her parents, to whom she had trouble relating. I saw a flash of guilt on her face—promise, in my mind.

"I did? I guess I'm mad that my dad doesn't get that guys ask for your number at the end of the dance."

I waved my hands. "Okay, that's an issue we can actually address. Playing the 'murderer of love' card sends your parents totally mixed signals. Remember, anger and upset are two different emotions. You have to display the one that is genuine, to get a more genuine response. I think you freaked your dad out a little."

She waved her hand lightly in my direction. "Nah, he's used

to it. He always plays strict dad and then I play emotional teen and we end in a compromise of fifteen extra minutes." The use of the word "play" triggered something for me. Both members of the family were *playing* certain roles. Even though the daughter had a legitimate reason for wanting the extra time, she decided to "play" anger—what she thought she was supposed to display. This was the first of many interactions that led me to focus on how we model our behavior after media examples when interacting with our family members.

How often have you seen movies portraying rebellious or moody teens who break the rules and roll their eyes at everything their parents say? Or songs sung by teens (usually written by adults) who are angry and resentful? When we watch family arguments on TV or hear about them in songs, we laugh because they remind us of our own experiences; they are familiar and touch on some of the heartache in our own life, whether it is about groundings, drugs, or the laundry. Media stereotyping happens when real people perform in life the way characters act in sitcoms—usually highly dramatic, overly emotional, sarcastic, and unfeeling.

The real problem with media stereotyping is that it teaches us—especially teens—that it is okay to be snarky, mocking, and dramatic in our interactions. Teens love to act in real life by imitating what they see elsewhere—at their friends' houses, on TV, or in the book they are reading. When younger children especially are exposed to the attitude-heavy tweens on the Disney Channel, viewers think they *have* to behave like the actors when they turn that age. This is part of the reason why Melissa applied the line from *Dan in Real Life*, because without even thinking about it, she thought it was normal.

Here's another example of how media stereotyping affects our daily interactions. I call this the "whatever" dilemma.

One day, a parent called me about her problem with the word "whatever." Her child was saying it all the time. "It's a relatively new thing," she complained to me. I thought about my own "whatever" period.

"I get that; it was one of my favorite responses to pretty much everything my parents said for a while."

"Exactly!" she exclaimed. "I ask her how her day was. 'Whatever,' she responds. I ask her to empty the dishwasher, and I get a 'whatever.' It's infuriating."

"Does the communication always end with 'whatever'?" I asked.

"Well, it is usually accompanied by an eye roll. But the thing is, I don't think she feels 'whatever' about what I ask her about. She will say 'whatever' and then a few beats later respond to the question I asked."

"Have you asked her about her initial 'whatever' response?" I wondered out loud to her.

"Oh, yes, and she looks at me blankly and says it's the 'cool' thing to say. But, Vanessa, none of her friends say that. At least, not yet."

I asked this mom to watch TV with her daughter over the next few days and look at the books she was reading and take note for me of all the "whatevers" mentioned in these media. A few days later we had a follow-up call. I had barely said hello when the mom said, "You are not going to believe how many times 'whatever' came up."

"How many?" I asked.

She gushed her reply: "Forty-two mentions in four days. Forty-two! I asked my daughter if she even noticed they were doing it, and she consciously had no idea. She was just mimicking what she was hearing."

This story is a great example of how mimicking what we see and the ways we believe we should be acting simply takes less thinking. This makes it easier for parents and kids to respond on autopilot with prepackaged answers than to formulate more genuine responses. The stereotypes we see over and over again on TV, in movies, and even on blogs—the surly teen and the sarcastic, exhausted parent—make it especially difficult for adults to recognize the unique differences in our children.

·········

In a 2001 study looking at screen media and language development in infants and toddlers, two researchers, D. L. Linebarger and S. E. Vaala, revealed that infants and toddlers do actually learn from screen media. The interesting part of this study is that toddlers and infants *only* learn if the media content resembles their real-life experiences.

In this study, "real-life experiences" included stories, objects, and household routines the kids were familiar with. Because the majority of TV is based on real-life dilemmas, situations, and experiences, it is extremely easy to watch television families and believe that is how everyone behaves. This is startling. Teens might have been learning to model their current behavior after television interactions as early as infancy.

Teens are also becoming more and more aware of the external forces affecting how their parents behave. In an interview about how and why she does not get along with her parents, my seventeen-year-old intern Rachel poignantly confessed:

"I think my parents act based on a warped view of their own childhood mixed with what they see in the media. This combination is deadly for making any progress in our relationship."

—Rachel, 17,
Radical Parenting intern

Media stereotyping is especially attractive because, as humans, we have the innate desire to fit in and want to do "what everyone else does." I cannot tell you how many parents use the "but other people don't do that" excuse as an argument for not following a piece of advice that could potentially save their family in crisis. It is in our nature to model our behavior on what we think our friends are doing, how our own parents behaved, and what we see on TV. *Yet what we perceive everyone else to be doing and what everyone else is* actually *doing are very different.* The lure of the *Dan in Real Life* comeback for Melissa had to do with the fact that it seemed like a normal thing to say when your father says no. In reality, it was hurtful, disrespectful, and completely ineffective.

Media stereotyping also makes it hard for adults to realize that all teens are unique. Every child is different, yet we see the same teen stereotypes everywhere.

> *"We are all different! We do not all sleep late, eat bad, and hate our parents."*
>
> —Dana, 17, Radical Parenting intern

The last type of programming is called lensing. We all view our family, ourselves, and situations through mental lenses. If you have a child who is always the teacher's favorite, you might also see the child through a bright mental lens—his or her behavior always has a positive spin, and you often expect the best. But what if you have a child who never seems to follow through, who is always late and sloppy, and who never appreciates what you and your spouse provide? It is very hard *not* to see this child through that negative mental lens, to start fresh with each interaction. Yet, as we know, acting with expectations, or through a lens, almost guarantees a person will respond back *through that same lens.*

Lensing is a type of programming that helps us organize or sort behavior in our minds and prepare for an automatic response. So when that unappreciative child asks you for extra allowance, you can click on that lens and say, "No, not until you finish your homework!" This answer is easier; it takes less mental work than actually checking in with the situation. This is why programming is so appealing. Acting from programming saves us thinking time.

We also can see how our minds are attracted to the kind of mental categorizing that lies behind lensing and the other emotional programming we've been discussing in a study done by Daniel Levin and Daniel Simons at Cornell University. They wanted to test the mind's ability to categorize and how that affects perception. Levin and Simons hired actors to pretend to be strangers on a campus asking passersby for directions. Yet as the actor and pedestrian talked, Levin and Simons had two men walk between them carrying a large door to temporarily block their view of each other. During the two or three seconds of interruption, one of the men carrying the door would switch places with the actor who had asked for directions. When the door finally passed, the new actor continued the conversation as if he were the original person.

Most people are certain they would notice the new person. Yet only seven out of fifteen pedestrians realized that there had been a change! The rest of the pedestrians—about half—had no idea the person they were speaking with two seconds earlier was gone, replaced by another stranger. This is a fascinating experiment, but it becomes even more useful to us in the second version the researchers tried.

Levin and Simons repeated the experiment, but this time

they had the actors dress as construction workers. This time, even fewer pedestrians detected a change. When one of the pedestrians was interviewed after the interaction, she said that she saw the actor as a construction worker, not as an individual. Her mind had categorized him. This categorization was so strong, she failed to notice that the second actor was a totally different person! When she placed the actor in a category or stereotype, she gave up her visual detection abilities that pick up on other details of the event—and not noticing the person you are talking to is a pretty big detail.

This study is relevant and important for parents and teens because it is a perfect example of lensing and how easy it is to slip into a mental expectation or categorization. This happens to parents and teens all the time. Parents assume their teens will be uncommunicative and therefore they hound them with questions; teens think their parents will say no to the party on Saturday night and consequently they plan to sneak out rather than simply ask. When the mind slips into categorizing rather than noticing, it shuts off its ability to pick up on small details like facial expressions, body cues, or vocal tones.

Yet the small details of each situation are the most important clues for finding a solution or understanding the true meaning behind what your teen is talking about. When our minds categorize our teens, like the pedestrians putting the actor in the "construction worker" category, we lump the current argument or behavior together with all of our previous interactions. This causes us to miss the essentials of this communication. Also, when we use lenses, we are unable to change the patterns of our arguments because we miss the clues to show us how. So, over and over again, we have the same disagreements at home. Categorizing our family members, or lensing, makes it very difficult to pick up on clues to their individual needs and emotional intent—therefore making it nearly impossible to find a solution.

What we can organize, though, feels less threatening. We usually hate feeling confused or ambiguous; it makes us feel vulnerable, indecisive, and lost. Yet confusion serves a very important emotional purpose. When we are confused—without a category—our senses are heightened and we notice more, so we can find the answer. It is our brain's way of telling us, "Pay attention!"

Being a confident parent means having the ability to be okay with your confusion and using it to pay closer attention to what your child needs, what your limits are, and how to best respond. Confusion means you are keeping an open mind and steering clear of expectations.

This is why programming, expectations, and lensing are so appealing. It lessens our confusion and makes us feel more emotionally confident. In Levin and Simons's experiment, participants who missed the switched actor had taken a mental shortcut instead of actually noticing the person they were talking to.

I often watch this happen to parents as well. Both Daphne and Sarah in the previous examples were victims of blinding expectations that caused them not only to misread their teens, but also to produce the exact behavior they were trying to prevent!

I stumbled upon my own emotional programming and negative expectations while working with clients. I would come into a home or family situation with a preconceived notion about the kind of misbehaving teen I would encounter. I was mentally categorizing the teens I was working with and actually shutting off the skill I needed most: my ability to read them! This blinded me to what was actually going on so that I could not implement the right solutions. But once I learned to open my mind and think differently, it was easy to ignore the stereotypes, deprogram myself, and see the situation for what it was. Parents can do that, too.

· · · · · · · ·

First, we need to *eliminate the expectations.* While working with teenagers, I developed a set of three rules:

1. If you expect the worst from teenagers, you often get the worst.
2. If you expect the best, you are often disappointed.
3. If you have open expectations, you always see clearly.

If we brace ourselves for the worst, it makes it much more difficult for the teen years to be anything but that. It closes our minds to the possibility of creating a positive time of growth and learning—which the teen years can absolutely be. Yet over-expecting can also be disappointing and blind us to potential problems because we do not want to see that anything is wrong. Always expecting the worst also explains why so many parents go to lectures and read blogs, yet still feel lost when they get home. In other words, even if you learn the best solutions that work, if you do not get rid of the stereotypes, negative thinking, and faulty programming, your interactions at home will always revert to bad behavior and embody those negative expectations. What I've learned over time is that no matter how many solutions I teach, if parents do not get rid of their programming and negative lenses, nothing holds. This is why, at the end of this chapter, I will assign you challenges to help identify and strip away the negative programming in your life.

The second way to combat programming is to choose to *make authentic responses over automatic ones.* These are the two kinds of responses we have to every action in our family life. *Automatic responses* are how we think everyone responds to certain stimuli. These are reactions to situations, behaviors, or people that happen without much thinking. They are responses that have been programmed or modeled for us by our own parents, friends, TV, movies, or books. They often do not take into account a specific situation's nuances, a person's needs, or what the responder is actually feeling.

> "**S**ometimes when I'm tired and my kids ask me something I snap at them. I immediately go into martyr mode, where everyone asks of me and I get nothing in return. Yesterday, my daughter began to ask me something and I yelled at her before I realized she was asking me if she should set the table—I felt terrible."
>
> —Heather, mother of one

Teens also have automatic responses. Sometimes all it takes is a specific word, action, or body language to trigger an automatic teen response—often in the form of begging, whining, or threatening. For example, when my dad used to insist on playing oldies in the car on the way to school, my siblings and I would complain bitterly. "Oh, come on, Dad, this sucks!" we would whine from the backseat. Dad would simply turn the music up louder and yell to the back, "My car, my music—get used to it." Grudgingly we would settle down and hide our heads bobbing to the upbeat melodies. When I was finally allowed to download my first album on iTunes, I picked a Beatles album. "Ha!" my dad exclaimed, "I knew you liked my music. You just think you *should* hate it, but you don't." In our minds, anything that our dad would listen to should be horrible, lame, and stupid. We never paused to think—or admit to ourselves—that we might actually agree with our father on his music taste. Instead we did what we thought we should do and automatically complained and whined, turning the first few minutes of every drive into a silly but derisive argument.

A more harmful automatic response that teens have is the

belief that they should not talk to their parents. There were many times growing up when I wanted to open up to my mom in the car on the way home from school, but I felt like I was supposed to play hard to get. *I can't be too available*, I would think to myself as she asked me how my day at school was. *If it's too easy she won't appreciate me, or worse, she will come to expect this every day*, I worried. This started our usual car-ride conversation dance:

> "**A**ll my teen son does is ask me for more allowance or spending money. It has gotten to the point where I don't even listen to the reasons, I always just say no."
>
> —Rod, father of three

"How was your day?" she would ask.

"Fine," I would respond.

"Really? What did you do?"

"Same old, same old," I would say, even though I was thinking I wanted to tell her about how the teacher fell out of his chair and that I got an A on my Spanish quiz and that at long last I had decided where I wanted to have my birthday party. But I let the tiring back-and-forth continue until I felt I'd put up enough typical teenage resistance. After a few more sighs and exasperated pleas, I would finally tell her my updates.

It wasn't until recently, hearing many other teens do this same perfunctory dance with their parents, that I realized this back-and-forth was purely an automatic response because I thought that was the way I was supposed to act.

Authentic responses require more thought, attention, and awareness. This is when a parent or teen looks at the situation she is in, thinks about the person she is interacting with, checks in with her own needs, and then makes a response.

Parents can learn to turn their automatic responses into authentic ones. For example, I was working with a mom named Allison who was having a very difficult time with her child's curfew. The problem was not that her son was breaking curfew, but merely that he was always questioning it. She explained to me that every Thursday she woke up with a feeling of anxiety. "I began to dread the weekends," she told me. "I never knew what Blake would want to do and was petrified it would require a later curfew." I wondered why this was causing her so much anxiety that it ruined her weekend.

"What happens when he asks you for a later curfew?" I asked.

"I say no. Then he gets upset with me and I feel guilty the whole weekend and worry he is going to break it anyway," she said.

"Why do you always say no?" I wondered.

She replied, "I feel like if I teeter at all, he will disrespect my rules and think I'm not serious about them. I want him to respect me."

This is very common. I explained to Allison how this kind of response was automatic: "I get that you want him to respect your rules, and therefore respect you. I also understand that you don't want him to think he can negotiate with you every weekend. But this is an automatic response because you don't take time to check in with yourself or your son's situation to see if 'no' is the best reaction. He might have a good reason for wanting a later curfew—possibly a late movie or special birthday party. In addition, by automatically saying no, you are not rewarding his past adherence to the rule. That is one of the reasons you probably feel so guilty."

Allison immediately caught on to what I was saying. "I think that is true. He has given me no reason to mistrust him. Mostly I'm unsure of myself and my decision because I'm not thinking it through—so of course I'm questioning my choice and feeling guilty about it." Allison also realized that she would be showing her son respect by at least listening to his reasons for wanting a later curfew. In the end, whether she said yes to the extension or not, thinking about her response and making it authentic also lessened her anxiety over Blake breaking the rule. Blake, too, shared that when Allison actually gave him a reason for saying no to his request for a later curfew, he was more likely to follow it and resent her less, therefore strengthening their relationship all around.

The third way we can learn to turn off our programming is to *heighten our ability to have protoconversations.* This is a way to help ourselves see each teen for his or her unique, individual characteristics. In Levin and Simons's experiment with the construction workers and the door, we looked at how when our brain uses lenses, we have trouble noticing details about who we are interacting with—or in some cases, who we are talking to altogether.

However, there is hope in learning to combat the blindness that lensing causes. Psychologist Daniel Goleman analyzes what happens when people get into tense situations and arguments. He explains that when we get into heightened emotional situations, a specific part of our brain, the amygdala, becomes more vigilant and extremely active. The amygdala is where we process the facial expressions of those around us. This is our brain's way of helping us make authentic responses by picking up on cues in the person we're talking with. Biologically, the brain knows that the only way to make it through a difficult discussion is to pick up on the other person's verbal, tonal, and facial cues and signals. I call this being able to have a protoconversation or building emotional literacy. This is actually a course I teach to teens and parents.

Protoconversations allow you to communicate beyond the actual words spoken. Understanding more than just words is important because 55 percent of the meaning people glean from conversations comes from what they see—e.g., facial expressions or body tension; 38 percent comes from sound—e.g., tone, volume, or speed; and only 7 percent comes from the actual words spoken!

Facial expressions are one of the best ways to read teenagers. When I was working with Derek and Daphne, I used Derek's flash of an angry microexpression—a jutted-out chin—to know how to best respond. A microexpression is a short, involuntary expression of emotion in the face. Dr. Paul Ekman is a researcher who deciphers physical manifestations of emotions and has explored the idea of the microexpression in depth. Teens, especially, will often flash their emotion in their face when responding to questions or communicating. When asking a teenager if he knows about the marijuana bust at school, your greatest piece of insight will come in the nanosecond following the question. Does your teen exhibit fear? Worry? Surprise? Anger? This expression will tell you far more about his feelings (and possible involvement in the situation) than the calculated words to follow. After all, 55 percent of the meaning people get from conversations comes from what they observe.

If you have trouble reading or understanding the meaning of a facial expression, try mimicking it. Arranging your facial features to mirror someone else's can actually cause you to feel the emotion of that facial gesture, because most microexpressions are universal. For example, look in a mirror and lift your upper lip as high as it goes, showing your teeth, then crinkle your nose and lift your cheek muscles. What emotion do you feel? Are you disgusted, grossed out, repulsed? This is the universal facial expression for disgust.

Physical cues or body language are another way to see if your teen is nervous about what you are speaking about. Does she fidget or develop a tic when she is feeling unloved or stressed? Does she place objects—like a remote control, chair, or table—

between the two of you? This is usually a sign that she is trying to end the discussion quickly or is afraid of what you might ask her because she might have to lie about it. I often see this when a parent accuses a teen of not getting a chore done.

For example, a mom might say to her son, "Did you forget to run the dishwasher *again*?" The son crosses his arms over his chest and widens his stance before answering, "It wasn't my turn!" This is a very physical hint, the battle stance; it says that if the conversation carries on like this, there will be a huge battle. You can usually subdue aggressive body language cues by changing the physical position of how you are talking. In this example, it would be in the mom's best interest to say to her son, "Hey, let's sit down and talk about this." This would let him relax and realize there is no need for a standoff, merely a discussion about a miscommunication.

Tonal emphasis is another way of gathering information on emotional intent in order to form authentic responses. Once you know what to listen for, you will be surprised how often teens use tonal emphasis when they speak. Teens often put vocal stress on the words that are most important to them. Let's look at a popular whine that I handed my parents when I was a teenager:

"But I want to go to the mall with Lisa."

Now let's look at it with tonal emphasis.

"But I want to go to *the mall* with Lisa."

In this case, the mall was the biggest concern for me. I would get it in my head that I wanted to do some shopping and maybe go to the food court. Who I went with, or when I would go, was not the big issue. Oftentimes, my parents did not want to pick Lisa up, so they would refuse. This would result in an argument. Hearing my stress on the word "mall," it became much easier for them to respond, "We really do not want to drive to pick up Lisa. If she wants to meet you there, we're happy to drive you to the mall."

"But I want to go to the mall _with Lisa_."

Another excuse I got from my parents was that the mall made them nervous because we were two girls alone at night, or that it was too expensive. My emphasis on _with Lisa_ let my parents know that it had nothing to do with the mall, and they did not even need to bring up these excuses—which always ended in a battle of logic. They could simply say that Lisa could come over, or suggest an alternate, more comfortable activity for the both of us.

"But I want _to go_ to the mall with Lisa."

You often hear this in teens who feel like they "never get to do anything." This emotional need is about wanting independence. My parents could have addressed this by saying yes to some other activities that they were comfortable with, helping address the emotional need for a little bit of freedom outside the house.

Being able to have protoconversations is one of the most important skills adults can develop because oftentimes teens are difficult to read when all you have are their words. Not only do they not always feel comfortable saying what they need to say to their parents, but sometimes they simply do not know how to express themselves. Ultimately this is one of the best ways to avoid programming and the lure of lensing because it requires paying attention to your children and giving them authentic responses.

Learning to listen beyond words encourages transparency and authenticity in your relationship. Having a protoconversation is just another way of listening with your whole being. You are listening to their tone, watching their body movements, and empathizing with their emotions. This helps us be intuitive as humans, as well as parents. Many people pick up books or start therapy when they are already in crisis or too stiffly programmed, and this is the hardest time to make changes and see your issues clearly because emotions and adrenaline are already running high.

This kind of listening does take time to learn. The challenges at the end of this chapter will help you build up these skills. Building up your skill finesse and learning to respond specifically, not automatically, is all part of deprogramming. This will help you evoke the response you want instead of pushing your child away.

Now, let's see how eliminating expectations, using authentic responses, and the art of protoconversations can help Derek and Daphne from earlier in this chapter. Derek had just told me that he stopped playing piano because it made his mother angry. This was very disappointing because they were on the same side! They both wanted Derek to pursue his passion, but their expectations had tripped them up. We talked about expectations and I taught him the teen version of how to read facial cues, body language, and vocal emphasis. Most important, this made him aware of his own verbal, physical, and tonal responses. "Like earlier," I explained, "when you touched your forehead, demonstrating embarrassment. I knew that we could fix the issue so both sides would win because you did not like how it was going either."

He laughed. "Cool! You knew what I was thinking without having to ask me." I left Derek's room but asked him to think about how not playing the piano at home just to make his mother angry affected him just as negatively as it did her.

I spent the next few hours with Daphne. I also taught her the art of protoconversation and we examined the lenses and expectations she had adopted as soon as Derek turned thirteen. I did not tell her about Derek's secret playing. I was hoping that his telling of that secret would help them rebuild trust. I called Derek from his room and brought them both into the kitchen for a family meeting. "Okay, open space. No judgment. Time for a reset." I looked them both in the eye and got head nods in acknowledgment.

Daphne took a deep breath and looked at her son. "I owe you an apology." Her hand slunk up to her forehead and Derek and I glanced at each other.

Derek smiled at his mom and said, "You do not need to be embarrassed."

She peered at her own hand and rolled her eyes. "Oh, right. Well, I am embarrassed because I realized I projected some incorrect and unfair expectations onto you. I thought you would be a lazy, changed teenager, so I treated you like one, and that was unfair."

Derek held up his hands, palms up, and said, "All of a sudden you started nagging me to play and never gave me a break."

I watched Daphne creep into a defensive position and I stopped her before she could respond. "Daphne, I know that felt like an attack, but it wasn't. He was merely offering you how he felt. Do you see how he held his palms up? Derek, did you realize you did that?"

He shrugged. "No, what does it mean?"

I demonstrated. "The palms-up gesture is typically an unconscious response used when a person wants to offer, show something, or request the reception of an idea. It also shows a withdrawal of negative intervention. He is not challenging you, merely offering you his opinion."

Daphne nodded. "Okay, I hear that. But, you *have* stopped playing. Why?"

Derek bowed his head and shifted nervously. I reassured him with a nod. "I actually have been playing," he said.

His mother's eyes brightened and a smile formed on her lips. "That's wonderful!"

I pointed some cues out to Derek. "Do you see her genuine smile? She has the little eye crinkles. She wants you to play piano because when you're happy, she's happy. This is not just about college applications."

She confirmed my comment. "That is true. If piano did not make you happy, I would never ask you to play. But you are playing again? Where? When?"

"It still does make me happy. I actually never stopped. I play at school in the practice room and have been using the Schwartzes' piano after school." Daphne clasped a hand over her mouth, covering genuine surprise. I saw Derek register it and he smiled at me, happy that I had not given away his secret, as I'd promised.

Daphne recovered and said, "At the neighbors'? Oh, God. It's because of my pressure?"

"I think part of me wanted to spite you. I also didn't want to turn it into another chore. I do still like playing."

I turned to Daphne. "What is your authentic response?"

She thought for a moment and then said, "I don't need to ask you about playing. I don't need you to play every day. All I ask is that if we pay for lessons again you do some of the recitals."

"That's easy," Derek replied. "And you'll promise not to ask as long as I follow up lessons with the semiannual recital?"

She smiled a genuine smile. "Absolutely."

THINGS TO REMEMBER

- We often succumb to programmed responses out of fear and anxiety because they feel familiar and more secure.
- We get what we expect.
- Treating every single interaction, argument, or behavior as a unique situation is important for picking up on our teen's cues.
- Media portrayals teach us to accept stereotypes, sarcasm, and emotionality in our familial communications, even though this does not benefit our relationships.

- Teens especially model their behavior after what they see in the media even if they do not understand how harmful it can be.
- Categorizing our family members, or lensing, makes it very difficult to pick up on clues about individual needs and emotional intent—therefore making it nearly impossible to find a good solution.
- Being a confident parent means being okay with your confusion. Confusion helps us actually look for answers, as opposed to responding automatically.
- We can choose to respond automatically or authentically.
- Being a reader of protoconversations means reading facial microexpressions and body language and listening for tones. These tactics can be essential for more meaningful communication with teens who are difficult to reach.

Challenges You Can Do Right Now

Family Challenge: Have a family discussion about stereotypes and programming.

1. Ask your kids what they think are the typical teen and parent stereotypes. Do they feel those are correct?
2. Have everyone give an example of a time when their actions were affected by a stereotype.
3. What are some negative or positive expectations you have in your life? For each family member? Which ones do you want to change?

Family Challenge: Examine your media.

1. Explain to your kids the effect that sitcoms and other media have on people's ideas of normal behavior.

2. Pick your favorite TV shows or movies together. It can be one for each family member or four shows the whole family watches.

3. While watching the shows, have everyone keep his or her own log.

4. Each family member should make a note every time a typical teen or parent stereotype is reinforced—a teen rolls his or her eyes, a parent says, "Just because I said so," etc.

5. Discuss which stereotypical actions or portrayals were successful and whether you think anyone in the family also does that: Did the dad get his way? Did the teen look silly? Can your teens relate to the teen on TV?

Personal Challenge: Learn the art of the protoconversation.

1. Take note of your teen's facial expressions. What does he look like when he is angry? Sad? Afraid?

2. What expression does he display most often?

Personal Challenge: Take note of your child's responses.

1. How does your teen sound when she is happy? When she is stressed? What kinds of words does she use—or not use?

2. Does she fidget or develop a tic when she is feeling unloved or stressed? Does your daughter dress differently with certain groups of friends?

3. Begin to take note of your child's facial expressions, tones, and body language when she is in different moods.

CHAPTER 2

Stop Fighting the Same Fight

In the last chapter, we talked about how to approach your children without negative programming, stereotypes, or expectations. Many of the examples I used show teens and parents wanting to be on the same page, but not knowing how to express those emotions or read each other. But what happens at the next level, when you and your child are in the throes of an argument and neither side knows how to get to a solution? In this chapter I will review teen and parent fighting—how it happens, why it happens, and how you can disengage to resolve the issues.

Four months ago Margie, the mother of one of my precocious new clients, Laura, called me in desperation. "Please, you've got to take her to get her semiformal dress for the school dance," Margie said. "I know she's thinking about boys and how she looks and she just hates me right now." I agreed to try my luck with Laura. Driving to the mall, I observed my thirteen-year-old passenger busily texting.

"You're a pathetic fatty," typed Laura, reading aloud from her glittering pink BlackBerry. "Don't you think Emily is such a slut?" Laura asked, turning to me and flipping her smooth blond hair over her Gap-clad shoulder. I gripped the wheel and furiously ran through my options. *If I agree . . . I'll be on her good side, but I'd be encouraging an awful behavior. If I disagree . . . I'd be stick-*

ing to my morals, but instantly I'd become just like her mother—you know, the one I have been trying to get her to compromise with for the past three sessions. . . .

I looked over at my long-limbed young client biting the nails on one hand and scrolling through my preset radio stations on the dashboard with the other. I stuck with my usual modus operandi: transparency. "I'm trying to decide which is better: agreeing with you for the sake of being cool, or telling you not to be mean and sounding like an old person. Which would you prefer at this moment?"

She peered over at me through her honey-colored, side-swept bangs, breaking into a toothy grin that reminded me she was still a kid under all of that drugstore makeup. "Uhhh . . . I guess I want the truth."

I turned into the mall just as Laura settled on one of my Red Hot Chili Peppers CDs. I grabbed a perforated paper ticket from the machine. "Honestly, I'm pretty sure you think she's a slut because she made out with your ex last night. A pathetic friend—yes; a fatty—not at all; and a slut . . ." I twisted so she could see my face clearly. "If making out with a guy at a party makes you a slut, then I think all three of us fit into that category."

I couldn't help but wonder what would have happened if her mother had not called me. How would this conversation have gone? I imagined a stressed-out Margie and an irritated teenager making a forced trip to the mall. I have split the scene into two different versions below. The Mom version is how this conversation can sometimes go when a teen daughter is talking to her mother. I wrote the second version, or the Vanessa version, to show how the same conversation and situation can go a totally different—and more positive—way.

The Mom Version

"Could you *please* put the phone away? You have been texting all morning," Margie pleaded with Laura as Margie turned right onto Olympic Boulevard.

Laura rolled her eyes at her mother. "I have not been texting *all* morning. Remember, I helped you mail *your* invitations?"

Margie sighed in exasperation. So far it had been an atrocious morning. Dad and Luke had been late for the basketball game because the invitations for the school auction crowded the kitchen. And Laura woke up so sour that vegetables would pickle next to her. No matter what Margie said to her daughter, it was the wrong thing.

"Oh, right . . . ," Margie said. "*My* invitations for *your* school auction. Sorry it was such a burden for you. We're going to the mall to get an outfit for *your* dance coming up," Margie reminded her less and less gracious daughter.

"No one asked you to sign up to run the auction. Who knows if I'm even going to the stupid dance anymore," Laura grumbled, slumping down in her seat.

Margie ignored the auction comment. Signing up for PTA and volunteer opportunities at the school was important to her. She wanted both of her kids to feel that she was involved in their world. "Of course you're going to go! You love the dances and everyone is going—Emily, Casey, *Ethan*." Margie singsonged the last name, knowing that Laura and Ethan were an item—as she had been informed two weeks ago by her authoritative daughter. Laura had explained, "It's official because we finally updated our Facebook status to 'In a Relationship,' so it's, like, really serious, Mom."

Laura put her feet up on the dashboard, because she knew her mother hated it, and slumped down lower in her seat—another thing her mother hated. "Seriously, Mom, can you not act like you know what you're talking about? Because you don't—you so don't!"

Margie bristled at the voice tone, the scuffed dashboard, and the posture that was so slumped Laura was practically lying down in the front seat. "First, watch the tone and put your feet down. Second, did something happen with Ethan?" Margie wondered if that was what was triggering the bad mood. Laura had come home after Emily's birthday party last night and gone straight to bed. Margie sighed, wondering when it had gotten to the point where she no longer knew anything about her daughter's life. Hadn't it been only a year ago when a simple "What's up?" during a car ride sufficed to get Laura to begin a soliloquy about school, boys, girls, and recess?

Perhaps it was the introduction of Facebook into their already screen-obsessed lives. Margie attempted to reassure herself, remembering all of the seminars she had gone to about teens online and the hours she had spent setting up her own Facebook page to reconnect with old friends. She had also wanted to get acquainted with the features of Facebook before Laura was old enough to get a page herself.

Puberty? Eighth grade? The looming threat of high school? Margie flicked through other explanations in her head before she realized the reason she was having trouble thinking was that Laura had set the car radio to a deafening volume. As if the loud music would make Margie forget to ask again about Ethan in her quest to obtain the answer from her only daughter about her "serious" relationship. Margie slammed off the blaring rock music and relished the silence for a moment. "You want to explain why you've been so cranky lately?"

Laura spun in her seat. "I'm cranky? *I'm* cranky? You're the one who's always yelling at us to clean up, do our homework, and do whatever you say. You won't even let me listen to music in the car. You are the strictest mother I know. I wish you could see some of my friends' moms . . . then you would know."

Margie missed a parking space near the elevators. "Whoa, whoa, that's so unfair. I'm the only one doing anything in the house. Maybe if you looked up from your phone every once in a while you'd realize that there are some things going on around you that do not always have to do with you! And I know that Emily does not act this way around her mother."

"Oh, my gawd! Emily! You, like, *love* her. Do you wish she was your daughter because she is, like, so perfect? I wish she was your daughter, too, let me just tell you that." Laura snapped open her phone and started typing a text to her other best friend, Casey, about how ridiculous her mother was being. She furiously hit send, willing the text to go through, despite being four floors down in an underground garage.

Margie, seeing her daughter texting again during their conversation, quickly pulled into a spot and threw her keys into her purse. "Unfortunately for both of us, we do not have that choice. And since you're being so snotty, unappreciative, and rude while I am coming to the mall on *my* Saturday for *your* dress, I'll be confiscating your phone for the week."

"Are you kidding me? You are so unfair! I hate you! *Everyone* texts as much as I do . . . maybe even more. You're lucky with me, and you don't even know it! Uggghhh!!"

Margie plucked the sequined pink phone from her daughter's hand and shoved it into the glove compartment. "Ready for some mother-daughter shopping?" Margie asked in a falsely sweet voice.

Laura made a noncommittal grunt and slammed the car door behind her. Margie hustled behind Laura into the elevator. "Please don't pout. I really can't deal with a stormy you today," Margie said to her daughter.

Laura crossed her arms over her chest and stomped into the

air-conditioned mall. "I'm not pouting. I'm just mourning the loss of friends that will happen after this weekend once they think I've abandoned them."

Now it was Margie's turn to roll her eyes. "You're kidding me, right? It's less than two days until you see them at school. I think you'll manage."

"You would say that, since you don't have any friends anyway," Laura snapped.

Low blow, thought Margie. Margie had lost touch with many of her old girlfriends from college after the move to a new city, and she'd had a falling-out with her ex-roommate after an uncomfortable miscommunication about husbands and salaries. Mother and daughter walked icily around the mall shops, occasionally stopping to check the price on a dress that would be suitable for the dance. Finally finding one emerald green strapless dress that was not too short or too low for a school function, Margie sat on a stool outside of the Forever 21 dressing rooms, wondering, *Who is this person in my daughter's clothes?*

The Vanessa Version

Laura sat silently for a moment, twirling her hair around her finger and nibbling on the ends. "It's just—it's just so unfair. I have liked Ethan forever. We finally say we're in a relationship on Facebook and then Emily, my quote unquote best friend, starts video chatting with him on iChat."

I circled the fourth floor of the underground garage. "What happened?"

She threw her phone in her purse as if tired of the drama emanating from it. "Two hours before her birthday party I get a notification from Facebook that we are no longer in a relationship. I get to the party and he and Emily are all cozy."

"Oh, my God, did they make out *in front* of you?"

"Worse!" Laura said. "Emily took a video with my Flip of them making out on a lawn chair in the backyard and then left the camera in my purse. Then, of course, I take it out to show some other friends my videos from last weekend's barbecue, and it pops up."

I pulled into a space by the elevators. "No. Don't tell me . . ."

Laura nodded and covered her face with her hands. "I watched it for the first time in front of everyone. The guys started hooting, and you know how much I hate Natalie? Of course she was there and just smirked and was like, 'Oh, yeah, I saw your breakup on FB.' Seriously, I could not have been more mortified."

"First things first: let me have it," I said.

Laura looked back up at me. "Have what?" she asked slowly.

I rolled my eyes at her and gestured down to her handbag. Laura pursed her lips and gazed guiltily down at her brown leather Target clutch, which she had cleverly disguised with a bright red scarf to make it more expensive and unique looking. "I'm not ready yet," she said quietly.

I nodded. "How many times have you watched it?" My client leaned her head back against the leather headrest. "Only four or five times."

I raised my eyebrows and waited.

"Ugh, fine," she continued stubbornly, "maybe ten or twelve."

I picked up her purse from the floor. "And that's not even counting how many times you watched it last night after the party."

Laura looked at me knowingly, and I could see the lack of sleep under her eyes.

I went on, "You know we have to get rid of it. We'll deal with the sleazy ex-boyfriend and terrible friend next. But first, we have to cleanse. *That* is toxic." I pointed to the side pocket of the clutch where she kept her Flip camera within easy reach

to capture any sudden YouTube-worthy moments. She reluctantly snapped open the leather flap and pulled out the tiny
camera.

"Do you want to do it, or should I?" I asked.

Laura gulped. "Do you want to see it first?"

"Do you want me to see it?"

She nodded yes. "But don't let me see it again." She pressed
her face against the passenger-side window. "You're right. It's
freaking toxic. It is, like, burned in my brain." I swiveled to the
other side of the steering wheel and booted up the tiny machine.
Sure enough, the first video in the library had a thumbnail snap-
shot of two teenagers touching lips. I hit play and covered the
speaker with my thumb to spare Laura any further suffering
from hearing the soundtrack to this heartbreaking scene.

There was Emily, the girl I had seen many times smiling
back at me in dozens of photos on the corkboard above Laura's
desk. She sure didn't look like the little kid in overalls playing in
the mud or the child in the freeze-frame of a second-grade kara-
oke birthday party. In this dark, muffled video she looked like a
thirteen-year-old girl trying to be eighteen. She sported heavy
eyeliner and straightened hair. At one point she quickly glanced
at the camera as if to say, "Gotcha!" or "Got him!" Laura did not
need to be reminded of that.

The unconscious message was also clear to me, although I
had yet to explain this to Laura. The sad girl in the video was
screaming, *I am jealous. I don't know how to be a real friend. I think*
this is what girls are supposed to do. I think this makes me attractive.
I think this makes me special. I think this means I'm lovable. I think
this means I'm loved.

The video was blurry, short, maybe three or four seconds,
probably because Ethan seemed unaware that she was secretly
filming them with Laura's camera. *At least he wasn't in on the*
planning, I thought hopefully. *Still a scumbag, but at least not a*

malicious one. The screen went black, and I asked permission: "Can I do it?"

Laura breathed deeply. "Yeah. Do it." The tiny cartoon trash icon danced playfully, blissfully ignorant of the enormity of this action. Once the thumbnail dissolved from the video library, I tapped the camera in my palm.

Laura stomped her foot. "I hate them! I hate them both. And she is such a b—"

I held up my hand. "Laura, you lost a best friend and a boy-friend in the same day. You have a right to be upset. And you have the right to be angry." She began to sniffle. "But," I added, "don't mask those with meanness."

She pushed some tears across her face, smudging her makeup. "But being mean to her makes me feel better."

"Okay, then what?" I pushed.

"When I'm angry and mean instead of just angry?" Laura tried to clarify the question before she answered. ". . . I guess she gets angry, too."

I took my keys out of the ignition and said, "And then she feels like she was justified in stealing your boyfriend."

Laura widened her eyes. "Nothing justifies that."

I grabbed a box of tissues from my backseat. "Right. So your being mean to her just gives her more fuel to get away with some-thing she never should have gotten away with in the first place."

Laura grabbed a tissue. "I see that," she said slowly. "I *can* be just angry and upset. But what can I do to feel better?"

"Well, I'm proud of you for admitting that you act mean as a way of feeling better—"

Laura interrupted, "But—but that doesn't even work. I'm mean and then she's mean even more and I feel worse."

"Exactly. So what I think you need to do is strengthen your other friendships. Reach out to people who care about you, so they can pull you out of being upset and angry."

"Like you?" she asked.

"Like me." I smiled. "And who else?"

"My mom?" she asked questioningly.

"For sure, your mom. Moms have this amazing way of making ex–best friends seem insignificant, picking the best ice cream place, and finding great girly movies to watch on Saturday nights."

Laura laughed. "My mom doesn't really get the whole Facebook thing. But she is good when I'm upset. I was so mean to her this morning, though."

I shrugged. "It happens. Apologize for being cranky and tell her you had a really bad night last night and that you need her. Moms love to be needed and hear what's going on. I bet it'll even cheer her up. You mentioned she seemed stressed."

"Yeah, the school auction thing has her acting crazy."

I had spoken to Margie about her stress. It was partially the school auction, but mostly the overwhelming fact that she felt she was losing her daughter to the vortex of texting, Facebook, and thirteen-year-old boys.

I tapped the wheel. "I don't know . . . call me crazy, but I think another thing that's stressing her out is her sudden lack of connection with you. Talking to her about this might kill two birds with one stone. You both need some cheering up."

Laura laughed. "I know I give her a hard time, and she *always* wants me to tell her things." Laura looked down at her chipping polish. "This time I actually want to. . . ."

"How about we go upstairs, call your mom, and ask her to come meet us at the mall. You guys can grab a snack together after we shop, and she can take you home."

"You think she'll come?"

"Of course! And here's a tip: stay off those text messages. Girls like Natalie are going to try their best to rub it in."

Laura leaned down and fished her cell phone out of her purse.

"Totally. Good call. I don't need to hear from anyone today," she said, pushing the pink "power off" button.

· · · · · · · · ·

Too often this is not how conversations go with parents and teens. In the Mom version both Margie and Laura got into a downward spiral until it degenerated into hurt feelings, low self-esteem, and passive-aggressive fighting.

How could Margie have gotten Laura to open up to her despite the surly, cranky, cloistered attitude being leveled at her by her angry, defensive teenager? Or, for that matter, how does any parent prevent the downward spiral of a passive-aggressive argument and get an adolescent to open up? This is a code I have cracked. It takes a few tries, and it certainly takes more flexibility than one would imagine, but it can be done.

First we need to examine why fighting is such a common problem for teens and parents. Many parents have expressed to me that they fear family conflict and that they are uncomfortable asking questions to gather information or clarify intentions. They worry that asking too many questions actually makes teens feel more challenged and forces conflict, which sends them into rebellion! Yet, by fearing conflict, parents are actually spurring their teen to lie to them.

One of the reasons teens have such a slippery tendency to argue is that they actually feel it is a productive way to communicate. In a fascinating study headed by Nancy Darling at Penn State University, researchers asked teenagers about why and how they fight with their parents. They also examined the correlation between the amount that teens lie and the frequency of fighting in the home. The researchers made a deck of thirty-six cards. Each card displayed a topic that teens might lie to parents about, such as using drugs, hanging out with a friend Mom does not approve of, or not finishing homework.

Researchers asked the teenagers in the study to set aside the cards that had topics they lie to their parents about. Investigators also contacted parents and asked them how often the family argues. Researchers thought that the kids who lied more would also argue with their parents more often. However, this was not the case. The families with teens that lied less had more in-house arguing and disagreement.

Why would this be the case? Darling and her researchers found that, for teenagers, arguing is a way of working out difficulties and telling the truth to their parents. Lying is simply another way for them to avoid an argument and pretend to give in to their parents' demands. Arguing, on the other hand, is their way of telling the truth and working through the disagreements. This is shocking to most parents, but not to most teens.

I wish teens like Nehat would not choose arguing as the only way to get their parents' attention, but it shows a teen's different perspective on conflict in the home. For teens, it is a means to communicate. For parents, it prevents communicating. Dr. Tabitha Holmes undertook a study of over fifty pairs of mothers and daughters with difficult relationships. When Holmes interviewed the mothers, she found that 46 percent of them believed that their ar-

"Sometimes I egg my mom on to get her to talk to me. She thinks I'm trying to fight with her, but I'm not trying to fight with her, I'm trying to talk to her. I don't want to have to ask for her attention, so I get it in a way that is not so nerdy—I pick a fight and then hope she asks the right questions."

—Nehat, 15, Radical Parenting intern

guments were destructive to their mother-daughter relationship.
After an argument, the mothers said they felt more stressed and
disrespected and that the fight had made the issue more confusing. Yet, when Holmes asked their daughters about those arguments, only 23 percent of them found the fights to be destructive.
In fact, the daughters believed that the arguments actually
helped to strengthen the mother-daughter bond!

The only time the arguments were not constructive for the
daughters was when they felt they were not heard or when the
mother was unreasonable and would not budge on any point.
This is an essential distinction. Arguments can be helpful to
your relationship when teens feel heard and there is a mutual
feeling of compromise. When parents will not compromise,
teens go into logistical mode—instead of asking, "How can I
communicate my needs to my parents?" they begin to figure out
"How can I get around my parents?" In other words, facing unbending rules and arguments where they do not feel heard encourages teens to lie and plan for risky behavior.

The second reason teens view fighting as a way to communicate is that they have an underdeveloped "secondary emotion."
When adults are angry, we feel this in both our bodies and our
minds. Then, anywhere from a millisecond to a minute after the
anger begins, we are able to take a step back from this primary
emotion and have what I call a secondary emotion. A secondary
emotion is where you reflect on your primary emotion. You think
about why the feeling happened, how long it might last, and how
it is affecting your body and judgment. After seeing many angry,
fearful, sad, happy, and overwrought teens, I have learned that it
takes them much longer to go from primary emotion to secondary emotion—sometimes skipping it entirely.

An easy example of this shows up in the addictive nature of
texting. Texting exacerbates this undeveloped skill in teens. We
saw this in action when Laura wanted to continue watching the

hurtful video; staying in her primary emotion of shame and fear, she couldn't help texting her friends about the drama until she literally had no reception in the parking garage. She was not ready to start thinking about why her friend had done this to her or what she could do about it, instead preferring to wallow in the upset.

HERE IS HOW THE TEXTING CYCLE WORKS:

- Teen gets a mean text message from a friend.
- Teen gets angry.
- Before teen thinks about the anger or the validity of the text message or what to do about it, teen is writing a nasty response.
- Still in anger, teen then texts other people about the mean message.
- Teen gets another mean text message back from the original instigator, thus starting a texting war.
- Teen gets angrier.
- Before teen thinks about the anger or the validity . . .

It becomes a very bad cycle. Teens are used to staying in their primary emotion because it is easier than really feeling and resolving a conflict. That's why so many teen friendships and relationships are now ending via cell phone and Facebook. These are the perfect vehicles for staying in primary emotions and forming quick, unresolved reactions and exaggerated conflicts. Facebook miscommunications, cyberbullying, and text wars are perfect examples of how teens have a tendency to stay in primary emotions longer than adults, before they enter into the secondary emotion and evaluate the credibility, solutions, and aspects of their feelings.

Finally, with teens, their fear often sounds like anger. While working with teens I have learned that what sounds like anger to most adults is actually fear in disguise. Sometimes, as adults, we take their disguised fear as a bizarre desire to argue with us.

I often have to teach teens to say, "I'm mad and I'm afraid I might say something I don't mean." This is a powerful tool for both parents and teens because many teens are afraid to show they care and often disguise their fear as anger—yelling, cursing, or door slamming. I hear many parents complain about two seemingly contradictory statements:

> *"Teens do worry about what their parents think; we just don't want them to know that. We're afraid of what they'll think, so we act like we don't care."*
>
> —Rachel, 17, Radical Parenting Intern

Teens are emotionally unavailable.

Teens are overly emotional.

How can these both be true at the same time? I believe we compare teens' emotional availability to our own.

Yes, teens are emotionally unavailable—but only when compared to adults. We often contrast the way teens talk to us with the way we talk to our friends. This is not fair. Teens are emotionally available in a different kind of way. We cannot compare how we emotionally relate to our teens to the way we emotionally relate to our adult friends.

It's also important to keep in mind that teens do not place high value on why they feel how they feel—the secondary emotion of assessing their emotional state. Rather, they prefer to stay in the primary emotion. This explains why we believe teens and tweens are overly emotional, but not emotionally available at all. They are very emotional, but when asked to talk about their actual feelings, they shut down—either for lack of interest or for lack of skill in judging their own emotional state.

Teens also want independence. Independence means having control. When they are emotionally available to you, they often feel less in control, and therefore less independent. This is why they can be afraid to connect with you, and why fighting is so common in a teen and parent household.

So how do we disengage from anger, help teens move into their secondary emotions, and learn how to communicate without fighting? Let's use an example with Stephanie and her son Trevor to explain the antifighting prevention techniques. In Stephanie's eyes, Trevor never seems to follow through. She insists he is always late and never appreciates what Stephanie and her husband give him. When he asks her for extra allowance, she wants to click on the usual lens and automatically respond, "No, not until you finish your homework."

But Trevor crosses his arms and braces for battle. "I did finish my homework!" When he says this, Stephanie shakes her head and remembers the C he brought home last week.

"I don't think so. You're always asking for extra money."

Trevor's voice instantly goes up on the whin-o-meter by two octaves. "I need it, though. You're so unfair."

"You want to know what's unfair? That's me having to clean up after you and you never saying thank you. Maybe if you earned your allowance I would give it to you."

Trevor stomps his foot and runs upstairs. "You don't even care what I do. I hate you."

How could either person have changed the trajectory of this argument, turning it into a discussion with a solution? We asked this exact question of our teenagers in this scenario. In fact, the fight was written by our intern Trevor, based on a real-life interaction he had over and over again with his mom. Their answers showed us how *teens* view fights with their parents—and what they wish would change.

We can conclude from these answers that teens recognize

that their parents have triggers and that when they are set off, communication is almost impossible. Our children often feel like their voices aren't being heard and that it's easier to live up to their parents' expectations rather than fight against them— whether that's good or bad. Also, we can see from Alyssa's comment that the harder each minor communication is, the more teens are encouraged to find a way not to talk at all. We can also tell from Emily's quote that teens themselves can distinguish between an automatic response and an authentic one. What I've learned as well is that when teens do not understand your answer, or feel it is not thought through, they feel more entitled to disregard it.

"Ohhh, this totally happens to me. Except my mom's thing is that she hates when I ask to stay out later. I just have to mention the idea of a later curfew or a few extra minutes and she blows off the handle. After that, nothing I say gets through and I am definitely not going to be able to go out."

—Emily, 15

Many parents would find these conclusions surprising. Do you? As adults, we often forget that our kids recognize trigger areas as well as—perhaps even better than—we ourselves do. It also helps us learn how to approach a trigger comment or action differently, so it does not end in the same old fight.

After collecting these answers in my teen interviews, I constructed an outline for how parents could approach a trigger topic with more success and I reviewed it with the original teens. This approach, the interviewed teens agreed, would help both sides slow down, take a step back, and see each other as allies,

> *"I know I give my parents a hard time and they have trouble depending on me. But that gives me a lot of leeway to continue being 'difficult,' and not needing to be 'accountable' to them—in the words of my parents. They expect me to fuck up, so why should I surprise them?"*
>
> —Trevor himself

not as opponents—making compromises easier. Most important, it helps us use authentic responses even during our tensest communications. There are four steps to this approach, which will help stop you and your teen from reliving the same fight over and over again.

> *"I guess this is how it usually goes. What sucks is she didn't even ask him what he wanted the allowance for! I hate, hate, hate when parents make rules or decisions without thinking about it. It is so frustrating it makes me not want to ask them at all and find a way to do it behind their backs."*
>
> —Alyssa, 17

1. Recognize Your Triggers

Most arguments happen when you and your child experience some kind of trigger. A trigger can be an undone chore, a needy demand, or anything that causes tension. Every parent (and child) has his or her triggers. Determining what your triggers are is the first step. In my household, a dirty microwave set my mom off. Other frequent examples I hear from parents include asking for money, not saying thank you, demanding last-minute scheduling changes, and leaving toys or dirty clothes on the floor. Laura pushed those triggers consciously and subconsciously with Margie by putting her feet on the dash, rolling her eyes, and making loaded comments without follow-up. Laura did this because she wanted to connect with her mom but did not know how to ask for positive engagement, so she egged on the negative kind: a fight. With Stephanie, her trigger was Trevor asking for money. For Stephanie, it didn't matter what the money was for, just that he had asked for money at all.

2. Assess Your State

Once you recognize a trigger has been set off, before you respond, check in with your needs.

Realize if you're tired, hungry, or angry

One of the teens I interviewed mentioned that everyone in her family avoids Mom when she hasn't eaten or gotten much sleep. As I've worked with clients, I've realized this is a problem for everyone. A study done at Florida State University, led by psychologist Roy Baumeister, looked at the effects of blood sugar levels on performance and self-control. He had a group of students perform a mentally challenging activity. Half of the students were then offered lemonade prepared with real sugar, and the other half got lemonade with a sugar substitute (Splenda). After a few minutes, students were asked to make important decisions about apartments. Students who had the real-sugar lemonade were better able to tap into their intuition and instincts to make their decisions. The Splenda students made financially and logistically worse decisions because their brains did not have the energy to process thoroughly.

Our self-control, intuition, and instincts are processed in the prefrontal cortex areas of the brain. This takes a lot of energy. When we are low on food or tired, this part of the brain does not function well. This makes our fights worse because we cannot pick up on our teen's clues, we have a short temper, and we have trouble finding a solution because that part of our brain is literally too tired to figure it out.

Differentiate between your feelings and their feelings

Psychologist Daniel Goleman analyzes how the mind deals with other people's strong emotions in an argument. He writes:

> When someone dumps their toxic feelings on us— explodes in anger or threats, shows disgust or contempt—they activate in us circuitry for those very same emotions. Their act has potent neurological consequences: emotions are contagious. We "catch" strong emotions much as we do a rhinovirus—and so can come down with the emotional equivalent of a cold.

He quotes an experiment done in Germany where students listened to two tape recordings, one in a sad voice and one in a happy voice. The content of each recording was the same, but students came away from each recording with the mood that was presented to them, though they could not explain why. This is why the first part, checking in with your own state, is so important when an argument is triggered. You need to make sure you are responding with your feelings, not the ones your teen is trying to pass—or dump—on to you. Remember, this is not a conscious dumping. It is good for our teens to want to vent to us, and we just want to make sure we are not adopting their emotions along with them.

3. Review Your Teen's State

Once you have checked in with yourself, it is time to look at what is going on with your son or daughter.

Remember what has happened recently

With teenagers, patterns often arise. Looking at past behavior can be important in making your decision or resolving how you would like to reply. Stephanie could have asked herself: *Did Trevor help me with the dinner dishes?* Or, *When was the last time he asked for extra allowance, and what happened?* Or even, *What did the school e-mail say about tests this week?* When we asked Stephanie these questions, a number of issues shifted her expectations, and she commented:

> "When I asked him those questions after the fight, I realized there were some new issues I should have considered. For example, he *had* helped me with the dishes and I had forgotten it was a no-homework weekend. However, I did remember that the last time he asked for extra money, he spent it appropriately, but he never said thank you. I realized that was what was really bothering me."
>
> —Stephanie, mother of Trevor

Get clarification

Once you have examined past behavior, you can get clarification. When Stephanie realized what was tripping her up, she could have asked Trevor about it. Remember, he had only just asked her for more allowance. Instead of responding out of anger, Stephanie's first response could have been a clarification dialogue:

> "Okay, let's talk about it. When was the last time you asked for extra allowance?"
>
> Trevor thought. "I think for Brian's birthday party, so I could have enough for a movie ticket and dinner."
>
> "Right, I remember that. And that is what your allowance is for, but I remember why I was upset, though, and that is making me consider not saying yes again."
>
> "What?"
>
> "I know it might seem silly to you, but you never said thank you for that extra money. Your dad and I kind of felt like you didn't notice or care that we gave it to you."

Clarification is an important step for you and your child. The teens above expressed that it was extremely important to them that they felt like their parent was actually listening to them and thinking about a specific answer. When they felt like their parents made a hasty or automatic decision, they were more likely to disobey. Making clarification statements and questions lets your child feel heard.

Even if Stephanie decides she does not want to give Trevor any extra allowance, it is this clarification process that will make *him* feel heard and have a better understanding of the reason behind the answer. This also makes him more likely to follow her decision.

Read the cues

While clarifying your child's needs and the situation, this is the perfect time to use the protoconversation techniques. You can listen for verbal cues and tonal emphasis. Let's look at Trevor's response to Stephanie's question: "Why do you need extra allowance?" He responded, "All of my friends are going to the Earth Day concert this weekend and it is twenty dollars admission. I really want to go because everyone is going to the concert and there are some cool bands."

While listening to his answers you can also ask yourself what kinds of words he is using and what that says about his emotional intent. Clearly, Trevor is very interested in the people going and the concert he might miss. He puts emphasis on these words and references these two reasons most. He could have said something like "I need it because this weekend there is nothing to do, so a bunch of people are going to a concert. It's all day Saturday and if I don't go there will be nothing else to do."

That answer would tell us that his request is really about having nothing better to do. The emotional intent is fear of being bored. In this case, if Stephanie does not want to give him extra money, she could offer another solution, something else he can *do* instead—go to a game with his dad or call other friends doing something closer to home. This would also satisfy the emotional need. This takes the focus off the money—which could end up causing a huge argument—and puts it back on finding a mutually acceptable solution.

Stephanie could also have used tonal emphasis to find an acceptable solution. Stephanie expressed to us that Trevor got very whiny when he was arguing with her. This set off alarm bells in her head about his neediness and subsequent lack of appreciation as soon as he gets what he wants. This was an important clue and

Stephanie could have addressed it head-on by responding in this way:

> Trevor's voice instantly went up on the whine-o-meter by two octaves. "I need it, though. You are so unfair."
>
> "Whoa, whoa. Take it down a notch. Explain to me in a calm voice why you need it."

4. Make Your Final Check

After gathering all of the information you can about your child's state, it's time to make a decision. This requires you to check back in with yourself. This is what I do when communicating with teens on a tense subject where we need to find an acceptable solution. I ask myself the two questions below.

What are the emotional needs here?

Often there are two emotional needs in an argument: yours and your child's. See how two emotional intents are competing in this example:

> **Child:** Mom, I hate going to Grandma's house!
>
> **Parent:** Sweetie, we have to go tomorrow and you know it.
>
> **Child:** But then we miss *all* of our Sunday fun time.
>
> **Parent:** Your Grandma is lonely! We need to go see her; she has been looking forward to this.
>
> **Child:** But I had soccer games all day today and a ton of tests this week. Sunday is my only day to relax.
>
> **Parent:** We have to go to be a good family to her. It's our obligation to see other family and your Grandma has done so much for us.

Here the child is speaking with his emotional need—wanting a break from the week. And the parent is thinking about her emotional need—feeling obligated to see her mother and make sure she is not lonely. It is best for the parent to recognize both with a response like this: "I know you want some free time tomorrow because you had sports yesterday and school all week. How about this: we won't leave until everyone wakes up, so you can sleep in, and I promise we'll be home in time for you to hang out with a friend. Maybe Steven can come over and hang out so you have something to look forward to after Grandma. You want to text him?"

Once you have both emotional needs addressed, you can ask yourself the final question.

What are my limits?

Ultimately, it is your home, your money, and your family, and as a parent, you make the decision you are most comfortable with. This is your last check-in. Using the information you have taken about historical behavior, your child's emotional cues, and current context, what are you comfortable with? I asked Stephanie this question and she said that had she stopped to think about her limits, she would have come to this conclusion:

"I didn't realize the concert was an Earth Day fund-raiser. I want to encourage kids to realize that being good to the Earth can also be fun. I was okay giving him twenty dollars for the ticket and I was okay letting him go for the day. I just wanted him to appreciate it more."

We then talked about how Trevor could attend and Stephanie could feel he appreciated the money and time she granted. We settled on having Trevor volunteer for two hours of the event so that he actually earned a free pass. His friends ended up joining him and they all got community service hours for their school, free tickets, and a fun time together—while appreciating the opportunity and the Earth.

With this mental checklist we can disengage arguments, address everyone's emotional needs, and reply authentically—which, as we saw in chapter 1, is an essential part of building strong communication. I call this responding out of design, not by default. Fundamentally, this mental checklist encourages us to be more intuitive. Rejecting automatic responses and searching for our inner limits and outer context helps us hone our intuition. It also teaches us that we can evoke the responses we want from our children and ourselves.

I use this mental checklist when I work with families and teens and even in my personal relationships to find compromise and make sure I am responding with authenticity.

Luckily, I had taught this mental checklist to Margie before her daughter Laura got into her emotional funk. Laura and I were at the mall, and she had decided to leave her primary emotions of anger and upset behind by turning off her phone and being willing to talk to her mom about what had happened.

I called Margie and told her to meet us at the mall. "Is everything okay?" Margie asked on the other end of the line.

"She had a rough night. But I want to let her tell you about it." I glanced over at Laura, who had settled on a simple black dress that she could wear to other events just in case she decided not to go to the dance.

This did not produce relief in Margie. "Do you think she will tell me?"

"Listen," I said, "I prepped her, and she knows you are on the same side. But it is an emotional situation for her and will probably test some of your limits, too. You are going to have to use the mental checklist on this one."

"Right, right." I could literally hear her nodding her head on the other end. She continued, "I know I need to pay attention to the smaller details because she is hard to read, and I have to make sure I'm comfortable with whatever we agree on."

"And don't fall for the triggers with automatic responses. She is calm now, but once you start talking about it again, I don't want her to try to bait you into an argument to distract you from the real issues."

The call ended, and we got the dress and met Margie at the curb. I hugged Laura good-bye and peered at her purse. "Don't turn on the phone until you are ready, okay?"

Laura's eye's widened with panic as she realized I was not coming back with them. She began to get teary. "But we didn't even talk about what I should do." Her voice began to rise in panic and I noticed fear lines across her forehead.

"We don't need to. You have someone else who can help you with that." I gestured toward her mom in the waiting car.

She looked at it skeptically and then her face softened. "Yeah, if she actually listens to me and doesn't blame me because she loves Emily so much."

I gave her a look of disbelief. "Give her some credit—she is not going to pick your friend over you. Deep breath. Give her a chance and remember the mental checklist." I had taught Laura the teen version of the mental checklist a few weeks earlier.

Laura gave me a small smile and got in the car with her mom. In the car, Margie shifted out of park and asked, "How was shopping?"

Laura rolled her eyes at her mother. "Fine."

Margie turned on the music, sensing her daughter wasn't in the mood to talk yet. "Oldies? CD? What should we listen to?"

Laura looked up from her nails. "What CDs do we have?"

While stopped at a red light, Margie glanced up at the CD holder on her sun visor.

"Hmm, we have the *Grey's Anatomy* soundtrack—you want

to play that? They have some young, hip songs and some old-folk songs."

Laura laughed. "Yeah, sure, that's a good idea. I can't believe what happened on the show this week."

"I didn't get to see it. I've been so busy with the school auction I feel like I haven't taken a breath, and I just have not had time to watch it."

Laura shrugged. "I won't ruin it for you, but it's good. Why did you sign up for that stupid auction, anyway? It's so much work."

Margie brushed her hair out of her face. "I know . . . you're right. I just really want you guys to feel like I'm involved in your world. Plus, no one else volunteers, and I don't want the event to just get canceled."

Laura looked over at her mom and felt a pang of guilt mixed in with the bad feelings she had had in her stomach all day. "Mom, you know you don't have to do that. Luke and I don't care if you volunteer at the auction. We know you're involved in our stuff. It's worse when you're cranky at home, even if you are involved."

Margie thought about how this comment would usually send her into a "no one appreciates me" tirade. But she took a deep breath and checked in with her limits. *Laura is not trying to be mean to me; she is trying to talk to me.* "I think we've both been pretty cranky lately. But you're right. I've just been stressed, and it does help me to know that you guys wouldn't feel bad if I don't volunteer again—you know I love you, and I just don't want to disappoint anyone or make you feel like I don't care."

Laura didn't respond to the mutual cranky comment, so Margie tried another subject as Ben Lee started singing through the speakers of her car. "What kind of dress did you get for the dance today, anyway?"

Laura sighed. "I don't even know if I'll end up wearing it."

"Why?" her mom asked slowly.

Laura started biting her nails as her mother stopped at another light. "I just . . ." She hesitated. "I'm in a fight with Ethan."

"Oh, that is the worst. Anything you want to talk about?" Margie secretly cringed inside. She hoped that nothing sexual had happened in their brief two-week relationship. She looked over at her daughter. Her shoulders were slumped, mouth pulled down in a frown. She was sad, upset—thank goodness not scared.

"I mean, it's not even worth talking about. It is more than just a fight. We broke up."

Margie looked over at her daughter and put her hand on her shoulder. "Oh, honey, I'm so sorry. What can I do to help?"

Laura tapped her feet to Ben Lee and nudged her purse with her foot, eyeing the flap with the dreaded camera. "I don't know, it sucks. It all sucks. He sucks, Emily sucks, and I hate everyone."

Margie had no idea what Emily had to do with her daughter's breakup with Ethan, but she did know that whenever Laura started in with the "everything sucks" attitude, she was feeling insecure and unloved, and Margie knew that this was not the time to push it. "Mm-hm."

"Sparing you the horrific details, *Emily* is now dating Ethan," Laura said, throwing her hands up.

Margie saw Laura's face flash with anger at the vocal stress and mention of Emily's name. "Emily, huh? What did she do?" Margie could not imagine little Emily stealing her best friend's boyfriend, and Emily and Laura had been best friends since first grade. But if Margie had learned anything through her own experience of middle school and now her daughter's experience of it, it was that girls can change . . . and they can be mean.

Laura nodded emphatically. "Emily stole my boyfriend. And

everyone knows because of Facebook and the party last night. I'm just miserable."

The light changed and Margie pulled over, unhooked her seat belt, and faced her daughter. "How can I help you?"

Laura rubbed her eyes and felt the sting of tears gathering, burning in the back of her throat, and threatening to unleash themselves in a torrent. She held back the floodgate and sniffled. "I'm not sure. I guess it just feels good to talk about it."

Margie stayed quiet. She waited thoughtfully to see what else her daughter would choose to tell her, if anything. The door was open to the dialogue, and it was Laura's choice to decide what to do next. Margie's decision not to push or prod was a sign of respect to her daughter and a cornerstone of Laura being able to trust and communicate with her mom.

Things to Remember

- For teenagers, arguing can be a way for them to communicate honestly with you. In households with more fights, there tends to be less lying.
- Teens spend more time in their primary emotions—fear, anger, distress from an outside stimulus—before being able to take a step back and evaluate their feelings.
- Emotions are "contagious." Your teen's bad mood, or your stress, can easily be transferred back and forth, exacerbating arguments.
- Teens often cover up fear with anger.
- Using the mental checklist when a trigger is set off can help us respond in the best possible way and resolve potentially problematic situations and behaviors.
- Finding the emotional need of each family member is essential for deciphering their actions and finding resolutions to problems.

- We can avoid arguments by examining historical behavior, getting clarification, identifying emotional needs, and deciding on our limits.

Challenges You Can Do Right Now

Family Challenge: What are your and your family's triggers?

1. What are the triggers that put you into a frenzy, a bad mood, etc.?
2. Can you identify triggers in other family members?

Personal Challenge: Keep a log of your conversations with your children for three days.

1. Are your conversations mostly neutral, positive, or negative?
2. What are the majority of your conversations about—logistics, feelings, the past, the future, the present?
3. Think about what your typical communication style is now. Are you satisfied with the tone and topics of your communications at home?

Personal Challenge: Reexamine an old argument.

1. Think about an argument that happened with your child.
2. What was the trigger?
3. How could it have changed if you had used the mental checklist?
4. Would there have been a different solution?

PART II

....

Learn About Their Life

CHAPTER 3

Figure Out Friendship

A teen's social life can be riddled with nuances, pleasures, and complications. In this chapter I review how friendship has changed—online and offline—and I outline solutions for parents to encourage healthy relationship maintenance. I believe as the value of friendship decreases for many young people, the need for parents to talk to their children about the necessity of true friends becomes even more essential. In this way, we can help our youth understand that, unlike some of the current friendship trends, deep relationships with their peers can be rewarding and reliable.

I was able to observe the true nature of friendship for twenty-first-century teens when I was asked to host a workshop for a small clique of ninth-grade students at a school I will call Central High. These kids, the school counselor informed me, were the "cool kids." They dominated the playground, got their first choice of cafeteria tables, and were constantly causing drama—among their own group members as well as for outsiders.

The school counselor paused outside of the classroom door and turned to me. "There is something going on right now. I suspect the clique is thinking of splitting. I'm not sure because they will not talk about it. All I know is they refuse to partner with each other in class, and parent complaints about playground and online bullying are through the roof. We are praying you can at least get them to acknowledge the problem so the school can figure out how to move past it. Honestly, if there isn't some progress today, we are going to ask you who you think is causing the most problems and have that person temporarily suspended."

As if I wasn't already nervous, this severely intensified the situation. I did not want to have to pick one of these students to suspend. I was also not a cool kid in school. In fact, I might have been the furthest thing from popular in elementary school, and I prayed these teens couldn't smell it on me. I peeked in through the door's small window. There was a group of eight students—five girls, three boys. Most of them looked sullenly silent, a few were playing on forbidden cell phones, and two girls were whispering in a corner of the circle—yes, I noted, somehow they had made a corner in a circle. I stepped into the room and took a seat in the circle. The tension in the room was simmering, literally on the verge of boiling. I knew, very quickly, that either no one was going to talk or, if they did, a war might break out and no one would be able to say anything productive. I decided to cut to the chase and change their perspective on the situation so they would realize how serious it was. "The school has asked me to figure out who in this group is the cause of the drama, so they can suspend them."

This caused a ripple of concerned murmurs, grunts, and hushed whispers around the circle. "However, if we can solve the drama, I do not need to give them a name. The good news is, I'm on your side. My name is Vanessa Van Petten and I'm a human emotion detector. I specialize in reading your face, your body language, your tone of voice, and the words you use to figure out the underlying emotion."

The boy next to me murmured, "Cool." And then went back to looking at his shoes.

I continued, "Now, this can be good for you—if you tell me the truth. Or not so good for you—if you decide to lie. Plus, you all will keep each other accountable. If you exaggerate or do not tell the truth, the other people in this room will call you on it. So let me be clear. If you lie, you will not only lose out on keeping your record clean but, most important, you will miss the chance to rebuild the relationships you had with the people in here. Because, let's be honest, we all know that something has changed."

I let a few people nod in agreement before moving on. "Look around the room. These used to be your best friends. From my understanding you all went to elementary school together and have gone to every birthday party for each other since kindergarten. Your school did not bring me in here to ruin your life or destroy your friendships. They brought me in to help you rebuild them. But I will not—let me repeat, will not—do that for liars. Second, if you do not want to rebuild these friendships or if telling the truth is not worth it, then you can leave right now."

I peered around the room and was satisfied when no one looked up at the door, meaning everyone wanted to try to make this work. "Okay, so here is how it is going to work. Today, I'm going to pass out a piece of paper to each of you. On this piece of paper you will have your chance. You will explain your side of the story and why you think you should not be suspended. At the end, I will collect and read them—I will not share your answers with the school. Once I have read all of them, I will expose any discrepancies and we will work from there. You can start your sheet with this sentence: 'My name is ____ and I should not be suspended because . . .' Then halfway down the page you will also finish this sentence: 'However, the things that I'm not proud of are . . .'"

I like using written explanations in peer groups with high tension because it makes participants be accountable for their accusations and claims. It also gives them time to calmly reason out what happened; this in itself can provide relief and answers. I guessed that someone was lying and that other group members were trying to cover it up. I would soon learn I was wrong on one account. After about thirty minutes of silent writing, I began to read some of the responses:

> "My name is Chloe and I should not be suspended because Justine is the one who started this whole thing. We all used to be super close and then all of a sudden Justine goes out with Suchin and DJ without the rest of us! They started to have their own little chats and I think, honestly it's because she likes DJ because they are all over each other. Plus it was Justine who wrote really awful things on my Facebook and made other people at school send me awful messages, too. They were terrible and I swear I couldn't even come to school the next day—I pretended to be sick.
>
> "However, the things that I'm not proud of are that I made an anonymous page for Justine and people wrote mean things on it."

> "My name is Justine and I should not be suspended because I don't even know why this is happening. Chloe started a really awful page about me, and DJ and Suchin stood up for me. She thought that meant we were, like, breaking up the group, but they were standing up for me because we all knew she was the one who started this anonymous website that called me a slut. She accused DJ and me of going all the way in the locker room and DJ and I are just friends, we just touch a lot—I swear. I feel like I'm being bullied by her and she is spreading rumors about me online.

"However, the things that I'm not proud of are that I told other people to be mean to Chloe back because I felt like she deserved it. I also am trying to convince Jim, Chris, and Sally not to hang out with her because she is mean. I also have been planning events and leaving Chloe out even though she hears about them on Facebook."

"My name is Jim and I should not be suspended because I'm in the middle. Justine and Chloe are having a war right now and I don't know whose side to pick. It sucks that Justine invited Suchin and DJ out without the rest of us. But also Chloe is being really mean to the three of them. To be honest I am so tired of the drama and I feel like I constantly have to check Facebook or my phone to see what people are writing. I have always had our group and the past few weeks I have just felt lost.

"However, the things I'm not proud of are my not choosing sides and agreeing with both of them. I knew about Chloe posting a page about Justine and commented on it. I also did say some bad things about Chloe and laughed about the bad pictures Justine posted of Chloe from the pool party last year."

"My name is DJ and I should not be suspended because I do not think standing up for a friend is wrong. Chloe posted a mean website about Justine even though none of it is true, we are not hooking up. When I stood up for her it only made it worse. Justine's parents are getting divorced and Chloe is awful to be doing this to her while that is going on. I only wanted to support her and I'm trying to ignore the mean stuff online and not talk to her at school.

"However, the things that I'm not proud of are

excluding Chloe and trying to convince Jim and Chris and Sally to not talk to her as well because she is attacking Justine."

The reason I gave the students this exercise is that I wanted them to acknowledge what they did right and what they did wrong. In social situations today almost no teen is totally guilt free. In fact, the passive-aggressiveness and secret "frenemies" make it nearly impossible for anyone to be without blame. As you will see at the end of the chapter, when I mediate between the clique members, even ignoring mean comments is a way of contributing to the wrongdoing. This workshop provides us a perfect window into how friendship has changed for youth today. It exemplifies the two major changes: how friendship and identity have become too closely linked, and how teens crave closeness to their friends, but have more and more trouble depending on them to show loyalty.

First, the need to belong has morphed into a digital and personal identity crisis. The fundamental problem for the Central High clique boiled down to the question "Where do I belong?" The entire friendship battle started when Chloe felt that her group—the clique she felt defined her—was threatened. Peer groups are incredibly important for a teen's self-worth and identity formation. Unfortunately, like most teens who fear their friendship is being threatened, Chloe and Justine responded by actually pulling their relationships further apart. Chloe felt left out so she attacked the other members of her group; if they weren't already wanting to separate, the aggression would surely alienate them. Some of the members who were "stuck in the middle" also expressed a desperate desire to "just work it out" and "get our group back" because, as Jim said, he was feeling lost without them.

Many teens respond as Chloe did—by getting revenge—

while others try to find ways to fill the void of not having their usual peer group. We already learned in chapter 1 how tempting it is to categorize others, but teens also have the tendency to categorize themselves.

This poignant comment by Sybil explains why teens gravitate toward tools that help them gauge how others feel about them. Teens do this so they know what to feel about themselves. An extremely popular Facebook application called Honesty Box is a way for users to post anonymous comments about one another. There are also a number of websites that allow users to post profiles and invite their friends to post or pose anonymous questions. Websites like Failin.gs encourage users to answer the question

> *"There is a new obsession with 'what people think of me.' It seems like everyone wants to know what other people think of them so that they can know what to think of themselves."*
>
> —Sybil, 19,
> Radical Parenting intern

"What is wrong with me?" on their friends' pages. A quick search on this site revealed these horrifying comments on some teenagers' profiles:

"ura fat ass and u should stop eating cause ur 2 ugly."

"no1 likes u even if u think ppl do, hahahahahaahaha. Its bc ur annoying in class and make stupid comments all the time. Ur not fuckin smart dude!"

These comments are devastating—to both adults and teens. When I ask my teen interns about these websites and applications, many admit to having a profile and finding the pull irresistible. One teen boy said, "I feel like I have to know what people think of me. It helps me know which category I fall into at school." But when I asked him how awful it feels when he gets bad comments, he said, "It's worth it to see the good comments and you get to know what people really think of you." This obsession with knowing what other people think speaks to the larger trends shown in the Central High clique: teens rely heavily on each other to form their own opinions about themselves. In addition, they fear losing their solid block of friends as much as—if not more than—they fear losing their identity. This is what caused all the members of the group to be so incredibly mean to each other as the clique was falling apart. Unfortunately, these students turned their hurt and fear of rejection into revenge, which only pulled the group further apart.

I see this over and over again with teen relationships. They base the majority of their personality on their friendships and who they hang out with. When their peer group or relationships are threatened, instinctively they respond from fear and lash out. This only further alienates their friends or group, and a terrible downward spiral begins. This cycle threatens young people's ability to develop not only healthy relationships, but also their self-esteem and identity.

Loyalty is the second major way friendships have changed. Friends have become the new family, and a slew of slang terms shows this trend:

Friendiversary *n.* A celebratory event between two people, honoring the day they first became friends. This can be celebrated with gifts, dinner, or a party.

"It's our two-year friendiversary next week—where are we going for dinner?"

Bromance *n.* A term describing the nonsexual closeness of two males in a friendship.

"Nick is always Brian's partner in science. You know they have a really serious bromance."

Nonsexual crush (NSC) *n.* A term describing one person's extreme liking for another. Often used to describe the way someone feels toward a best friend or their bromance.

"I can't wait to hang out with Marie this weekend. I have such an NSC on her!"

Friendtervention *n.* An intervention done for one person by their friends on an issue or behavior of concern.

"I am really worried about Sasha's grades; we should plan a friendtervention."

Cuddling for funsies (CFF) *v.* Engaging in nonsexual activity between two people that encourages closeness and intimacy without being aroused.

"I swear we were CFFing, but then he tried to kiss me—he so knows he can't do that!"

Male best friend (MBF) or female best friend (FBF) *n.* Terms used to describe a person's opposite-sex best friend.

"We aren't dating. He is just my MBF."

I believe this trend has emerged because friendships have become more fickle, making teens crave more closeness to reassure themselves of the connection.

> "Sometimes I feel like my best friend today is my enemy tomorrow."
>
> —13-year-old female

Why have teenage friends become less dependable? The realm and rules of digital friendships have greatly influenced how easily they can be sacrificed. Teens do report that social networks and instant messaging clients have some positive effects. Many shy kids are able to use technology to approach and talk to new friends. Students have also used social network groups to discover mutual hobbies with other classmates. However, these benefits only go so far. The iPhone application text-Plus recently did a survey of its teen users. It found that 71 percent of teens aged thirteen to seventeen say they have more friends on Facebook than they care to communicate with. Teens seem to be obsessed with having a large quantity of friends, not quality friends. After a speaking event, one boy came up to me and explained, "I really wanted to be the first in my grade to have five hundred friends on Facebook. It doesn't matter if I'm actually friends with them."

The author T. S. Eliot said of television, "It is a medium of entertainment which permits millions of people to listen to the same joke at the same time, and yet remain lonesome." It is tempting to feel that watching the same YouTube videos, reading each other's statuses, and spending hours online together constitutes an intimate relationship. But, as I explain to teens, it is not about quantity time, it is about quality time. Teens always argue with me about this. Here is an example of a conversation I had with a teen about this topic:

Teen: No way, I do know my friends. I know what my friend had for breakfast. I saw her pictures from the time she spent with her sister this weekend right after she posted them, and I talk to her every night.

Me: Well, that's all great. But when was the last time you asked her how she was? And I don't just mean "what's up" or "how are ya," but really asked her *how* she was doing with her life, not just *what* she was doing in her life.

Teen: I guess . . . well, I just know. She is happy . . . I think.

The ease of digital friendship has actually lessened the value of our friends because we do not need to put as much effort into maintaining the relationships. As a member of the Facebook generation, I often trick myself into thinking that spending hours connecting with friends on chat means I actually have a connection with them. However, I quickly learned that the moment the friendship gets difficult—I ask for advice or want to talk about something deep—my "friend" either does not know how to respond or pulls back, knowing he or she has hundreds of easier online friendships to fall back on. These online friendships are not fulfilling and are very hard to rely on—after all, there is less and less face time in which to observe voice tone and body language. When talking to someone through technology, you have no idea if he or she is talking to four other people at the same time or watching TV or if you are even talking to the person you think you are! Unfortunately, when you doubt your friends, you don't feel like you have a stable system of support, and then you doubt yourself.

I liken online friends to cotton candy. At first, it looks exciting and filling—kids are sure that they will eat the huge stick of cotton candy and it will tide them over until dinner. Yet twenty minutes after eating the sugary puff, they complain that they want real food, their hands are sticky, and there is a fake chemical taste clinging to the back of their molars. Online friends also seem quite satisfying and exciting at first, but after a few monotonous conversations, we become lonely, hungry for real connection. The friendship might taste or feel fake, and inevitably a sticky situation arises when someone posts a bad picture, leaves a conversation early, or makes a joking comment that seems mean, not funny. Online friends, like cotton candy, are not nutritious—the soul becomes hungry for sustainable, dependable relationships. In the end, like the clique at Central High, these time-consuming but unfulfilling relationships make users feel lonesome, lost, and hurt.

An example of this is when I graduated from Emory and returned home to Los Angeles. I was sure I would be able to sustain my friendships from college online. I decided to forgo many of my childhood relationships in Los Angeles and instead relied on the digital connections I had with my college friends. Although I was constantly on chat, messaging with them, and looking at their pictures and videos, I felt lonely. I didn't have anyone to call on a bad day and I soon realized that even though I was constantly in "contact" with my friends from college, I no longer knew them and they no longer really knew me. This is exactly why young people crave closeness, celebrate friendiversaries, and stage friendterventions—because in reality we doubt the true depth of our friendships and fear being attacked or misunderstood at any moment.

Using the story above as an example, I was surprised at how quickly Chloe turned on Justine when she felt like she was being left out. As soon as the group started to fall apart, Chloe turned on her, viciously and cruelly. Despite being friends since elementary school, all members of the group had very little confidence in the loyalty of their friends. In addition, both Chloe and Justine were victims and bullies at the same time. This is very common when friendship loyalty is low—which, today, it often is.

Sharon's comment, as well as Justine and Chloe's behavior of hurting and getting

> "The other girls in my grade made a website about how fat I am. So then I was mean to them back. I hate them so it feels good, but it also feels awful."
>
> —Sharon, 15

hurt by each other as soon as the friendship got threatened, shows how confusing and fickle current relationships can be. Since teenagers get much of their identity and self-esteem from friendships, this can have enormous repercussions for their self-perception.

So how can parents help their children develop lasting, nourishing friendships? I spent much of this chapter talking about the intricate nature of friendships today because I think it is important for parents to have a background idea of how tenuous and complicated the social life of an adolescent can be. However, we can help teens positively link friendship and identity formation, while maintaining their independence and individuality. We can also encourage offline friendships to balance out the online ones. This in turn will encourage teens to build lasting, dependable relationships.

Since the majority of teen relationships are unpredictable and change daily, the first solution demonstrates how you can talk to your teens about their social life and, most important, how to keep the dialogue open. If adults can let their children know that they will always be there to talk without judgment, teens will be able to get help with their friendships and therefore feel more secure in their relationships. As a parent, think about those times you have tried to get your teen to open up, but there was some kind of block. Teens either do not respond at all, change the subject, or answer with vague statements and grunts. Parents report this happens most often in the car, during a meal, or right after school. Often a parent can sense that something is going on with their teen, but does not know how to broach the subject or, worse, the teen starts to open up and then a disagreement starts. Usually it sounds something like this:

Mother: How was school?
Daughter: Fine. Things suck with Casey right now.

Mom: Why, honey?

Daughter: She is just awful. She said she was going to host everyone before the dance and now she is backing out, so we have nowhere to go.

Mom: Well, maybe her parents are being strict.

Daughter: No, she already checked with them. She is just being a flake.

Mom: Well, I am sure she didn't mean it. Someone else will host it, I'm sure.

Daughter: No, Mom. God, you always stand up for her!

The daughter took her anger at Casey and began to direct it at her mom. Mom was trying to calm daughter down by reassuring her it would be fine and Casey didn't mean to offend anyone. This only made the daughter feel like her mom wasn't really listening to her and was choosing to support Casey instead of her. To avoid this kind of argument and to encourage teens to open up, there are three steps I use when working with young people.

1. Let them be extreme until they are empty. I often joke with my parent audiences that teens love to speak in super-superlatives. Everything is the "most," the "best," the "worst," and there is no end in sight. As adults, we fear this kind of black-and-white extreme. We prefer to be in the gray and never get too angry or too irritated or miss the pleasant middle ground. Teenagers like to put situations and relationships in black-and-white terms. It makes it easier to categorize their surroundings. It is important for adults to take the extremities with a grain of salt and let teens stay in the extremes before pulling them back into the gray. I have also found that upset teenagers are like a contaminated well. Once they start pulling up buckets of emotions, they go deeper and deeper until there is nothing left. Many parents hear this toxicity and they try to stop it. But this does not let teens get all of the toxic emotions out and therefore makes it impossible to heal and move forward. In the previous conversation, the mother first tries to come up with an explanation for the friend's behavior and then she attempts to lessen the damage. To the daughter, this feels like her mom is not listening to her and does not believe what she has to say. More important, the daughter is not ready to find solutions or feel better—yet. She is in dumping mode. She wants to vent all of the extreme feelings first. Then her mom can help refill the well with healthy, clean, drinkable water. We will get to how to refill the well in a moment, but let's look at how we can encourage kids to empty that well of emotions so they are ready to refill it with more healthy ideas and solutions. Here is how the mother could encourage her daughter to vent:

Mother: How was school?

Daughter: Fine. Things suck with Casey right now.

Mom: Why, honey?

Daughter: She is just awful. She said she was going to host everyone before the dance and now she is backing out, so we have nowhere to go.

Mom: When did this happen?

Daughter: Today. But we have been planning it for weeks.

Mom: What else happened with her?

Daughter: She is just selfish. I'm worried about her at the dance, too. She invited her old crush and I think there is going to be a lot of drama.

Mom: Oh, wow.

Daughter: I know. Ugh, it is frustrating.

Notice that the mother is not encouraging her daughter to be negative, nor is she passing any judgment or sharing opinions.

She is simply letting her daughter get everything out. This is also a way for the mother to get the whole story so when they enter solution mode, she will know all the background and will not have to dredge up the extremities again. Friendships can be incredibly complex and emotional for teens. This is why letting them stay in extremes and vent is extremely important. It helps them get everything out and gives you a peek into the issue so you can help them. Using protoconversation skills here is also extremely helpful. I take careful note of the facial expressions flashing on the teen's face. Sometimes you see more anger—this can be a tip that there has been an injustice in the friendship. Other times it is fear or jealousy. All of these clues can help you ask the right questions so your teenager keeps dumping and updating you on the situation.

2. Let them come to their own answers. It is important not to push opinions on a teen. There are two reasons for this. First, they often don't really "hear" your advice—even if it is very good. Second, whatever they are dealing with will most likely come up again in their life. Helping them come to their own answer, instead of telling them what to do, actually helps them own and learn from the experience if it happens again. If you feel they have reached "empty"—this can come in the form of a large sigh, a letting go of muscle tension in the shoulders or jaw, or a long period of calm silence—you can begin the solution period. I often will ask questions like "What do you think you should do?" or "If your friend came to you with this situation, what would you tell her or him?" These are great ways for them to think about their own answers. It also shows them that you respect their intelligence and want to give them space to think on their own—so they come back to you with issues later. If they are truly at a loss, you can also ask how they could help the situation a little bit. Typically teens are not yet in forgiveness mode, so they cannot envision solving it, but they can guess how to alleviate some of the stress. Let's look at how this would have gone in the previous conversation:

Daughter: I know. Ugh, it is frustrating. [Sigh]

Mom: What are you going to do to make it better?

Daughter: I'm not sure. . . .

Mom: Well, what do you think could help with this situation even a little bit?

Daughter: Maybe I should call her later and figure out without everyone else around what is going on. See if it is about the crush or her parents. I bet Jesse would host if we asked her. I should check in with both of them, I guess.

With these phrases the mom makes it clear to her daughter that she is not trying to belittle her opinions or impose her own thoughts.

3. Finish well. Once you have started to brainstorm solutions, you can also take the opportunity to ask if they want your advice. This is a way of asking them if they would like to hear what you have to say and it shows you respect their opinions. I usually try something like "How can I help you with this?" or "What can I do to support you?" or even "What do you need from me right now?" These also work if you were not able to get them from venting mode into solution mode. It shows them you are there for them and have ideas if they want to talk. If they did open up and you found a solution, it is essential to capitalize on this feeling of mutual satisfaction to keep the door open for future communication. For example, I might say, "I feel really honored you came and talked to me about this. Is there anything else I can do?" or

"Did I answer or help enough?" If there was a miscommunication or the conversation did not go smoothly at first, you can also say, "I want to make sure I respond the best way when this happens. What would you like me to do next time?" This also calls their attention to the fact that you want to respect them and communicate on their terms. Consequently, next time they are upset and you respond exactly the way they asked you to, they are much more likely to respond positively.

These three stages of conversation are a great way to get teens to talk about sticky situations with friends and relationships. The second way to help teens build and communicate about having healthy relationships with their peers is to use teachable friend moments. I think it is imperative to have conversations with your teens about empathy, standing up for your friends, and being loyal in your relationships, but it is also important to demonstrate this. You can do this a number of ways. I encourage parents to talk about and have positive relationships with their own adult friends.

> *"I know I'm supposed to have 'great' friends and be really loyal and all that. But my mom has no friends. So how important could they really be?"*
>
> —Jen, 14, Radical Parenting intern

This is a very positive way of demonstrating the importance of friendship and how a good relationship works—a balance of online and offline, building trust, and standing up for each other. Teens tell us that when they hear their parents talk about their best friends, or see their parents spending time with their friends either on adult nights out or on joint vacations, teens also feel happier. Parent friendships actually help your teens feel more secure. Our teens have also told us that seeing that their parents have other adults who enjoy spending time with them reminds the teens that their parents are actually "cool" in someone else's eyes.

Having strong friendships not only is a great way to demonstrate healthy relationships to your kids, but also makes you feel like you have other adults who support you. Moms tend to put their own needs last and then friend time falls by the wayside. However, when you put your own friendships and mental health last, this sends a powerful negative message to teens: friends are not important, and relationships do not need to be maintained. Putting more emphasis on building your support system shows your teens that everyone, at any age, needs to maintain healthy friendships.

> *"When we go on vacation with our family friends and I see my dad hanging out with the other guys and my mom goes out with the other moms I am always shocked at first. I forget that my parents are my parents, but also other people's friends, too! If other people like them, then maybe I should, too."*
>
> —Benjie, 16,
> Radical Parenting intern

I also like to flip the negative influence the media has on kids by using TV shows, movies, and even music as ways to teach teens about relationships. Watching TV and movies together with your kids can significantly decrease the negative effect.

This is because you are able to talk through some of the sticky scenarios or mean behavior on TV. Here are a few movies you can watch with teens and a few discussion questions you can also ask to address some common teen friendship dilemmas:

MEAN GIRLS

- How would you feel going into a new school?
- Has there ever been a new student at your school? Were people nice to that person? Were you?
- If you were mad at a friend, would you try to get back at him or her? Is there any justification for Lindsay Lohan's character when she is trying to get back at the mean girls?
- Who are the bullies and who are the victims?
- Are there cliques at your school? Do you encourage or discourage them?

10 THINGS I HATE ABOUT YOU

- Which character do you think you are most like?
- What do you think about the rumors that were spread?
- Do you think the teens should have been honest with their parents? Would that have helped or hurt?
- How would this movie be different if the characters had used Facebook and texting?

BRING IT ON

- Do you think this movie is based on real experiences? Could it be?
- Does the drama going on between the groups seem stressful or exciting?
- Do you feel bad for any of the characters?

Commercials and TV shows are also a great way to do this. You can watch or rent old episodes of *The Secret Life of the American Teenager* or *Gossip Girl*. Both of these shows portray the mean side of teenagers and technology, which we will discuss at length in the chapter on bullying.

Parents should explain these tactics to their teens, and then tell them to address this kind of behavior directly. Friendship pacts are another way parents can help teens address these kinds of bullies. I encourage all of my teens to form "pacts" with their friends. This means that they agree not only to stand up for each other in front of others, but also to call each other on these kinds of tactics because the friendship is more important. If there is a bully that your child is having to deal with, or a "mean girl," parents should ask for as many specifics as possible. This helps the teen think through the details and lets parents examine whether they need to get the school involved. If someone's mental or physical well-being is threatened, explain to your teen that reporting an incident can often be anonymous and it is not the same as "tattling." Friendship pacts can come in handy here, as teens can stick with close friends at school, on the bus, or while walking home. Overall, teens need to learn that acting with meanness will not be tolerated by others and will surely destroy fulfilling relationships in the long run. Additionally, they should not have friends who are unkind to them.

Modeling appropriate behavior, using teachable friend moments, and having open communication will help teens begin to build positive relationships. If friendships are still a problem, or your teen is feeling lonely or left out, encourage them to socialize with friends outside of school so they can maintain a strong social support system in another area of their lives.

Let's revisit the workshop I hosted with the clique from Central High School. After reading their letters, I quickly realized that a simple miscommunication had spiraled out of control, feeding on the insecurities and fears already percolating in the group. Everyone was on the extreme defensive after the first exercise and I knew I needed to shift the mood to make any progress. I quickly paired up the most controversial duos: Chloe and Justine, Monica and Suchin, DJ and Jim, and then Chris and Sally. Since Chris and Sally were the most neutral pair, I had them go first.

"I would like you to stand up and tell the room your partner's three best qualities." Disgust flashed across Chloe's face. Justine showed fear and DJ covered his face with his hand. *Good*, I thought, *a different kind of thought process*. I also thought it was a bit poignant that the group was more nervous about saying nice things about each other than saying mean things about each other. The first and second pair went easily. Monica and Suchin, whom I had designated as the queen bee's helpers, choked out some very nice praise, but constantly glanced at their leaders for forgiveness—or approval, I was not sure which. Finally it came to Chloe and Justine.

Justine started, "Um. I guess Chloe is pretty. And, uh, she is really good at making me laugh when I'm sad." She giggled a little and Chloe nodded. "Last, I guess she was a great best friend." With this, Justine wiped her cheek with her sleeve.

Chloe took in a deep breath. "Justine is amazing at lacrosse. Like, amazing. She has really cool fashion sense and I love borrowing her clothes." Both girls laughed at this. "And she is a great best friend, but I know we can't copy, so I will say she is a really good listener." I wanted this exercise to remind them of why they wanted to keep these friendships.

I addressed the group. "Thank you for being so open during that exercise. Okay, I read all of your letters and it put a lot into perspective. There were two things I learned from them. First, all of you said you want your friends back. So I know we can work this out today. The second thing I learned is that this whole war was based on a small issue. Oftentimes fights can be built on simple miscommunications, and I want to clear this up. Justine, may I ask you something?" She nodded yes. "Why did you take DJ and Suchin out without inviting the rest of the group?"

Justine looked down at her feet and I could see fear. This is how I knew it was not as simple as "I forgot." I went over to her seat. I said in a low voice, "Is it something personal? If you need to take a moment, you can."

She wiped her nose. "No, these are my friends and they should know. I should have told everyone at first, but it was such big news I couldn't bear telling everyone at once and I needed help from people who had been through it first. Um . . ." She looked up at the group. "I should have told you all first, but my parents are getting a divorce. I invited Suchin and DJ because their parents are also divorced. I wanted to get their advice on what I should do. I never thought it would offend everyone. I just wanted to talk to some people who had gone through it. Chloe, I was going to call you the next day, but then the website went up and . . ."

Chloe put a hand on her chest. "Why didn't you tell me? I mean, I can understand you wanting to talk to them. Oh, my God, I'm so sorry." She put her head in her hand. "I can't believe I started that website and the whole reason you went out with them was because of the divorce. Oh. My God." Chloe showed deep shame.

"It's okay," I said. "Do you see how there can be huge misunderstandings? More important, do you see how easily I solved it? I just asked her why they went out alone. That was it."

Jim, one of the quieter boys, laughed. "Yes, can we please just do that in the future?" Everyone relaxed a little and agreed.

"Now, if that were the only problem, we could move on. But I know that some other things happened because of this miscommunication. I'm not going to rat anyone out. But if you have something to apologize for, I would like you to do it now. This is all about empathy. Everyone did something they were not proud of in the past few weeks, but I'm also sure many of you felt wronged. Please stand up and ask for forgiveness from someone you wronged, the same way you wish another would apologize to you."

For the next twenty minutes or so, each member of the group stood up and admitted to their wrongdoings. Some sugarcoated or added excuses, in which case I had to interrupt and ask them if they would want their apology riddled with excuses and half-truths. Jim was the only person who had trouble coming up with something to apologize for. "Jim," I said, "I know you feel like you were a neutral party. But I have to ask you something. If someone made a website about how terrible they thought you were and one of your best friends saw the page on Facebook and didn't say anything, wouldn't you be upset with them?"

"Yeah, I guess I would."

"As far as your school is concerned, as far as you are all concerned, ignoring mean comments can be just as hurtful as making them."

Jim did make his apology and I decided to end with some preventative measures.

"Are we all okay? When we leave this room, are we good? All websites and comments will be deleted later?" Mutual head nods all around. "Okay, so we need to talk about how this does not happen again."

"Yes, please," said a puffy-faced Justine—she had been crying a lot during apologies.

They all waited for me to speak up. "Hey, it's not for me to come up with. You guys need to figure out how you are going to work *together* not to do this. I'm not going to be here when you guys are fighting."

They looked around at each other. DJ spoke up first. "Can we just make a deal, that Facebook and IM and texting are great for sharing and chatting, but fights get worked out in person? I think technology just added another layer to everything. I never knew if people were joking or who was sending things to who."

Chloe sat forward. "And no more anonymous sites."

I had everyone in the group state agreement. Justine added, "Also, can we just, like, keep an eye on each other? If someone posts something mean, I don't want to just stand around. I know I can promise that if anyone says anything mean about you guys, I will either tell you or ask them to take it down."

I nodded. "That's called a friendship pact, and if you guys want to protect each other online and at school, I think it is an awesome idea."

Jim added the last comment. "Also, I like Vanessa's idea of just asking what is wrong. I know it is way less exciting, but seriously. If someone does something that upsets someone, just ask them about it instead of assuming and reacting in the worst possible way."

"Sorry, sorry, sorry," Chloe said, putting her head on Justine's shoulder.

"It's okay," she said, patting her friend. "I should have called you to let you know. And then I should have cleared it up right away instead of reacting to your reaction and reacting to that and to that, you know."

I looked around and saw everyone was calm. "I think we are about done. Is there anything you guys need from me? Any way I can help?"

Suchin crinkled her eyes. "Are you going to tell the school a name?"

I shook my head. "No way. You guys were awesome today.

The only thing I will be telling them is how they will not be having any more problems with this group, right?"

THINGS TO REMEMBER

- As a teen's identity becomes more closely associated with the amount and quality of friends he or she has, social support structures become even more important and precarious.
- Many teens are becoming obsessed with having their friends categorize them, or hearing anonymous comments—both good and bad—about themselves.
- Teens desire to establish connections with their friends, but are having more trouble avoiding disappointments and betrayals in the shallow digital world.
- Having open communication and encouraging teens to find their own solutions to friendship problems are great ways to help youth with their relationships and make sure they can come to you if they are in need.
- Reverse the negative effects of media by discussing its bad social behavior examples with your teen and modeling healthy relationships.

Challenges You Can Do Right Now

Family Challenge: Discuss friendship.

1. Ask your teenagers to describe their friendships. Are they part of a clique? Do they have a best friend?
2. Talk about your history with friends, cliques, and groups.
3. How has texting and the Internet helped or harmed friendships?

Family Challenge: Implement friendship solutions.

1. Pick one or two movies or TV shows about modern-day friends and watch them with your teen. What issues come up?

2. Talk to them about your friendships. How do you support yourself with positive, healthy relationships with your friends?

CHAPTER 4

What Happens Online, Stays Online

"I found my wardrobe, my boyfriend, my job, and your Christmas gift all online."

—Jessica, 16, Radical Parenting intern

In today's age, technology pervades almost every area of a teen's life—school, friends, family, and their futures. I will review how this is both scary and beneficial. Parents can learn how to avoid the negative effects of technology and capitalize on the positive influences of the Internet.

Last year I was helping a school integrate technology into academic life—making safety rules as well as advising them on ways they could actually utilize technology in the classroom to engage kids. On my first day, I was sitting in the principal's office when a horrifying scream filled the corridor. We both leapt up out of our chairs and ran into the main office, where a teacher stood, arms crossed, looking down at a girl curled up in a ball on the floor.

"Is she hurt?" the principal asked. "What happened? Did someone call 911?"

I grabbed my cell phone from my pocket and looked furiously for an injury on the girl. *Is she bleeding? Did a stomach ulcer rupture?* My mind started to assume the worst.

The teacher tapped her toe and raised one eyebrow. "Lacy, would you like to tell the principal what's wrong?"

The girl on the floor rocked back and forth; muddy tears smudged her face and baby blue polo shirt. Her lower lip trembled and the inner corners of her eyebrows pulled up into the most pitiful expression of sadness I had seen in a long time. Her voice was shaky as she pointed up at the teacher. "She . . . she took my cell phone!" With that she buried her head in her arms and continued to weep, her small rib cage racked with loud, honking sobs.

Slowly I could see the anxiety drain from the principal's face and turn into scorn and exhaustion. "Thank you, Mrs. Saunders. I will take it from here." The teacher placed an iPhone wrapped in a flame-covered case in the principal's palm and stepped over the heap of teen girl on the floor.

Despite the girl's seeming safety, I was still alarmed by the whole episode. The principal, seeing my shock, waved his hands lightly. "Don't worry, it happens all the time." I nodded in disbelief. He bent down. "Lacy, when you are done, please come into my office. This is the third time this month. I need to call your parents." Upon hearing that comment, a muffled groan came from the tangle of arms, legs, and iPod earbud cords on the floor.

I followed the principal into his office, where he flipped through the student directory. He tossed the iPhone in his hands and chuckled while he examined the red and orange flames. "The teachers and I joke that the iPhone should be called iPrecious because it turns kids into little technology golems. This happens to us every day with different kids. Tearing kids away from their cell phones has become a part of my job description."

"Cell phones aren't even allowed at school, though. They must know you are going to take them away. And who could they want to be texting with—everyone else at school is under the cell phone ban, too, right?" I asked.

Lacy plopped down in the chair next to me and answered my

question for the principal. "*Everyone* has them anyway. I just can't believe I got caught. I need to know what my friends are saying. You don't even know what I'm missing right now." I saw genuine terror in her face—eyebrows high, eyes wide. This was no drama queen moment; she was really scared she might miss something.

The principal called the parents, who seemed just as exasperated as the school administration with the problem but agreed to come in at the end of the day and sign out Lacy and the phone; confiscated phones require parent signatures for release.

I hung around waiting for her parents and watched the interaction. Everyone in that room was miserable. Lacy had missed a day of socializing and was beginning to show shame and embarrassment at her own cell phone obsession. The parents were at their wits' end and could barely make hollow promises to the principal, saying things like "Yup, it won't happen again," and "Right, we know, we know. We are trying." And of course the principal felt this should be the last thing that needed attention in a school of more than three thousand students.

The mom put iPrecious into her purse and Lacy crossed her arms and sniffed. "Maybe if you let me get on Facebook and were more reasonable, I would follow your rules."

The mom glanced at me pleadingly. "Not this *again*." Both parents had attended one of my previous lectures on supporting kids through academic pressure and social stress.

The dad turned to me. "Vanessa, any advice for us or for Lacy? We cannot settle on compromises here."

I looked at the anguish in Lacy's face and the exhaustion in the parents'. "How about I come over later today? We can have a family meeting and talk about how to best approach the phone and Facebook."

Later that day I entered the Clarks' household. The fighting had already begun. "Lacy," the mom, Sandy, said, "I need you to be doing homework on your computer, not chatting. Are you actually doing homework?"

Lacy rolled her eyes. "Gawd, Mom, I am. I'm just asking Jessica about the homework. And later we will have an iChat study session!"

David, Lacy's dad, harrumphed in return. "I don't think that counts. It's just an excuse—"

"Okay," I interrupted before a fight started. "Sandy, can you tell me some of your concerns? And then I can talk to Lacy about hers."

"Ha! I wish Lacy had more concerns. Her grades are slipping because I think she is chatting instead of doing homework. We fight about the phone and the computer. . . ." She trailed off, rubbing her temples.

David, who was a bit calmer, but just as frustrated with the situation, explained in greater detail, "Safety is a concern. The amount of hours she spends online and texting instead of studying and sleep; who she is talking to; and, of course, Facebook is a huge discussion."

Lacy cut in, "Everyone is on it. Just because I'm not thirteen yet doesn't mean anything. My birthday is in summer. It's so not fair!"

I didn't want the discussion to escalate too much and put Lacy on the defensive. "Why don't Lacy and I go upstairs and we'll chat?"

I followed Lacy upstairs and she glared at me as we sat on her bed. "Go ahead," she said. "Tell me how bad technology is, like everyone else."

I put my hands up in a gesture of innocence. "Are you kidding me? I check my iPhone more than anyone. I thought we would start by you showing me your favorite YouTube videos."

Her eyes widened in surprised delight. "Really? Okay!" We scrolled through a few videos of kittens playing with toys and watched one of the hottest new music videos, and I showed her some of my favorite prank videos. "I love YouTube," she gushed.

"Me too, it totally sucks me in and I spend hours watching videos."

"I know. I hear Facebook is the same way, but my parents suck. If they don't let me get a Facebook page I'm just going to set one up on my own. I don't care what they say."

I nodded. "Have you talked to them about their concerns?"

Her chin jutted out in anger and her eyebrows furrowed. "Everything is a concern. I don't even listen anymore. I'm going to text as much as I want and I swear I'm going to go behind their backs and get on Facebook if they don't start listening."

Technology, like rock music, television, and antiwar rallies of the previous generations, is the new cause of the perpetual widening gap between parents and teens. In the Clark household, the Internet, Facebook, iChat, and texting rolled into one big, continuous argument where both sides felt they were being misunderstood. Sandy and David were grappling with technology's ease of use for their daughter and the growing dangers of being online. Not to mention how much technology had affected their daughter's home behavior, school time, social life, and health. Along with both parents, I was also concerned about Lacy's lack of sleep, her studying habits on the computer, her lack of face time with friends, and her nonexistent respect for school and house rules. On the other hand, Lacy was feeling misunderstood, left out, and anxious about her friendships and parents.

Although the players might be different, some form of these arguments is happening in households all across the globe. For some kids, gaming, virtual worlds, and Xbox tournaments are their ultimate escape. In other families texting and cell-phone Internet browsing are huge issues. Ultimately, all teens and parents are dealing with privacy issues, cyberbullying, and making rules in an area that never existed before.

Danah Boyd and Eszter Hargittai examined Internet use for eighteen- and nineteen-year-olds and found that they spent an average of 17 hours per week online in 2009. In just one year, from 2009 to 2010, average Internet use went up 2.3 more hours per week!

Many parents wonder what teens could possibly be doing on-line for so many hours when they also have to go to school, eat, and do homework and extracurricular activities. According to the Norton Online Family Report from the Symantec Corporation, maker of the popular Norton security software, kids' top searches in 2009 were as follows:

	Boys	Girls
1	YouTube	YouTube
2	Google	Google
3	Facebook	Facebook
4	Sex	Taylor Swift
5	Porn	Sex

YouTube, Facebook, and Google, together with chatting programs such as iChat, AOL Instant Messenger, and Skype, are by far the most-used sites on the Internet for teens. In this way, technology provides a number of outlets for teens and continues to draw them into higher and more serious usage. Lacy loved using YouTube to entertain herself and share content with her friends. Many parents also found it surprising that both boys and girls were searching inappropriate terms like "sex" and "porn." Before we look at the negative effects of increased media use and exposure, let's examine some of the positive reasons youth use technology.

First, teens love technology because it allows them to try new things. The Internet provides a new experimental area for young people.

> *"I don't want to do bad things online. Most parents think we are trying to go on the Internet to break rules. They don't realize how many cool things you can do. I can play games and actually donate real money to my favorite causes on some websites. On one, FreeRice.com, I donate rice to poor people in Africa by learning vocabulary. My parents were probably never able to do anything close to that in high school!"*
>
> —Channing, 14

Although we do address some of the negative effects of technology below, using it to try new things is not all bad. I have worked with teens who made YouTube videos for their favorite community service cause and went on to raise thousands of dollars from strangers that they never would have been able to reach had it not been for the Internet. Websites such as Score.org and TeenInk.com encourage teens to try new experiences like working with nonprofits, writing poetry, and starting their own businesses. The Internet can give teens opportunities and practice in areas they never dreamed possible. Take for example an experience I had with a seventeen-year-old named Michelle. I was speaking at a rural school in Missouri about Internet safety. Actually, I refuse to call my technology talks to students "Internet Safety," and prefer instead to call them "Internet Savvy," as I review both the good and the bad parts of technology. After my talk, a tall female student walked up to the podium.

"Thanks for that," she said.

I looked up from my notes, expecting to meet one of the many similar-looking girls I had seen milling around the halls all morning—average skin tone, medium-length hair, some kind of brightly colored sweater. Yet when I glanced up, I gulped—loudly. "Tha—ahhnk you?" I cleared my throat. "Thank you, I mean."

She shrugged her leather-clad shoulder. "Usually people come here and talk about how awful and unsafe the Internet is, but for me, it saved my life."

The girl in front of me had jet-black dreadlocks to her hips, more piercings than I could count, and dark black eye makeup caked over painted-white skin and large spiked boots. A couple of the students who had been waiting to talk to me shuffled off upon seeing her. I reminded myself to have no expectations and smiled. "Wow, it saved your life? What do you mean? And what's your name, by the way?" I put out my hand.

She shook it gently. "I'm Michelle, and I'm a Goth. I always knew I was different. But I live here." She gestured around the large auditorium and I looked at all of the students who—though I was sure they were unique in their own ways—looked strikingly similar. "Everyone here is *the same*. It used to drive me crazy. I don't do drugs or have sex. I'm a good girl, I go to church, but I really like to dress this way. I like Goth makeup and music. But it doesn't matter that I don't do anything bad, because when I dress like this, people think I'm bad."

"I can't imagine what that would be like. How did the Internet help, exactly?"

"When I was thirteen I went on MySpace. It was the first time I realized not everyone was from Missouri." She laughed. "You know what I mean. I knew that before. But I found people who were like me. People who loved Goth makeup and heavy metal music and they didn't do drugs or anything. I finally started to feel like less of a freak. I felt like I was normal— different than people here, but normal somewhere."

I had never thought about this aspect of identity searching before. "So, it actually gave you a community and self-esteem about who you are?"

She flashed me teeth that matched her white skin. "Self-esteem, don't even get me started. Before the Internet, to be honest, I was thinking about killing myself. I hated who I was and was tired of pretending. I met a girl in a Goth chat forum who convinced me not to take the pills I found in my dad's medicine cabinet." She looked down at her spiked boots. "I might not be here now if it wasn't for the Internet."

I often tell this story when I speak, not only to demonstrate the importance of accepting people for their differences, but also to address the fact that technology provides new access to both good and bad experiences.

There are also many technological programs that give teens access to new opportunities and information. Teens who live in rural areas with rare diseases or psychological problems are having digital doctor visits with therapists or specialists in faraway cities when they cannot afford to travel. A company called the Birds and Bees Text Line, started in North Carolina, delivers sex education to teens via text messaging. They send questions to teens, like "If you have sex underwater do you need a condom?" Teens can also send in their questions, like "Why do guys think it's cool to sleep with a girl and tell their friends?" and get a response in twenty-four hours or less. This is a new kind of sex education that delivers information on staying safe that kids might not get elsewhere and offers them an anonymous way to ask questions they are worried about.

The second major reason youth are attracted to technology is that it allows them to connect with others. In the story above, Lacy wanted to be on Facebook because it was a way to talk with friends. The reason she was so distraught—albeit overly so—on the floor at school was because she could not stand missing out on the opportunity to connect with her friends via text. Other teens constantly list the virtues of texting, Facebook, Club Penguin, and other online social areas.

I love how Chelsea feels bad for her parents' generation because, poor them, they could only talk to one person at a time! Teenagers also love that technology allows them, as Sam points out, not only to check in, but also to have new and more frequent ways to just "hang out." Lacy argues this point with her parents in the previous story. Her lack of Facebook access literally meant less hanging-out time. For many parents, they could swap out "Facebook" for any website their child is begging to use because "everyone is on it," and you would have the same story and lines as Lacy used with her parents.

> "It must have been so hard for our parents! I mean they could really only talk at school or if they had to they could talk on the phone—but that was only to one person at a time. I couldn't imagine that! I love being able to check in with my friends and get updated."
>
> —Chelsea, 16,
> Radical Parenting intern

Even parents recognize connecting and hanging out as major incentives for kids to get online earlier and earlier.

I showed an example of toddler video playdates in one of my presentations, and at the end a man stood up and told a story about how he uses technology to connect with his kids. He explained that he travels for work almost constantly and he realized

> "Of course I love technology to be with my friends. But it's not all about knowing what they are doing, it's also like a grown-up play date. You know, we like to hang out—we watch videos together, do our homework on video chat. Sometimes I bring my computer in while I'm making a snack so I can chat with my friend. I get to hang out with them through technology, too."
>
> —Sam, 12, Radical Parenting intern

that he was quickly losing his relationship with his oldest son. Every time he went out of town and came back, it was like starting all over again to get his son to open up—which is a challenge for any parent, let alone one who is always traveling. When he called home all he would get was short, terse responses. The dad knew he had to do something. So, he told the group, he began to learn how to play World of Warcraft. He knew his son loved the game and as long as he had a computer and Internet connection, which he always had in his hotel rooms, he would be able to play with his son from anywhere in the world. His son was shocked when his dad proposed that they both get headsets and log in to play together remotely. This started their tradition where, after the son's school day, whether it was morning or night where the father was, the two would conquer worlds together. Slowly, he said, they built a special kind of communication. During the slow parts of the game, the son would open up about school, grades, and even girls. The man finished this amazing story by saying that this kind of connection never would have been possible without technology.

Another benefit of connecting through technology is that it

"My daughter is two and a half years old. She has a cousin the same age who lives halfway across the country. We used to have to wait until major holidays for them to see each other until we realized the Internet could help. We set up a Skype session with cameras and now my daughter and her cousin have video play dates every Wednesday. My sister and I cook and chat in the background and the girls play dolls, blocks, and make-believe through the camera. Sometimes she even swipes her fingers across the screen because she thinks it's like my iPhone screen. Talk about a digital generation!"

—Mother of a two-year-old

gives shy kids a chance. Many teenagers have told me that social networks have allowed them to talk to people—crushes or the "cool" people—that they never would have had the opportunity to connect with otherwise because they were so intimidated by them. Chatting online or via text allows them to say things they feel they could never say in person. For example, it has become quite popular to ask your date to the prom on YouTube. I love watching the videos of nervous, smiling teenagers popping the prom question to their would-be dates and then sending them the video or posting it on their profile pages.

This is a wonderful side to technology. The opportunities it affords teens allow them to connect with each other and new experiences in different ways. But what about the negative side of all this connecting and access? Now that we know why teens use technology, let's look at some of the negative results of grow-ing up digital before we begin to explore the tips and solutions.

· · · · · · · ·

Despite the positive effects of the Internet, as teens search out these benefits, they also get stung by the negative aftereffects. First, access to new information, new people, and new opportu-nities can also expose youth to issues they are not ready for, such as at the many websites about sexuality, drugs, violence, and rac-ism. As the list of search terms we saw from the Norton Online Family Report showed, "sex" and "porn" rank in the top five for teens.

> *"I sometimes use the Internet to do things I'm not supposed to do. Like I look at porn or talk to strangers. I know it's bad, but Google makes it easy."*
>
> —16-year-old male

Technology makes it easy for teens to learn about risky be-havior and then engage in it with strangers or friends. More-over, the Internet has a tendency to make scary, dangerous things seem normal to teenagers. Take for example a female cli-ent I was working with. Kendra was an incredibly anxious teen-ager before we started working together. Her mother had originally called me because her stress levels about school, friends, and her future were through the roof. Our first few sessions went well and we began to work on better planning for her homework so she had more time for relaxation and sleep. On our third session I had planned to tackle the time-suck that inevitably happens when kids spend time online. I wanted her to balance online chatting, watching funny videos, and browsing the Web—all good in moderation—with face-to-face time with friends and family and being active. I knew this would help her combat the feelings of stress and depression.

"Hey, will you load up Internet Explorer for me? I want to make some bookmarks of good sites and we can make a time log."

"Okay," she said, pulling up the window and rolling her desk chair to the side so I could use the keyboard.

"Let's see." I opened her bookmarks folder—a place where users can save their most frequently visited websites for quick access—and my heart stopped. Quickly, I skimmed some of Kendra's bookmarks. I recognized them immediately. If you did not have previous knowledge of these websites, you would have no idea what names like "Butterfly Girls" and "Go Ana" mean. Fortunately I had been alerted to this small teen niche by one of my interns a few months before. "Hey, Kendra? Let's go through your bookmarks and sort them, okay?" I realized she clearly did not recognize I knew what these websites meant, and I did not want to make her feel attacked if I jumped right on her about them.

"No problem." She rolled over and started clicking on different icons. "That's my school's website. That's a game I sometimes play with my friends. Um . . ." She paused over the three or four websites I had immediately flagged. "Those are some other websites I sometimes go to." She swallowed deeply—she was lying, and her eyebrows raised together: fear. I was a little glad that she was not angry I was looking at her private websites. I have found that sometimes, when you accidentally stumble into something private, teens can get very angry, protective, and defensive. Fear, on the other hand, can be gently dealt with.

"Hey, isn't that site about eating and stuff?" I asked casually.

She looked at me questioningly, unsure of how to respond. "Kinda, yeah."

I rolled back from the computer, feeling the tension in the room rise. "Look, Kendra, I know you have some things that are private and that's cool. I'm here to help you feel better and have less stress, not make you feel bad or embarrassed or get you in trouble. All I know is that you are unhappy right now. If those websites are a part of that unhappiness, then let's talk about it. If not, I can respect that, but I don't want to assume anything that's wrong."

"Um . . ." She touched her forehead, a sign of embarrassment. "You know what they are, don't you?"

"Yes, I do," I said simply. I was not going to pretend I did not know that the websites she had bookmarked are social networks that encourage eating disorders. Members come together and list the best ways to purge, starve yourself, and overexercise. Users give each other encouragement and often celebrate extreme thinness by posting pictures of emaciated models and themselves.

She began to shake. "I can't help it. I thought was sick and ugly, but the people on there make my . . . my eating stuff seem kinda cool and normal. It makes me feel normal."

It took many hours to get Kendra to the point where she was willing to tell her parents and enter into a clinic. The hardest part for me was making her understand that just because thousands of girls on these websites are anorexic and bulimic and have somehow embraced their disease, it does not mean that it's normal or healthy. Although this is an extreme example, I think it shows how the access and information that technology provides can be healthy, but it can also make dangerous things seem attractive and normal.

"Sexting" is another huge issue with technology. Sexting is when someone sends a sexually suggestive comment, video, or photo through technology. It happens most often through texting, hence the name. According to a survey by Cox Communications in 2009, 9 percent of teens between the ages of thirteen and nineteen had sent sexually suggestive pictures via text or e-mail, 3 percent had forwarded one, and 17 percent had received one. Most teens, if asked, would never dream of getting undressed in front of their English classroom, yet when they think of taking a seminude picture of themselves in the privacy of their bedroom with their personal cell phone, there is less reservation. It is difficult for teens to make the connection that a sext might end up in the wrong hands or be seen by their whole English class.

> *"I just sent the picture of me in my underwear to my boyfriend. I didn't realize he could forward it with just a click of a button. I didn't think it was any different from when we hooked up in person or that it would last forever."*
>
> —Justine, 17

Technology can provide a method to experiment and give a semblance of privacy to teens who are already experimenting with their sexuality and attractiveness.

The second result the proliferation of technology has had on youth is that the importance they place on fame and recognition has increased greatly. One of the application questions for our internships is "What is the number one thing you want for yourself in the future?" Surprisingly, over the past three years, "fame" has slowly crept up the list of the most popular answers. YouTube, Facebook, Twitter, and a number of other sites have made fame a very real and palpable desire. We have seen this with the girls who beat up a fellow classmate to get a video with a million views, or the group of teens that set up a fake kidnapping in 2010 to get hits on their YouTube channel. Kids and teenagers often feel that they are only one video or one post away from a million people seeing them—that is a lot of power to give an adolescent. Unfortunately, this has made them hyperaware of their own importance.

> "I have forwarded some pictures. Just to my close guy friends. It feels like it is kept private, but then one of my friends' phones got confiscated by a teacher and he saw the picture I forwarded. I ended up getting into trouble."
>
> —Craig, 14

> "I took the dare from my friends to jump off the roof because the video would have looked really great in my news feed."
>
> —Teen male

We have seen the rise of "ego surfing," or typing in one's own name or screen name in a search engine to see how many results appear. Laptops, iPods, and smartphones have made a teen's online reputation just as important as his or her offline one.

Many youth have developed a kind of obsession with being constantly plugged into their technology. They fear missing out or seeming uncool.

> *"Technology has taken over the world. I can't go a day without Internet or phone. I think that is bad, but can't help myself. I tried to take a day off, but had to go to the library to get a fix."*
>
> —Victoria, 15, Radical Parenting intern

Internet addiction has become a very real issue as technology invades many areas of our lives. In a study done by Lawrence T. Lam, the more addicted to the Internet his teen subjects were, the higher their rate of depression. The Internet does help us stay connected and build relationships. But it also makes it even harder for relationships to be authentic so that teens can separate their online and offline identity, and this causes feelings of depression. I have sat with teens while they sent out an update or piece of gossip, and watched the painful, tense silence as they waited for someone to respond or comment on it. I like to call this "pingxiety"—the sense of dread, hope, and desire that teens feel while waiting for the "ping" of an important text response or the notification of an update via e-mail or IM.

One of our seventeen-year-old interns, Rachel, wrote an article called "Life Without Facebook." I think an excerpt of her experience best describes the type of addiction and attraction technology has for teens:

All parents wonder, "What's so special about Facebook? Why must teens go on it SEVERAL times a day?" We need to feel connected. It's becoming an instantaneous world, where everything can happen. You can speak to your pen pal across the world, share pictures with your family in different countries, even break up with your boyfriend in a click. You can "buy your friends" or cut old friends out of your life with just a click. The big reason is plain and simple: this new generation hates to wait.

I was grounded from the computer because I kept sneaking on my Facebook while doing my homework. That meant no Facebook, no instant messaging, no cell phone. After just the first 8 hours of grounding, I felt like an alcoholic that hasn't gotten his habitual drink. I couldn't update my status; how would anyone know what I was doing? I couldn't reply to my wall posts or retaliate on my bidding wars over my friends. I couldn't even visit my friend's Facebook group he made for help in math class. I felt cut off from the world. I get 15 notifications MINIMUM each day. How was I supposed to reply back? Let me tell you, that was the longest week I have ever had.

Rachel's experience is common. Even for teenagers who are slow adopters, they often eventually get sucked into the online world. How do we help kids enjoy the positive effects of technology while preventing the negative ones? Many parents' first instinct is to take the technology away. I hear parents tell me, "I don't know how to deal with the dangers of the Internet and cell phones, so I'm not going to give them a phone or let them online." Unfortunately, the Internet is the new playground. Not allowing your child to use modern technology is like not letting them onto the playground just in case they get bullied or fall off the monkey bars. We have to teach them how to enter the playground and make the right choices, stand up for themselves, and ask for help when needed.

The first way parents can begin to guard against Internet addiction and foster safe technology use is to embrace rules and systems. I cannot emphasize enough the importance of clear rules and systems in a household. Daniel Ariely, a professor at the Massachusetts Institute of Technology, did a study with three of his undergraduate classes to test the importance of unbending directives. For the study, he gave three of his classes different assignment schedules. In the first class, students had three papers to do over the course of twelve weeks. The students had to set their own deadlines—they could be evenly spaced out or all due the very last day of class. The second class also had three papers, but they had no deadlines and could turn in their papers anytime before the last day of class. The last class was more traditional. Ariely set their deadlines, evenly spaced out: one the fourth week, one the eighth week, and one the twelfth week. He also made sure all the students knew that if they turned in their papers early, there would be no reward and they would not be read early.

This is to very similar to the dilemma that parents have. Should they make strict rules, have their kids set their own rules, or have no rules? Once all of the papers were graded blindly, which class do you think had the highest quality of papers? The class with the strict rules, set by Ariely, did by far the best on their papers; next came the class that got to set their own deadlines; and the no-deadline class's papers were the worst. What does this teach us about teenage and human behavior? Clear deadlines and rules produce the best results.

Therefore, when thinking about technology use, media, and cell phones in the home, the most important tip is to have clear boundaries ahead of time. Researchers from a study published in

Pediatrics also found that parental control programs that allow parents to set limits do reduce the amount of time youth spend in front of screens. In the end of this chapter, we have a number of ideas to help you think about what clear limits you can set in your own household. I also recommend, in addition to setting rules about screen time, listing forbidden websites and online time budgets. Teens often completely lose track of time when they are chatting online or texting with friends. Setting up time logs can help all family members realize how much time they are actually spending with technology when they could be sleeping, eating, or interacting in real time with other people.

The second important way parents can take advantage of some of the Internet's benefits and avoid the pitfalls is to show children how to use it well. Not surprisingly, a study released in 2010 proved that parents' Internet use and behavior significantly predict the Internet usage of the children in the home. Take this story from one of our interns:

> *"My mom will literally turn to me from her cell phone and tell me to stop texting. That is so hypocritical! How can she expect me to have a conversation without looking down at my phone when she gives me that command while she herself is texting?"*
>
> —Jenny, 17, Radical Parenting intern

Jenny's point is important: you should model the behavior you would like your children to use. In most households, I suggest setting up "electronics-free" time periods—4:00 p.m. to 8:00 p.m. for homework, and the hour before bed, for example. Also set up electronics-free zones. The kitchen or dining room table is a great place to keep free of all such devices. I recommended to Jenny that she set up a basket in front of the kitchen table where both she and her mom would drop their cell phones before mealtimes. This not only helps family members use technology less, but also demonstrates to kids that we all have to sacrifice to maintain our real-life connections.

Being a good model for our children applies both to the amount of technology we use and to how we use it. A great way to do this is to show your kids that the same rules you would follow in real life, you also follow online. Many kids forget that their e-mails and their favorite websites and social networks can be quite public and that the same manners, laws, and etiquette—or "netiquette"—apply. Shockingly, 50 percent of teens actually think they act safer online than their parents do. The Norton Online Family Report surveyed 2,800 kids and more than 7,000 adults in fourteen countries about their online lives and experiences. It found that nearly half of the kids aged eight to seventeen "think they are more careful online than their parents, with 20 percent saying their parents have 'no idea' what they are doing online." This startling fact has two important takeaways. First, teens are grossly overconfident in their own safety online. Second, youth fear that their parents—the ones who should be teaching them Internet safety—are even less safe than they are! We can correct this by teaching them and modeling my five Cybercitizen Rules for both teens and parents to follow online:

1. **Do not steal.**
   Teens should always pay for their music and movies instead of downloading illegally.

2. **Always dress like you would at school.**
   Teens should never post naked or inappropriate pictures or videos of themselves online. I often explain to teens that you never know if a teacher or friend's parent is going to be looking at your pictures.

3. **Treat others the way you would like to be treated.**
   Teens should not bully or attack others through IM, on-line chat forums, virtual bulletin boards, or e-mails.

4. **Do not destroy public or private property.**
   Graffiti is the same online as it is in real life. Teens should never put graffiti on wiki pages, deface or hack into another person's website, or write inappropriate comments in online forums.

5. **Do not talk to strangers.**
   Never talk to random people in social networks, IM, online forums, or virtual worlds.

Encourage your teens to follow these rules *along* with you, not *because* of you. When they hear you talking about following these and then see you actually implementing them, they are more inclined to model their behavior after yours.

The last major solution I implement with parents regarding technology is getting real about privacy. I used to think that teenagers were pretty clear on what should be shared online, such as nonharmful updates or first names, and what shouldn't be, such as financial information or contact information. Yet technology has brought a number of new issues into the privacy debate—topics I never dreamed could be shared online. I believe in trying to communicate with most of my interns and inter-viewees via social network because I have found that they check these messages and status updates more often than e-mail or voice mail. I also pride myself in knowing about the latest and most interesting teen destination sites. It was these two factors that led me into the uncomfortable trap that three of my teen girls unintentionally set for me.

It was a regular Tuesday morning when I got a ping on my Facebook chat saying Lizzy wanted to chat.

> **Vanessa Van Petten:** hey
> **Lizzy G:** hiya you have to join our new network
> **Vanessa Van Petten:** lol no how ru?
> **Lizzy G:** oops ya how ru but this is the coolest site!
> **Vanessa Van Petten:** ok whats the link?

From there, I clicked on a seemingly normal teen girl website link and was taken to a sign-up page. I scanned the FAQ and tried to surmise from the smiling women on the page what the site was all about—and who I would be giving my e-mail to. A few lines into the "About" page, I gasped. *It can't be*, I thought to myself. I clicked back over to my Facebook chat.

> **Vanessa Van Petten:** lizzy whats the site all about?
> **Lizzy G:** its a social network for us 2 share our periods 2gether!!!!!!!!!!!!!!! <3

I wasn't sure if the heart and abundance of exclamation points were supposed to cover up for the fact that this was a freaking website for girls to track their periods together! My first thought was: ew. My second thought was: but why? And this is what I asked her—but in teen language.

> **Vanessa Van Petten:** but y?

It took a few painful moments, in which I hoped she was re-evaluating her own membership—perhaps she hadn't already thought about this question when programming in her ovulation cycle?

> **Lizzie G:** uhh like y not?
> **Vanessa Van Petten:** bc it's private and I don't really want 2 know ur period cycle?
> **Lizzie G:** ouch!   = (=—(=-(

Upon seeing the crying emoticons, I was beginning to have a bit of an existential crisis. *Am I being too harsh? Does not wanting to know this mean I'm not a good boss/interviewer?* My inner questions got weirder and weirder until her ping interrupted my thoughts.

> **Lizzie G:** Like its so gr8 we get to see if we are period twin-sies and I get pings when you are PMSing so I know not 2b l8 with my intern assignments and then i can send u a virtual hug and everything!

And so the conversation went for twenty minutes, until the amount of sad and crying emoticons she kept sending over pressured me into creating a preliminary profile. I couldn't help but think that I was peer-pressured into sharing my menstrual cycle—like a weird form of mensebullying. This interaction made me realize that the teen and adult views of privacy are vastly different.

Alessandro Acquisti and Ralph Gross did a study in 2006 that looked at what students thought they were sharing on their Facebook profiles versus what they were actually sharing. Only three-quarters of the Facebook users knew how open their profiles were and exactly what they were sharing. This was even before Facebook settings became as complicated as they are now! Not only do teens have a much more lax version of what is private, but they greatly underestimate how public their information is.

So how do we teach privacy to our children and monitor them? There are two approaches to win the privacy and safety battle online. The first set of techniques helps parents monitor their kids, while the second solution helps teach kids Internet resiliency, or the ability to make their own safe decisions online that will last even when parents are not around to supervise. There are a number of tools parents can use to monitor children's Internet use. Let's first review these tools and then talk about the consequences of using them. The first is *e-mail monitoring*. A number of e-mail programs can be set up to either send copies of messages to parents or withhold ones the program has flagged for inappropriateness. The second is *safe Web browsing*. Internet browsers can bring up a number of websites that are inappropriate for kids. There are a range of both free and expensive programs that allow parents to see and/or block what terms their kids might be searching. Finally, parents can use *parental controls*. Numerous different software programs can monitor, block, and alert parents to everything their teens are doing on their computers, cell phones, and gaming systems.

These tools can be helpful for younger teens or older repeat offenders of house technology rules. Yet it is important to consider the lack of trust that can be built on the child's side when these tools are used. I find that the threat of these tools works almost as well as the tools themselves. It can sound something like this:

> "Listen, honey, I trust you and know that you understand and follow the house rules. You know, no above-PG-13 websites, no inappropriate chatting or talking with strangers. But I have been reading recently about

some new parental control software and safe Web browsing tools. I am thinking of installing some, just to be safe. I want to let you know I might be putting those on the computers. I don't think you have anything to worry about or to hide, just wanted to let you know so you don't feel I'm going behind your back."

This is a great way of being transparent with them about the possibility of using some of the Internet safety tools, and it gives you a chance to gauge their reaction. Using your protoconversation skills, you can see if they are shocked, neutral, happy, scared, or even angry at your news. This can also help you decide whether you need to be worried about Internet safety and if tools would be a good idea. For example, if they seem scared, defensive, and worried when you tell them you might be putting parental controls on the computer, there is probably something they are hiding.

Monitoring is the first part of encouraging privacy and safety; the second technique helps them make their own smart decisions even if you are not around. I usually teach teens what I call the Teacher Check. In the heat of an angry, passionate, or bored moment, teens, as well as some adults, need to have a self-check system. Oftentimes, youth are unsure of what they should and should not be posting. Before posting or writing anything online, I have kids ask themselves this question: "Would I want my math teacher to see this?" This is a great gauge for them. If they can get in the habit of asking themselves this question every time, it will encourage them to make smart decisions, take pause before acting, and eventually learn to follow this principle naturally. Teens have told us that this technique is a very clear way to avoid posting potentially harmful information, pictures, or videos.

Now let's see how setting up technology rules and systems, being a good cybercitizen role model, and using privacy techniques can help the Clark family from earlier in this chapter. We left Lacy talking to me about her grappling with the decision to create a secret Facebook account behind her parents' back because of all the fighting around technology.

"Okay, let's play that out. What would happen if you created that fake account?"

She crossed her arms defiantly. "I would be able to actually talk to all of my friends and see their updates and not be so left out at school."

"Uh-huh, but how would you check it?" I knew that her parents monitored her computer and she hated it. But that meant they kept an eye out for Facebook.

She thought for a moment. "I guess I would have to do it at Hannah's house."

"Right, so not only would you have to sneak around and hope your parents don't find you on Facebook on their own, but you would also have to sneak around even to get on Facebook to check it."

The reality of her idea hit her. "Ugh, and then I would still be missing stuff because I couldn't check every few hours because I can't always be at Hannah's." She buried her head in her hands. "Another thing that I would have to check constantly."

"What do you mean?"

She looked up at me and suddenly looked very tired, as if the fight was draining out of her. "I like texting and everything, but sometimes it, like, never turns off. Sometimes I think Crystal is lucky."

"Who is Crystal?" I asked.

"She is in my group. Her parents won't let her get a phone, so she doesn't text or anything. Sometimes she misses out on gossip. But we talk about it all the next day anyway. And no one really gossips about her because she can't reply. Plus, she has never sent anything mean because she can't. I feel like I *have* to because I can't just be silent when someone sends a text, even if it is a little mean."

I totally get this. "Lacy, I also envy Crystal. See this?" I held up my iPhone. "I lose more sleep over this than anything else. When a friend texts me in the middle of the night, I feel like I have to respond to be a good friend."

"I know," she said, her eyes wide. "It is, like, peer pressure to text."

That was exactly the connection I needed her to make. "Have you ever thought that's what it's like on Facebook, too?"

She looked at me blankly. "But I thought it's all good stuff. Funny videos, photos, chatting, and even doing homework."

I find many teens idealize social networks and the Internet before they get it, not thinking about some of the bad that comes along with the good. Now that Lacy had made the connection between addicting texting and peer pressure, I knew I could make it for her with Facebook. As in life, they need to see both sides. "Yes, Facebook is great for those reasons—lots of time with friends, and you get to share cool links, videos, and sites. I also like that you can join causes." I looked around at the posters on her walls. "I'm sure you would be able to join some of the 'save the rain forest' groups." She nodded emphatically. "But I'm smothered by my Facebook. I feel like I have to check it all the time. Before Facebook if someone did something I didn't like or didn't want to talk about, I could say I didn't know about it. Now people say, 'I know you saw it on Facebook.' And I'm pressured to check it all the time."

"I so don't want that," Lacy said.

"Listen, that will be a huge plus for your parents. I'm sure we can work out some other compromises with them if you offer to wait until you are thirteen for a Facebook account."

"Okay, I can do that," Lacy said, and we both went back downstairs.

David and Sandy sat with us around the dining room table. Dinner was simmering in the background and it seemed everyone had calmed down a bit. I turned to Lacy. "Lacy, please tell your parents what we discussed."

Lacy took a deep breath. "We talked about it and I'm willing to wait for Facebook. I don't want to have another thing to check. But I really would like some more freedom in some of the other areas if that's okay."

Sandy sighed with relief and put her hand on her chest. "That's the best news we've heard. We can absolutely work with that."

David nodded in agreement. "What other rules do we need to discuss?"

Lacy traced a crack in the wood table. "I really do use chat and the Internet for homework and for approved games. Sometimes when you guys just come in and tell me to get off the computer, I feel like I can't do homework or just relax."

I interjected before Sandy and David could respond; I could see them tensing again. "Look, this is a trust-building experience. We need to get very clear on the rules and limits, and then you have to give Lacy a chance to follow them. Right now it is a day-by-day battle, so Lacy does not have the chance to prove to you that she can use the Internet wisely, and you guys cannot see the positive effects while avoiding the negative ones."

"That makes sense," David said. We spent the next hour drawing up a set of rules everyone agreed upon. First, a set of free parental controls would be put on Lacy's computer so she could prove she was only on approved sites and games. She also had no problem putting on the inappropriate site blocker, as a gesture to her parents that she really was not doing anything "bad." This would give Lacy freedom to go to her different sites without her parents constantly challenging where she had been, and David and Sandy could check the site log at any time. Second, Lacy agreed to a timer for her computer that disabled the Internet at 9:30 p.m. on weekdays, an hour before bedtime. This also turned off the Internet when the day's use reached two hours—a number Lacy came up with. In return, she got Internet until 11:00 p.m. on weekends, with a maximum of 3.5 hours on those days. This would cut down on arguments tremendously because Lacy knew exactly how much time she had left in her budget. She could choose to use it or not and the Internet would simply be disabled after the agreed number of hours. This removed her parents from the struggle. It also taught Lacy how to monitor and budget her own time.

Last, they got very clear on privacy and safety rules for the entire household. Both parents and Lacy agreed that chat rooms and illegal music sites were forbidden in the household. Lacy could also only have approved friends on her chat list. Sandy and David said they trusted her to do this on her own and would only check every once in a while, so she could build trust. They also made a list of information that would not be shared on social networks, game sites, or chats—such as social security numbers, birth years, addresses, and phone numbers—unless it was absolutely necessary for specific purposes, and even then only on sites the parents agreed they trusted, like Amazon or PayPal.

"Does that list make sense to you, Lacy? Are you okay not sharing that info? This also applies to texting."

"Yeah, totally. I wouldn't share it anyway, but it is good to have a list we will all follow."

"There are also some things that might come up that are not on the list, like when someone sends a mean text and you need to reply."

She rubbed her forehead. "I never know how to respond to those."

"So, there is something I do, called the Teacher Check. When I'm thinking about responding to someone or posting something, I ask myself, 'Would I have wanted my math teacher to see this?' If the answer is no, I don't post it, or I change it to make it more appropriate."

Lacy nodded. "I think I can do that."

Things to Remember

- Teens are spending increasing amounts of time online because it allows them to try new experiences and connect with others.
- There are both positive effects for youth using technology—making new friendships, giving back, learning—and negative ones: inappropriate exposure, increased self-absorption, and loss of privacy.
- It is beneficial for parents to set up clear rules and systems regarding technology use inside and outside the home.
- Learning to be a model cybercitizen is important for both children and parents to implement.
- Using tools such as parental controls, safe Web browsing, and e-mail monitoring as well as teaching youth the Teacher Check are ways parents can encourage online privacy and safety in their teens.

Challenges You Can Do Right Now

Family Challenge: Make your own systems and rules.

1. Make your own set of systems and rules regarding the following topics and share them with family members:

- Electronics-free zones in your home
- Electronics-free times
- Passwords and user names on social networks
- Strangers and chatting

- Amount of texts
- Allowed websites
- Information that counts as private

Family Challenge: Keep time logs.

1. Have everyone in the family guess how much time they spend eating, sleeping, doing homework, watching TV, playing online, spending time with friends in person, and spending time with other people offline.
2. Then have everyone keep a log of their time for three weekdays and one weekend day. Measure how accurate your guesses were compared to actual time spent.
3. Discuss the surprises that arise from this challenge, and possible goals for spending time better in the future.

Personal Challenge: Are you a good cybercitizen?

1. Look at the rules for cybercitizenship. Have you ever broken any of these in front of your children?
2. Do you think these are hard to follow?
3. Decide what kind of Internet role model you want to be for your children and talk to them about this.

CHAPTER 5

The New Bully

Parents and teens today still have to deal with traditional forms of bullying, but they also struggle to fend off digital forms of attack, through social networks and the like, on computers and cell phones. In this chapter I will talk about the new bully. The new bully can exist in both online and offline environments and oftentimes is even a victim of bullying as well. Finally, I will discuss what can be done to discourage meanness and how parents and teens should handle attacks. The story below of Jackson, his family, and his bully is all too common, but nonetheless shocking. Here I piece together the series of events and have laid them out for you in chronological order.

November 12, 2009, 3:42 a.m.

Fourteen-year-old Jackson was awakened by a soft buzzing noise. He rolled over and saw the bright blue light of his cell phone. He had one new text from a classmate named Sean. It read:

"Wait until ur fat ass gets 2 school. Well be waiting!"

For the third night in a row, Jackson responded, "Go 2 hell, u asshole!" And then he quickly deleted both messages. He sighed, pulled the covers up, and tried to go back to sleep.

November 12, 2009, 7:16 a.m.

Groggily, Jackson pulled on an oversized UCLA sweatshirt and went down to breakfast. His mom, Vicki, was hurriedly getting breakfast ready. "Come on, Jack! You got up late again. What is going on with you? Grab your waffle and get in the car."

Too nervous to eat and thinking about the "fat" comment, Jackson chucked the waffle in the trash and went to wait in the cold car. His mom got in and glanced at her ragged son. "Honey, maybe you should get to bed earlier or something. You are getting up later and later." Getting no response, she finally asked, "Is everything all right?"

Jackson thought for a fleeting second about telling his mother about what was happening at school, but reminded himself that she wouldn't understand that it was normal. And, of course, he figured she would just freak out when she saw some of his return text messages to Sean. He mumbled, "Fine," and checked his phone to see three new text messages from Sean: "I'm going to take you to hell fucker!" "Lilly says you make her sick," and "Hello? Getting all pretty 4 school, fag?" Jackson hit delete on all three and turned to his mom. "Can you drop me off in the back today?"

Vicki's forehead wrinkled. "Sure, but isn't that far from your locker, sweetie?"

Jackson groaned inwardly at the use of "sweetie"—he hated when his mom called him that. He said only, "I don't need any books for first period and the back is closer to English."

November 12, 2009, 10:07 a.m.

Sean and his friends gathered in the cafeteria during break. Upon spotting Jackson, Sean taunted, "Hey, sucka! Didn't see you out front today. Did your mommy drop you off in the back?" He continued, "Are you retarded? I'm talking to you, faggot."

Jackson glanced at Sean and his group of friends and wondered if they would actually physically fight him if he talked back. They hadn't hit him before, but they did shove him in the hallway. His palms began to sweat and he looked around desperately for one of his friends. He had noticed they had been avoiding him lately, and he was too ashamed to ask them for help.

Jackson sucked in a breath and hoped the girl from his English class might step in like last time and distract Sean. He saw her watching by the vending machines and looked to her for help, but wasn't sure what to say. He cringed when he saw her survey the scene and step quickly into a classroom. He began walking swiftly toward his next class when he saw one of Sean's friends, Thomas, snapping pictures with his phone. "Hey, don't take my picture!" Jackson shouted.

"Fuck off, fatty!" Sean said, laughing with his friends.

Jackson gripped his notebook with sweaty palms and yelled back, "Well, at least I'm not poor like you and your white-trash parents!"

November 12, 2009, 1:45 p.m.

Vicki picked up some dirty clothes from Jackson's floor and accidently bumped his desk. His MacBook sprang to life. "Oops," Vicki said to the empty room. She rolled her eyes seeing that it had been left on. A few weeks earlier the family had tried to "go more green" by shutting off computers, TVs, and other electronics when they weren't being used. With laundry basket in hand, Vicki leaned over to shut down the laptop. A window popped up saying, "Are you sure you want to quit iChat? All unsaved conversations will be lost." Vicki hit cancel and glanced at the open conversations to see if Jackson would mind if she deleted them.

Immediately her breath caught in her throat. Cusswords,

threats, and unflatteringly modified pictures of her son filled the screen. She put down the laundry basket and took her cell phone out of her pocket. After a few rings, she got my message machine and said quickly, "Vanessa, it's Vicki. We spoke a few weeks ago after the keynote for our fund-raiser. Well, I just saw something on my son's computer and I'm not sure who else to call. I think I have a serious problem."

Some version of this story happens every day around the world. Many parents have dealt with similar situations in their own household. Bullying, both online and offline, is a serious and growing problem for many parents and children. First, "bullying" is an extremely broad term. When I refer to bullying, I mean any behavior that is meant to harm or intimidate another person. Versions of bullying for young people can include playground threats, punches, exclusion from parties or groups, and spreading rumors, among other harassment. Cyberbullying or e-bullying is any type of bullying that happens through technology. This can include text threats, attacks on social networks or IM, sending inappropriate pictures through e-mail, or malicious exclusion from online groups or chats.

Jackson, in the story above, experienced both kinds of bullying. He was attacked by peers through text and IM and was also being harassed at school. This is not uncommon. In fact, two researchers, Justin Patchin and Sameer Hinduja at the Cyberbullying Research Center, conducted a study with approximately 2,000 randomly selected middle schoolers and found that 30 percent of them reported being victims of cyberbullying two or more times in the past thirty days. Among types of bullying, the most frequently cited, at 27.7 percent, was calling another student mean names, making "fun of or teasing him or her in a hurtful way." This is what happened to Jackson by the vending machines as well as through texts. Sadly, 34.1 percent, more than one-third of the students, also reported that within the previous thirty days they had engaged in traditional forms of bullying two or more times, and more than 21 percent admitted to cyberbullying others. In another study, published in the *Journal of Media Psychology* and focusing on 1,700 teenagers aged thirteen to eighteen, researchers found that the victims of Internet bullying are often also the victims of school bullying. This is demonstrated in Jackson's story. It's important for adults to realize that it is impossible to separate the two forms of bullying. Jackson's bully Sean attacked his victim from all sides—at school, on the phone, and through the Internet.

As Jackson's bullying got worse and worse, why didn't he tell anyone? Jackson contemplated telling his mom while sitting in the car with her, but convinced himself that she would not understand. Another article, in the *Journal of School Health*, reported that of the study's 1,454 twelve- to seventeen-year-olds who were cyberbullied, 90 percent did not tell adults about what had happened to them. I think there are three reasons that teens do not report bullying to adults.

First, both being mean and being bullied have been normalized, which

> *"Rumors are power. When I have a secret, I feel like I'm better than everyone else."*
> —Radical Parenting intern

> *"I learned how to get back at my best friend from Gossip Girl."*
> —Courtney, 15, Radical Parenting intern

> *"Everyone gets bullied at some point. You deal with it on your own and then you are a real teenager."*
> —Jessica, 16

causes teens to think that they don't need to report attacks because they are "just part of being a teenager." Unfortunately, though adolescents have always had mean streaks, today teens report that because of shows like *Gossip Girl*, cyberspace taunting and meanness have been glamorized.

Being mean has never been cooler or more "normal." In the car with his mom, Jackson worried to himself that his mom wouldn't understand that "this is just what teenagers do."

The entire battle between Sean and Jackson was actually quite subversive and passive-aggressive, done behind the scenes through text messages, anonymous IMs, and altered pictures. While working with both Sean and Jackson later, I asked Sean about the mean anonymous comments he sent via text to other people about Jackson. His response was "But that's normal!" The new slew of teenage programming on TV and in movies and books teaches teens how to use subversive aggression over outright attacks. Researcher Jamie Ostrov has studied "popular" kids. He found that the most popular kids use a combination of "prosocial" behavior—being kind and pleasing to others—and "antisocial" behavior: inflicting cruelty on others to get what they want. Their peers and teachers rate adolescents who use a balance of both behaviors as the most popular. More important, when researchers examined how these kids learned this behavior, they found that the popular students actually watched more *educational* television.

Unintentionally, par-

> "Drama is trendy. Reality TV makes drama seem cool and typical. People think it's normal to constantly be having drama and problems with friends."
>
> —Leslie, 17,
> Radical Parenting intern

ents were changing the channel from violent television to more docile programming, and this was actually teaching kids how to use more subversive forms of clique formation, bullying, and cruelty, such as passive-aggressive comments and rumors. This is exactly why we see kids like Sean, his accomplice friends, and Jackson experiencing a terrible mix of cyberbullying and mental playground drama.

The hype of drama and the under-the-surface nature of meanness make it incredibly hard for teens to deal with and move past problems. It also makes it even harder for adults, like Vicki, to step in and help. Jackson was not only receiving harassing texts, but also sending them back. This is why many parents struggle to gauge whether their kids are being bullied or *are* the bully! Not only has technology made being mean easier, but when kids get harassed, they question whether it is actually out of the ordinary.

> *"I guess I was upset when my bff wrote on my blog that 'my frizzy hair framed my face nicely.' I was like, 'wait, is that an insult?' She put a smiley face so I just figured that is how everyone talks and I'm supposed to be a little irritated with my best friend anyway."*
>
> —Blaine, 16, Radical Parenting intern

Digital meanness and cruelty toward enemies and friends alike has become acceptable behavior. This is a major reason why many bullying incidents go unreported until it is too late.

The second reason many teens are afraid to report attacks is

> "I have been bullied, but I can't tell any teachers because then she would tell them about the mean messages I sent to her last month. She is just getting back at me, I know that. But it still really hurts."
>
> —Julianna, 16

that in most bullying incidents today—both online and offline—teenagers get confused about who is at fault and are therefore afraid to report what is happening. This happened with Jackson. While worrying about whether or not he should tell his mom, he thought she would "freak out" if she saw some of his return text messages to the bully. Some would construe Jackson's defensive but attacking messages back to Sean as another form of bullying. In this way, teenagers are often unsure what to report because they are afraid they might also be at fault. More often than not, I see that bullies are also victims, and victims are bullies. This makes victims feel ashamed and confused. They do experience the attacks, but also feel like the threats might somehow be their fault or that they "deserve" to be bullied. Bullying is devastating to a teen's self-esteem, which is a major problem and often results in teens not speaking up.

The third reason many teenagers do not report or know how to handle bullying is that young people are having a more difficult time reading social cues. Due to the increasing use of technology among young people, there has been a rise in social illiteracy. Employers and college professors have flooded our website with e-mails about other symptoms of social illiteracy—namely, students who no longer look their professors in the eye or employees who cannot read social cues during office meetings, because they are used to only interacting with people through screens. With all of the opportunities to connect online, there are now fewer chances for people to build meaningful relationships offline and practice reading human behavior. With the birth of "never losing touch," in the next ten years we will see the death of the high school reunion. Many people already keep in touch with the old friends they still want to have relationships with—or they maintain those ties to spy on others—through social networks. The increase of technology has made teen life very virtual. For example, one time I was about to host an assembly called "The 10 Careers You Never Thought Of," on blogging, entrepreneurship, starting virtual non-profits, and tips on how to apply for jobs in the digital age, and I was waiting beside the bleachers in a school auditorium to be introduced. While there I observed a teen boy furiously texting in his lap.

> *"It's embarrassing to tell my parents I am being bullied. They will think I am a loser or that I did something to deserve it. On top of the bullying I don't need my parents making me feel bad, or worse, getting into trouble for somehow provoking it."*
>
> —Brent, 14

"What are you texting?" I asked casually.

The boy jumped and his eyes widened in terror; he had obviously not seen me standing there and knew I was the speaker we were waiting for. "Uh, please don't get me in trouble. I will put it away."

I laughed. "I don't care about that. I'm not a teacher. Plus, I'm about to give a presentation on technology, so I can't be too averse to it. I was just wondering what you were texting about, if you don't mind."

He smiled and sheepishly showed me the screen. He had responded "Cool" to the text "im behind u." I looked at the girl sitting behind him on the bleachers—literally two inches behind him. Her knee was practically in his back. "Wait," I said to her. "You texted him, 'I'm behind you'?" She giggled. "Why couldn't you just tell him? He is sitting as close to you as your phone is," I asked.

She looked at me with the same amount of confusion I was showing her. "Why not?" she said. This showed me that even real-life interactions are changing. It is becoming harder for teens to communicate with each other face-to-face, especially when it comes to emotional topics, such as confronting bullies or even expressing feelings of love or upset.

> *"It is almost harder to have friends now. I think before we all had phones and Facebook you felt bad if you gossiped about someone in the cafeteria because you could see the person you were being mean to in the corner of your eye. Now it is so easy to write something mean about someone on chat. It feels like you are talking to a screen."*
>
> —Alexandra, 14, Radical Parenting intern

It is much easier to be mean online because it feels less personal. Desensitization can be a devastating consequence of technology.

Why has it become so easy for young people to replace real

interactions with virtual ones? J. Marsh conducted a study in 2010 regarding kids who play in virtual worlds. While examining children aged five to seven, they found that "virtual worlds offered these young children a wide range of opportunities for play and that the types of play in which they engaged relate closely to 'offline' play." In other words, technology offers a better version of what happens in real life, and children have trouble distinguishing between offline and online.

Social illiteracy makes teens even more disinclined to report bullying. When bullying happens in real life, they do not have the social literacy to deal with it by standing their ground or reporting the incident. Instead, many teens, like Jackson, retreat inward, hoping it will blow over while they wait, stewing in their own shame and confusion over the meanness being perpetrated. Standing in the cafeteria, Jackson could actually not tell if Sean and his posse were joking with him or if they would physically threaten him. He wondered if they would hit him and ineffectively looked to a female student to come to his rescue. He also had trouble asking for help from his own friends. Later, I asked Jackson why he didn't even ask his friends for help. He explained that he never talked to his friends about "stuff like that." He insisted that they just played video games and chatted on Facebook and he was unsure of what to say to them. In addition, he thought Sean and Thomas were "just joking around" and that if he told on them, he would be made fun of even more. Jackson's comments, and his inability to read and talk to his friends, show us one of the major symptoms of social illiteracy and help explain why bullying often goes unreported until it spirals out of control.

Digital "slaps" are even more confusing for a socially illiterate teen. Jackson had no idea how to respond to the mean texts and IMs he was getting. Sometimes he attacked back, while other times he ignored their comments. This is because cyber attacks are often masked in emoticons, "jk's," or "lol's." When I give antibullying workshops, I call this "the problem with just joking." When accused of being mean, teens will often say that it was "just a joke" or that they were "joking" with their victim. Teens report that they fear being called a snitch for reporting bullying incidents, but they also worry about misinterpreting a joke and being seen as a poor sport. Snitching is an old issue, but teens today who already have trouble reading social cues have even greater difficulty deciding what is play and what is actual bullying.

When teens like Jackson do not report bullying, or they internalize meanness, or they assume attacks are just "normal" or inside jokes, there are serious consequences. In another report by Hinduja and Patchin, they found that all types of bullying were significantly associated with increases in suicidal thoughts. Sadly, 20 percent of respondents who had been bullied reported seriously thinking about attempting suicide. In fact, cyberbullying victims were almost twice as likely to have attempted suicide compared to youth who had not experienced cyberbullying. If bullying causes such devastation, we have to wonder, why do teens still do it? Additionally, why do so many teens who have been victims, and experienced the awful feelings of self-doubt and suicide themselves, turn around and bully others? I think there are three major reasons for bullying: low self-esteem; stress; and, for cyberbullying, the ease, access, and reach of technology.

Both bullies and victims report significantly lower self-esteem than uninvolved youth. When Patchin and Hinduja looked at cyberbullying in their group of two thousand randomly selected middle schoolers, they found that "cyberbullying victims and offenders both had significantly lower self-esteem than those who have not experienced cyberbullying. This relationship persisted even while controlling for gender, race, and age, though our results suggest that males, nonwhites, and older middle schoolers tend to have lower levels of self-esteem than their peers." What makes this even more relevant is that we already know that students who bully through technology also tend to bully in school, therefore technology and playground politics are not the problem. There has to be another common factor; I believe that factor is low self-worth. Unsurprisingly, low self-esteem is a huge predictor of both perpetrating bullying and receiving it. It makes sense that teens and tweens who feel poorly about themselves also lash out at others or seem vulnerable to bullies. Jackson is an unfortunate example of this. A bit overweight, Jackson was self-conscious about his body, and when Sean and his friends saw this weakness, they preyed upon his vulnerability, poking fun at his size, altering pictures of him by adding on extra weight. This, of course, made Jackson feel worse about himself, and he, in turn, made fun of something he thought Sean would have low self-esteem about: his economic status. We will see that Sean picked on Jackson not only because of his vulnerability about weight, which made him an easy target for Sean, but also because Sean identified Jackson as a "rich kid." Sean, on scholarship at the school, wanted to attack Jackson because of his own fears and insecurities about his family not being able to afford tuition.

Anger and stress are also major reasons why teens turn to bullying. In their article on traditional and nontraditional bullying, Patchin and Hinduja found that youth who are angry, frustrated, or experiencing stress are significantly more likely to bully or cyberbully. They also found that "adolescents between ages 11 and 15 increasingly cope with strain in maladaptive ways, such as resignation, avoidance, and hostility." This was absolutely true of Sean. He avoided his own feelings of inadequacy by openly attacking Jackson. Many teenagers who are feeling stressed at home or school have told us that this almost makes them feel justified in their surliness.

"When I get a bad grade or something and I'm in a bad mood, I can't help but take it out on my friends. They don't mind. They know that it's just the grade and they shouldn't take my insults personally."

—Daniella, 16,
Radical Parenting intern

The way adults argue or sarcastically attack each other at home is often replayed by teens at school because they feel the strain and anger of stressful home relationships.

The last reason I think bullying has become so prevalent is that technology makes cyber attacks easier. Before cell phones and computers, if teens got in a fight at school or found out they were not invited to a party, they were able to come home and vent about it to a family member, get a snack, and cool off. Now when they are mad at someone, they can instantly send a text message, update their social network profile on their phone, and post a mean comment. Now there is no "off" time. The second something happens, everyone knows about it because they all get alerts or texts from automated news feeds or plugged-in friends. Teens are checking these services constantly, so what once took a few days to

"I don't even realize it when I am being mean sometimes. My mom is a yeller and so I don't even think about it when I am doing it to people at school. When I got called into the principal's office for being a bully it was a shock."

—Lindsay, 13

spread and perhaps fizzle out can now take only a few minutes to explode.

Technology also provides a buffer between people.

> "It's really hard to walk up to someone and say to them, "You are a fat slut." It is much easier to write that on someone's Facebook wall. I write things through IM that I would never say in person."
>
> —Anonymous, 12

Technology is a way for students to be mean "behind someone's back." Many times, students can post pictures or videos or send messages anonymously! This has changed the face of bullying because it allows people to be mean without having to face the consequences. Teens are more harsh with online comments because they feel they can hide them from parents and teachers by posting anonymously and they do not have to say them directly to someone's face. Instead, they can type a comment in a moment of anger when they are alone in their room. Sean and his gang were mean to Jackson at school, but their text and IM comments were even more detrimental because Sean could type them on a screen without seeing the devastation on Jackson's face.

The bigger problem is that technology also makes these mean comments and actions more permanent. Even when wall postings or texts can be deleted, there is almost always a permanent record of it in a database somewhere. These can be accessed for court trials and by schools or parents who request full records from phone companies. When working with teens I also point out how easy it is for someone to print a chat, take a screen shot, or download a video or photo before it gets taken down. Before I discuss solutions, let's get clear on what the law and schools can do regarding bullying and technology.

Countries like the United Kingdom and Canada actually have quite strict laws regarding bullying both on and off school grounds. In the United States, at the time I'm writing this book, forty-four states have passed laws regarding bullying, and thirty of those mention electronic forms of bullying. Most of these laws only direct school districts to create their own bullying and harassment policies, though some do propose possible action plans. On the federal level, the Megan Meier Cyberbullying Prevention Act was put before the House of Representatives on April 2, 2009. This says, "Whoever transmits in interstate or foreign commerce any communication, with the intent to co-erce, intimidate, harass, or cause substantial emotional distress to a person, using electronic means to support severe, repeated, and hostile behavior, shall be fined under this title or impris-oned not more than two years, or both." This is a significant move to catch laws up to technology. Unfortunately, in most countries the enforcement of bullying laws is not sufficient in preventing or even punishing bullies. Additionally, we have seen that bullying cases are often not clear-cut—bullies are victims, victims are bullies, and many bystanders are indirectly involved. So how can parents deal with bullying?

One of my most popular workshops is an antibullying pro-gram for parents and students starting as young as second grade. In this workshop I address the issues I delineated above: why kids bully, why kids are afraid to report, and how to recognize the new bully—who is both online and offline, victim and per-petrator. I also explain how we can curb bullying and meanness at home and in the schools. To do this, I first encourage parents to teach their children what I call Bullying 101. This includes the basic bullying vernacular: types of bullying; the roles of bully, victim, and bystander; and then what to do if it happens to them. I think teaching your children the types of bullying is very important because it serves as a way to denormalize meanness. When we give attacks names and definitions, we teach kids that they are not normal. This is also helpful in encouraging them to report incidents, because they have concrete terms to explain to adults what is happening. Here are the different types of bullying:

Impersonation: Pretending to be someone else online by sending messages, posting material, or contacting other people under another person's name or image.

Flaming: Online fights using electronic messages such as IMs, e-mails, chat comments, or posts. They usually include angry and inappropriate language back and forth.

Reporting: Sharing someone's embarrassing images, secrets, or private information online.

(Cyber) Harassment: Repeatedly sending nasty, mean, and insulting messages or threats.

Denigration: Insulting someone by spreading gossip or rumors or posting pictures to damage their feelings, relationships, or reputation.

Tricking: Tricking someone into revealing secrets or private info in a public forum and/or revealing it to others.

Exclusionary: Purposefully leaving people out to insult or be hurtful to them.

Stalking: Repeatedly following someone or sending messages to him or her.

Many kids and teens do not realize that some of these actions are actual bullying. They think that purposefully being excluded or having someone spread rumors about them is "normal." As adults, it is important to explain to them that if someone is spreading a rumor that is false or could affect their reputation permanently, it should be taken seriously. I also take this time to explain how there are different levels of bullying. For example, there is a difference between excluding a fellow student from a birthday party at Disneyland because they only have so many spots in the car, and excluding someone from an end-of-the-school-year party for the entire grade. Helping teens identify the type of bullying that is happening to them and then having them gauge how damaging it might be to their self-esteem or reputation teaches them important self-evaluation skills they need for life. Teaching honest reflection is how we can instruct our kids to think consciously, not automatically, about their actions, and to be more adept at social literacy and cues.

The next part of Bullying 101 is teaching them the different roles:

Bully: The attacker or person who is harassing, demeaning, or attempting to harm others.

Targets, or victims: Those who receive the insults or attacks.

Enablers: Those who encourage and support the bullies who are harassing others.

Harmful bystanders: Those who know that bullying is going on, but do nothing about it.

Helpful bystanders: Those who know bullying is going on and report it.

It is essential for teens and kids to understand these roles. They also must understand that even when they are not the one perpetrating the attacks, if they encourage the bully or even just ignore the behavior, they can be just as guilty. If adults can teach kids about discouraging bullies and not slipping into passive by-stander or enabler roles, we can significantly reduce the amount of bullying, because bullies will be standing alone. When bul-lies, like Sean, do not have a posse, they feel less justified in their attacks and they often back off.

I would also like to mention here the importance of talking to your kids about what I call "guilt bullying." When I speak to teens, I spend a lot of time explaining that bullying comes in a variety of forms. It can vary from a small comment to an actual act of physical aggression. For instance, a guilt bully uses passive-aggressive behavior and guilt to attack his or her vic-tims. Take a look at this IM conversation between two teen girls:

> **Alyssa22:** Anyways, I have 2go study 4 my test, talk 2morrow?
>
> **Jackiesmiley:** Now? its not 4 another 2 days, =) ur such a nerd! Start 2morrow lol
>
> **Alyssa22:** Whatever, I have a game 2morrow so I got2 start 2nite
>
> **Jackiesmiley:** Nooooo! Half of the grade has stuff tomor-row, if u get off you might miss chatting with eric. . . . ;)
>
> **Alyssa22:** ahhhh, I know, my mom will kill me though! I go2go, talk to u tomorrow
>
> **Jackiesmiley:** Wait wait, im so sad, I will miss u
>
> **Alyssa22:** we can talk maybe on my break in like an hour
>
> **Jackiesmiley:** ohhh = (I love talking to u because ur my BFF!
>
> **Alyssa22:** OK, I will come on in an hour and checkin k? BBS [Be back soon]
>
> **Jackiesmiley:** before you go!!!!!! Alyssaaaaaaaa??
>
> **Alyssa22:** ya ya ya still here
>
> **Jackiesmiley:** I forgot to tell u I am deciding who is coming

to my skate night this Saturday. i can really only invite a few ppl u know?

Alyssa22: oh ya . . . I want 2 go!

Jackiesmiley: ru only friends with me because of my skate night? Now all of a sudden you want to talk? That's lame.

Alyssa22: No that's not true, I would talk anyway I just have to study!

Jackiesmiley: . . .

Alyssa22: Ok fine, im here, ill wait for Eric and we can plan outfits for skate night?

Jackiesmiley: I knew u were really my BFF!!! u want to get ready with me be4 on Sat?

Alyssa22: Ya, cool! Excited =)

I have seen, heard, and even been victim to this type of exchange before. This type of bullying happens with girls, but more often with teen boys when they are trying to get a friend to do something bad or when pressuring girls to have sex. It is important for parents to point out the nuances of guilt bullying because it can be just as dangerous as physical aggression. This conversation is not openly mean, but it is casually malicious. Notice the "lol's" and use of smiley-face emoticons. This is an easy way to pad the snide remarks like "you are such a nerd," etc. This makes it difficult for the victim to call the bully out on the negative behavior. With the smiley faces and "lol's" the bully can always say that she or he wasn't serious or that it was "just a joke"—a common teen excuse for bad behavior. Notice the shift in Jackie's tactics. First, she uses anger and meanness to bully Alyssa into staying online. Then, when she realizes it is not going to work, she pretends she is sad and appeals to Alyssa's sense of friendship. When that doesn't work, she uses a soft threat. Jackie's soft threat is telling Alyssa that she might not be able to come to Jackie's skate party on Saturday night and loosely linking it to her getting offline. This is not an overt threat, but it works—Alyssa wants to go on Saturday, and she sees that if she gets offline, she might lose her invite. Usually soft threats state something unpleasant without mentioning all the ways it could hurt the other person.

The last part of Bullying 101 is teaching teens the basic formula for what to do if they are being bullied or see someone else being bullied: Stop, Save, and Report.

Step one is to *stop the behavior*. Young people must learn never to write back to a mean message, whether to retaliate or even to gather more information. For example, with anonymous text messages, e-mails, or IMs, I always tell students that no matter how tempting it is, do not write back and ask who the sender is. This will only exacerbate things and fuel a bully's fire. Jackson got himself into a flaming attack when he wrote back messages to Sean. Even in the beginning when Jackson would text simply, "stop sending me messages," Sean engaged in the back-and-forth. Eventually, when Jackson began writing back mean messages, not only did this not stop Sean, but it also risked getting Jackson in trouble.

Next, students should learn how to *save the action*. This usually only applies to cyberbullying, as hallway threats cannot really be saved. I teach students how to take screenshots—shift + command + 4 on a Mac or the "print screen" button on a PC. It is important for parents to explain to teens that no matter how embarrassing or mean a message is, they should save it so when they report what is happening, teachers and adults have all of the history of what happened.

Last, I give students many options for how they can *report the action*. You want to give teens as many options as possible for this part. If they do not want to go to their parent, they can go to their English teacher, school counselor, basketball coach, aunt, cousin, brother, or another adult they are comfortable with. I also show teens how to use the "report" button to flag inappropriate pictures or messages for the webmasters of the social networks and websites they are on. This is helpful on Facebook or gaming sites when a fellow user posts something offensive in a public area online. This process works very well for teens who are being bullied. Bystanders can also follow the Stop, Save, and Report formula.

What should parents do if their child is the bully? The second set of tips I suggest are for parents of bullies. This is a very common problem, so, first and foremost, parents should not feel ashamed or embarrassed. If you find that your child is bullying, it is important first to gather all the information you can. Ask your child how long it has been going on; what forms it has taken—online or offline; who was involved; who else knows about it; and whether they have any record of their actions. Once all of the information has been gathered, it is time to look at the emotional intent behind the bullying. This is where protoconversation skills are extremely useful.

Parents who find that their child is bullying need to identify the emotional intent behind the attacks. I find that bullies are often acting from one of three emotional states: vulnerability, insecurity, or anger. I encourage parents to be transparent about these areas. Once you glean where your child is coming from, you can not only work to stop the bullying, but also deal with the emotional deficiency.

In addition, there are a few strategies I use with bullies who have trouble seeing the negative effects of their actions. I call bullies who cannot identify with one of the three emotional states "avoider bullies." These bullies instead insist that "it was no big deal" or "it was just a big joke." This is because these kinds of bullies are always trying to avoid blame, consequences, and the devastation that their actions and bullying have caused. I encourage creative and interactive strategies to help avoider bullies explore the seriousness and breadth of bullying and its consequences. I may suggest that they:

- Develop a website or blog on antibullying. Here they have to research the laws on cyberbullying, stories of bullies and victims, and the bullying terms and roles.
- Put together a program or workshop on antibullying for their own grade, younger grades, or the local library.
- Create an antibullying PSA to be posted on YouTube.
- Mentor younger students who have been bullied on how to have healthy confrontation and build back their self-esteem.

These are not only great educational activities, but they have success in reforming the attitude of an avoider bully.

In the antibullying workshop, I teach both teens and parents the art of protoconversation: how to read faces and pay attention to voice tone and word choice to find emotional intent. This is my third tip for parents trying to prevent bullying, because I believe the only way we can counter social illiteracy is to teach social intelligence. This is a totally new approach to preventing bullying, because once teens learn—and get excited about—reading nonverbal cues, I remind them that the only way to do this is in person. By encouraging teens to use protoconversation skills, we give them the incentive to take communication, confrontation, and relationships offline. In the resources section I have included a link to online resources that help parents teach their teens social literacy. I recommend parents explain to teens the idea of protoconversations and then watch some of the video demonstrations I provide from my antibullying workshops on the six universal facial expressions and how to spot them. They are anger, fear, surprise, happiness, disgust, and sadness. If you do not have a computer, you can also practice the expressions together and rehearse spotting them on each other. This teaches teens to pay attention to social cues and spend more time looking and really listening to the people they are interacting with, so they do not fall into the social illiteracy trap. It also teaches them skills for reading those around them to prevent confrontation and bullying.

The fourth tip I give parents is to help monitor their children's online actions and reputation. Sometimes teens do not realize people are posting things in the public domain online, or they are too afraid to tell parents. Therefore, I share some easy ways for parents to monitor their child's online reputation without invading privacy. For example, parents can set up a free Google Alert on their child's name. A Google Alert is a service that reports to you anytime a search term or phrase appears publicly on the Web. I have a Google Alert on "Vanessa Van Petten" as well as "Radical Parenting" to know when anyone posts or says anything about my blog or my name. I recommend parents set one up for their own name as well as for each of their children. Simply go to www.google.com, search the term "Google Alert," and enter your child's full name into the box that says "search terms." Then select how often you want to receive the update—I recommend once per day—and the e-mail address where you want the alert delivered (if you do not already have a free e-mail account, you first need to set one up). That's it! Anytime someone posts something about your search term publicly, whether on Facebook, Wikipedia, a public forum, or a website, you will be notified. This proved extremely useful to one of our readers, who wrote in this e-mail to us:

> "Hi Vanessa! I set up a Google Alert on my child's name and nickname a few months ago after I read your post on online reputation management. Nothing important really came through except for a lawyer who has the same name as my kid. But then three days ago I saw that someone had posted a public picture with my child's name underneath it. A boy from school had superimposed my son's picture onto a naked man and made it public! I was horrified and immediately reported it to Facebook. It was taken down within 2 hours. I have no idea if I ever would have seen it and when I brought it up to my son he told me that the same boy has been sending him awful text messages. I wanted to let you know that it was really helpful. Thanks for the tip!"
>
> —Alexandra R.

Other than monitoring your child's online reputation to observe any cyberbullying—or inappropriate posts by your own child—I also encourage parents to regularly get together with other parents to converse about offline activities. In the resources section I have many ideas for setting up your own community parenting group. I think it is essential for parents to work together to keep each other updated on what is going on. What one parent sees may be very beneficial to another. Additionally, this is a great time to get onto the same page regarding rules. For example, teens send on average thirty-four texts after bedtime! Trust me when I say *nothing* good happens after bedtime. When meeting with other parents in your community, you can talk about keeping the charging stations for phones downstairs so texts cannot be sent after an agreed-upon time. This cuts down on pressure and bullying after hours.

Another tip I give parents to prevent or deal with bullying is to let your teen know that you have had trouble with boundaries and meanness as well. If you lecture them, or pretend bullying is just a "teen" problem, they are more likely to shut down and not talk to you if and when something happens. The truth is, in the digital age, all of our reputations are at risk. At some point we ourselves or someone we know has had to deal with a real-life or online bully. If you commiserate with your kids, you can learn together. This is also the time to make a game plan for what happens if they experience bullying. Jackson said that one of the reasons he did not tell his mom what was going on was that he did not know how she would react and he thought she would most likely "freak out." If Vicki had sat down with Jackson and told him that she would not overreact or "snitch" on him without talking to him, he might have been more willing to approach her with the problem. One reason teens do not tell parents when someone is bullying them, or when they think they have gone too far in bullying someone else, is that they are afraid their parents will overreact.

A game plan I suggest, which both parties are usually comfortable with, is first to research the situation fully. This means gathering all messages and all sides of the story and background calmly. Too often when I am working with families or schools, parents jump the gun and accuse others, when their child might have also been at fault or information is missing. We never want to assume anything. Second, teenagers usually feel more comfortable if there is a "sanity check" put in place. This is a third adult who both parties feel comfortable talking to. It can be a spouse, older sibling, other family member, or a teacher or friend. The next step is to review the story and information with this third person. I find that in bullying situations, emotions are running high for both parents and teens and it can be helpful to have a third neutral person ask the tough questions and help craft a plan. Finally, make a plan to deal with the incident. Parents have a couple of options. They can approach the other child's parents, go to the school, or report to the police. Every situation is different and it is important to consider the repercussions of each solution. Parents might want to contact the school ahead of time to ask what its policy is regarding reporting bullying or cyberbullying, so that they are prepared before anything happens.

One final way I believe parents can help prevent bullying and build social literacy skills is to work on encouraging empathy. I believe empathy is one of the most important characteristics of being human. It is the ability to feel, read, and understand where people around us are coming from. Many teens understand the concept of compassion, but do not have the tools to act on their empathetic feelings or impulses.

In a recent study from the University of Michigan, researcher Sara Konrath and her colleagues asked students if they agreed with statements like these:

"I sometimes try to understand my friends better by imagining how things look from their perspective."

"I often have tender, concerned feelings for people less fortunate than me."

Shockingly, compared to their counterparts twenty to thirty years ago, *students showed a 40 percent drop in empathy* and agreement with the above statements. Teens also recognize this shift. One of our teen interns, Melissa, describes empathy as a matter of respect:

"Unfortunately, in this day and age, more and more teens do not give respect to those who deserve it. In my eyes, respect is the act of being empathetic and showing kind and considerate gestures to those around you. It does not matter if you dislike a person greatly, or if you do not know the person, if you would like to gain respect, you must first show it. When walking the hallways of my high school, I can point out hundreds of examples of teenagers acting inappropriately to not only their peers, but to teachers as well. They will talk back to their teachers and argue over silly things, when the teacher is rightfully correcting them in their speech or advising them on to the right path."

—Melissa, 16, Radical Parenting intern

Modeling and talking about your own feelings of empathy in front of your children is a wonderful first step. In addition, here are a few activities I like to do with kids and teens to encourage empathy.

Taking away a sense is one activity that helps remind teens how lucky we are to have our basic senses. You can challenge your kids to go without one of their senses for one day . . . or even one hour! Often the key to being empathetic is appreciating your senses and heightening them by focusing on a few at a time. I also started the "gratitude brush" when I was a freshman in high school, and I still love it. Whenever I brush my teeth I think about all of the things I am grateful for in my life. I also think about each person in my life and try to tune in to how they are doing, what they are going through, and what they might need from me. Now it is habit and a great way to start and end each day. You can also encourage your teens to write empathy notes. Sit down with your kids and think of three people who might want to hear from you and what they would like to know. This helps teens think about other people in their life and what they are going through. For example, if Grandpa feels lonely, telling him you love him and that you did really well in school would make him feel happy, loved, and proud. If teens are better able to empathize with bullies and victims alike, they are more likely to act with compassion. Teaching empathy is another way we can combat social illiteracy and help teens understand the importance of tuning in to those around them.

Now that we have reviewed how parents can address the new bully, whether that is their own child or not, I want to reveal how I dealt with Jackson, Sean, and Vicki. Four hours after Vicki's phone message I was sitting with Vicki, Jackson, and his dad, Bryce, in the kitchen. Vicki's eyes were puffy and Jackson's sullen expression seemed permanent.

"Okay, the hardest part is over. People have been mistreating you and that is going to stop right now," I said, patting his shoulder. He put his hand up to his forehead in shame. "Hey, Jackson. Please don't feel ashamed. I have been there. When I was in college someone set up a fake Facebook page and put some terrible things on it. I was so embarrassed, but then realized that unfortunately people can be bullies, but I did not have to put up with it. Neither do you."

"I don't even know what happened. It spiraled out of control."

"Let's go over exactly what happened. We'll make a list of what happened together, starting from the beginning."

Jackson's brows knit together in anger. "I guess it started at school. Sean and his friends would call me names in the hallway or move my backpack when I wasn't looking. Stupid stuff. Just joking around."

"Whoa," I said. "I'm going to just stop you for a minute. There is joking and then there is just being mean. Let's get really clear on the difference. I know you say that he was joking, but your face showed pure anger. Did you ever really think what they were doing were just jokes?"

He looked at his hands for a moment. "No, *I* never thought it was joking. After the hallway stuff he started sending me IMs and got his friends to do it, too. Then he got my cell phone number and sent text messages."

"Can we see those? Did you keep them?" I asked.

His eyes widened in fear. "Uh, no. No way."

"Why are you so afraid?" I asked. I looked at Vicki so she could register that I was using some of the protoconversation techniques she had learned from my keynote she attended.

She nodded and added, "Honey, Vanessa specializes in finding emotional intent—learning the emotions behind actions. She also reads faces, which she taught us how to do in her lecture. I think she is asking these tough questions because she sees you look a little afraid, and you were angry before."

"Oh, that's pretty crazy." He pressed his lips tightly together, a subconscious facial expression that indicates the speaker is trying not to say something or is holding something back. "I just . . . uh, well, some of them are really inappropriate. I don't want my parents to see. Maybe a little embarrassing, and I don't want to get in trouble, either. So I deleted them."

I stayed calm, wanting to reassure him that this was something we could deal with. "Okay, I hear that. So, maybe Sean was bullying you, but you also sent back some not-so-good messages that could be considered attacks as well?"

He rubbed his hands through his curly brown hair. "Yeah."

"First, it's really important that from now on you do not delete or respond to any messages or threats. Whenever someone gets bullied there are three things they should do. Stop the action; so do not retaliate or send anything back." He nodded while I continued. "Second, save it—even if it is embarrassing. It can help you get in less trouble later if we can see all of the history. Third, report it to someone. This is where we are now. Once you report it, we will work together to research everything that happened and piece together the events." We spent the next few hours going through as many incidents as Jackson could remember, recovering e-mails and Facebook chats from his computer's history files and getting a list of recent texts from the phone company. It was pretty dismal. I felt terrible for Jackson for being subjected to the awful bullying and knew he had been at a loss for what to do when he tried to retaliate with his own messages. In fact, it seemed he tried everything he could to get the bullying to stop—ignoring the messages, attacking back, pretending it was no big deal, even trying to befriend the group. Everything except asking for help.

We sat down over Chinese food and I brought up why he didn't ask for help. "Jackson, when everything was going on, I know you were afraid to ask your parents or a teacher for help because you were embarrassed and thought you would get in trouble, but why not ask your friends?"

His eyebrows went up in surprise. "My friends? I mean, I don't talk to them about stuff like that. We just play video games and stuff."

Bryce chimed in over an egg roll. "But you are always on chat with them on Facebook and IM. What do you talk about?"

Jackson shrugged and thought for a few seconds. "Nothing, really. Plus, I figured what was happening was normal. Everyone gets picked on. It was just my turn."

Vicki covered her mouth. "Jackson," she gasped, "no one deserves to be picked on the way you were. That's not right. It's not normal at all."

"Vicki is right. It's not normal, but I can understand why you feel that way, Jackson. I feel like I talk to my friends all the time, but it's never very serious, unless I force them to open up to me. And it feels like we see harassment all the time on movies and on TV. But just because we see bullying around us does not mean it's okay."

Jackson nodded sadly. "I'm realizing that now. I just did not know how to ask for help." I looked at Vicki and we both locked on the pronounced statement of social illiteracy. It is extremely hard for anyone to ask, let alone teenagers who are used to having most of their discussions via technology.

"I think we need to focus on our plan of action. We need to approach Sean and his parents about this and figure out why it happened and, most important, how we can get it to stop."

Jackson buried his head in his hands. "I just don't want it to get worse!" he lamented.

I reached over the table and touched his arm. "Jackson, we are all going to think this through and make sure it doesn't get worse. In a sense you also bullied him, even though it was retaliatory. The emotional intent for that, or the reason you did that, was because you felt vulnerable. Sean has an emotional intent as well. Once we figure that out, the bullying will stop."

"Okay, but if we can, I really don't want to take it to the school. Maybe just talk to his parents?" Jackson asked.

Bryce started clearing the table. "I'm okay starting with that. If they are going to take this seriously, I do not think there is a need to get the school involved."

Vicki wiped her hands on a napkin and said, "I know Sean's mom a little from parent events. I can call her. I think we should invite them over or go over to their house to discuss everything."

After a very long and difficult phone call, where Vicki as best as she could laid out the facts of what had happened, it was decided that we would all troop over to Sean's house to discuss the situation in person.

When we reached Sean's house, he and his mother, Millie, were waiting. Sean seemed furious already. I could see Jackson instantly tense up in response and I grew more worried that this would not go as smoothly as I had hoped. "Hi, Sean. I'm Vanessa. It's nice to meet you, although I know these are tense circumstances."

He limply shook my hand and scoffed, "And who the hell are you?"

Millie's eyes widened in shock and she said, "Vanessa, I am so sorry about that." She turned to her son and quietly said, "Sean, apologize, please."

"No! Why did you even invite them over here anyway? They are just going to make fun of our house." Sean crossed his arms over his chest in a defensive pose. Until that point I had not noticed anything about their house. I briefly looked around and realized it was smaller than Jackson's family's house, but still clean and nicely decorated.

Millie reddened. "Sean, you are going to have to get used to the fact that you are on scholarship. That is not why they are here and you know it." I glanced at Vicki and Bryce, who seemed just as surprised as I was at the outburst, but now I was beginning to see what was going on.

First, I wanted Sean out of his defensive stance. I have found that just changing hostile body language into something more relaxed can help dispel anger. "Let's all sit down, okay?" Once we had settled in the small living room, I turned directly to Sean, hoping that being direct and transparent was the best policy. "Sean, are you feeling uncomfortable about the fact that you are on scholarship and Jackson isn't? Is that the reason for all of the texts and IMs and threats at school?"

His nostrils flared in hostility. "Yeah, I'm mad about that. Him flaunting all his money around and acting superior." There, I thought, was the emotional intent: he was insecure about being on scholarship and angry about not having as much as his fellow classmates—Jackson in particular.

Jackson's jaw dropped. "I never flaunt that stuff. I don't care if you are on scholarship! I just want you to leave me alone."

"Oh, yeah? And how about your fancy ski trip over break?" Sean said, slamming his foot into the coffee table.

Jackson's eyes widened and I realized he had no idea he had offended Sean. "Ski trip? What are you talking about?"

"For weeks at school you were going around telling everyone you were bringing people with you to your parents' *ski chalet*," he said in a mocking tone. "But of course you could only bring people who had ski gear and knew how to ski. I, unlike you, have never been skiing and I definitely do not have the money to get my own ski stuff or whatever."

Millie blushed and Vicki looked mortified. "We had no idea it would have that kind of effect," she said, looking over at Millie.

Jackson put his hands up in exasperation. "I wasn't trying to make you feel left out, I was just freaking excited. Jeez, I mean, come on, that doesn't warrant all of the texts you have been sending me—"

"Whoa, whoa." I interrupted Jackson and looked at him. "Jackson, I know you probably didn't mean to, but that trip made Sean feel inferior and left out. The only way we can move on from here is by all of us being very honest and remorseful about the miscommunication and attacks that have happened in the past."

Jackson took a deep breath and said to Sean, "Look, I never meant to do that. I'm sorry if I did. If you felt that way, I wish you would have said something to my face, without your friends around, and then we could have dealt with it. Instead of all the texts."

I swelled with pride at Jackson's ability to apologize in a genuine way and stand up for himself. Sean's face softened and his mom gave him a stern look. "Yeah," Sean said, "I should have done that. I just . . . it just sucked."

As lame as the "it just sucked" excuse was, I knew we were getting somewhere. "Look, some serious stuff was said, Sean. I know that there were no physical attacks, but the way you were both talking is almost more harmful. From my understanding, you usually initiated, especially online. Am I right about that?"

Sean nodded. Millie interjected. "The conversations that Vicki read me—those were all written by Sean?"

Vicki nodded and, despite her anger, tried to keep her emotions in check. "Yes, they were all written by Sean." She handed over some of the printed-out conversations. "Look, we are not happy about what Jackson wrote, but some of the threats Sean sent are totally inappropriate and foul. We don't want to go to the school, and we hope we can resolve it together, but something needs to happen."

Sean read over the conversations and cringed. He looked sadly over at his mom. Millie said, "Absolutely. Believe me, there will be consequences. I don't even know where to start, but I can promise you phone and computer privileges are gone."

Sean sat back, resigned. "I know. As long as we can keep the school out of it, I will do whatever."

"I have a few suggestions—if you guys are up for it?" Nods all around. "I think this happened, just like other bullying happens, because of a few things. First, neither boy knew how to reach out. Sean was feeling bad, and he should have talked to Jackson directly. When the back-and-forth flaming first started online, Jackson should have asked for help before it got out of hand. These are tough social skills. I want both boys to practice with me at my next workshop on social and emotional literacy."

Jackson actually smiled. "Do I get to learn how to read faces?" He saw Sean was confused and explained to him what I teach.

"Yes, that is part of it. It is also about actually listening to people around you and being able to politely ask for what you need. The second reason I think this happened is because we are not well versed in what bullying is and how to prevent it. Plus, you guys are from different parts of town and don't know each other. I think we should change that. I do many antibullying presentations for third and fourth graders. I would like you guys to put one together. I'll give you an outline and I think you both should ask the school if you can cohost a workshop."

"Oh, that is going to suck," Jackson said. Sean rolled his eyes.

Vicki looked a little more relaxed. "An excellent idea for both of you."

"I'm sure your parents will have some other consequences at home and with electronics, but this will at least help you guys and maybe even others who are going through what happened to you. Are we agreed?"

"Yeah," Sean said along with Jackson.

I turned to the parents. "I also think there are some things you guys can do. First, you should set up Google Alerts online to help monitor anything in the public space. Second, maybe you should put together a grade-level parent group to get together every once in a while to discuss changes and rules. Some of the texts were sent after hours." Millie looked at Sean. "If parents worked together on consistency with phone rules, that wouldn't happen as much. Plus, then you can research what the school's stance is on bullying. It's just a way of working together on this kind of situation, which can be really hard."

After a few more minutes of talking, the boys apologized again and I realized that even though the current crisis had abated, bullying is a struggle that is a constant fight for parents, teens, and even schools. Giving our kids tools to deal with bullies as well as taking preventative, proactive measures ourselves is the only way we can encourage our children to be genuine and kind.

THINGS TO REMEMBER

- Cyberbullying and traditional bullying often occur concurrently and are both increasing in frequency.
- Bullying often goes unreported because students feel the meanness and attacks they are enduring are not out of the ordinary, they are confused about what should be reported, they believe they are partially at fault, and they are unable to read social cues or ask for help from peers.
- Bullying, both online and offline, occurs because of low self-esteem and stress on teens today, and because technology makes it extremely easy for teens to post instant, impersonal messages.
- Laws are slow to catch up to bullying issues and, therefore, parents must act to help prevent bullying from occurring.
- Parents should work with their teens to teach them about bullying terms, roles, and the antibullying formula: Stop, Save, Report.
- Parents of bullies should use protoconversation skills to identify the emotional intent behind the bullying, then implement creative consequences.
- Adults can help prevent social illiteracy by teaching teens social intelligence and helping them practice their own protoconversation skills.
- Adults should help monitor bullying by setting up Google Alerts and parent community groups.
- Teens often react well when they work together with parents to come up with a game plan in case bullying happens. This is a great opportunity for parents to share their stories.
- Encouraging teens to have empathy is incredibly important for them to combat social illiteracy and understand why threatening others through bullying is harmful.

Challenges You Can Do Right Now

Family Challenge: Bullying 101

1. Go over the types of bullying with family members and ask if they have ever experienced any type of bullying.
2. Go over the different roles in bullying.
3. Practice the Stop, Save, and Report formula for dealing with bullying and come up with a game plan that all parties are comfortable with.

Personal Challenge: Monitoring and Community Groups

1. Set up Google Alerts for your name and each of your family members' names.
2. Go through the directions in the resources section and think about who you would like to invite into your parenting community group.
3. Start the process to set up your group!

Family Challenge: Protoconversations and Social Intelligence

1. Read together the section in chapter 1 on protoconversations.
2. Watch some of the videos from my website on facial expressions.
3. Practice making and recognizing the six universal facial expressions.
4. Implement some of the empathy exercises.

CHAPTER 6

Risky Business:
Smoking, Drinking, Sex, and More

Every teen will engage in "risky" behavior. This can be experimenting with drugs, promiscuity, partying, or even breaking the law. In this chapter I review the two major causes of dangerous conduct: boredom and bad peer influence. At the end of the section, I will talk about how parents can create consequences and use other techniques to counteract the causes of unsafe actions.

The Yapsa family provides us with a fascinating look into "bad" teenage behavior. The Yapsa family is mom and dad—Clara and Bill—and twin daughters Sabrina and Natalie. Sabrina is a bubbly, sweet girl who struggles a bit in school and has a little bit of boy drama, but is overall happy and well-adjusted. Natalie, on the other hand, is teetering on "out of control." Her parents report her breaking curfew and dressing promiscuously and worry that she is dabbling in drugs. What makes the Yapsa family interesting is that the twin sisters could not be more different, despite growing up in the same home with the same parents and attending the same school. Neither is an extreme of golden child or black sheep, but they both have completely different personality traits. For the purposes of this chapter, I would like to focus on Natalie, but Sabrina provides an interesting comparison because it allows us to examine *why* these two are so different. During my preliminary meeting with the parents, I learned that most of Natalie's problems centered around her social life.

Clara started. "I think Natalie is on the brink of getting into serious trouble. She is constantly doing things that are just plain risky."

"Okay, can you give me some examples?" I asked.

"Yes. Some constant arguments we have are her breaking curfew and her wanting to go out to parties on the weekends. We say yes sometimes because we do not want her to sneak out entirely, but we are pretty sure she is drinking and probably doing pot, because we found a glass pipe in her drawer. I have smelled liquor on her breath. Last week we also found birth control in her purse. That's what made us call you—we are not sure if she is lying when she says it is for her skin. I feel like she could have come to me for that if that were really true." Her mom shook her head as if she was disagreeing with the arguments in her head.

"Does she have a boyfriend? A solid group of friends?" I questioned them.

Bill tried to answer; clearly this was an issue he was worried about. "She is on and off with different boys, I think. It's really hard to tell. She is not only very secretive, but she lies a lot. We can no longer tell if she is telling the truth."

"How do you know she is lying?" I asked.

Her mom shrugged. "Well, we catch her in the lies sometimes. She tells us she is going to be somewhere and then we check and she is not there. Also, a mom called me recently and told me that Natalie was sending mean messages to her daughter on the Internet. I was so embarrassed and ashamed. I mean, my daughter is the cool-girl bully." Her mom flashed fear and then anger—her upper eyelids went wide and then she pulled her lips into a tight grimace.

I made a mental note to unpack that later, but asked, "What do you mean?"

"She just"—Clara sighed and an expression of anguish flashed across her face—"she is that girl, that mean girl that I used to hate in school. She is mean to other girls, really catty and cliquey, and always has makeup on—"

Bill interrupted. "She wears promiscuous clothes. I have seen her use her allowance to buy designer things and she makes these 'haul' videos. It's really blatant materialism. Terrible." Bill curled up his lips in disgust. I knew a haul video is when someone buys new clothes and accessories and then comes home to make a video showing off her "haul" of goods on YouTube. Teenagers do it to show off to their friends and get fashion advice.

Clara nodded, her eyebrows pinched in an expression of sadness. "Really, she could not be more different from Sabrina. Sabrina has a small group of friends and is very into art; Natalie is all over the place and has no real passions about anything. Sabrina is not perfect, but they are in totally opposite worlds, even though they grew up in the same household, went to the same schools, and everything."

I wondered about the same thing. How could two girls with the same background be so different? I walked into Natalie's room for the first time and was arrested by the overwhelming smells of perfume, hair dye, and some kind of depilatory cream.

"Heya," she called as she sauntered across her room. "Sorry if it smells, I was doing my beauty routine." She glanced at my jeans. "What brand are those?"

Suddenly I felt anxious. I started questioning myself: Were my jeans cool enough? Was I dressed okay? Then I shook my head and realized that this was the feeling I had picked up on from the mom earlier. This girl was the "cool girl." In her mind, it was her job to make other people question themselves. I was not going to fall into that trap, and I was going to be myself—cool or not. "I'm not sure. I never really pay attention."

"Oh." Her face dropped. But she looked at me more closely. "Oh my gawd. Were you on *Real Housewives of Orange County* helping those girls?"

I laughed. "Yup, that was me. Do you watch that show?"

She bounded over. "Yes, I love that show. That was so cool! I can't believe you were working with them and now you're working with me." She squealed.

I held up my hand. "I'm glad you are excited, but we are not working together yet. I worked with the Curtin girls because they were also willing to do some work on themselves. You remember some of the serious stuff they told me? They took a leap, even if it was stuff that could get them into trouble, because we were going to turn a new page. I'm hoping it will be the same with you. But it is up to you."

She nodded her head vigorously and sat at her desk chair. "Yes. I'm ready. I do want to change."

Her face was honest, but I could see she had no idea how hard that might be. "Okay, that's awesome. Let's just get to know each other. What do you like to do?"

"I love clothes and shopping and hanging out with my friends. I also like to read and I used to play soccer, but I just don't have the time anymore. I still play with my sister occasionally. I'm really into fashion, though. I might do that, like, in real life."

"That's really cool. Do you have some styles or designers you like?" I asked. I could see surprise register on her face. "What? You seem surprised I asked?"

She sighed. "Usually adults don't really care what you say. I mean, they ask you and they are like, 'uh-huh, uh-huh,' and then they just ask about college and grades. I can't believe you actually care what designers I like!"

I put a hand on her shoulder—a universal indication of camaraderie. "Natalie, if you care, I care. And people should be interested in all aspects of you."

She pulled down a *Teen Vogue* from the stack on top of her
desk. She began flipping through the pages and stopped on one.
"I really love Roberto Cavalli's evening wear." She turned to another page that was dog-eared. "And I think Pucci scarves look
good on anyone." She glanced at my shirt. "Some of her fall line
would look amazing with your top." She flicked through some of
the glossy pages and briefly stopped on one. An expression of deep
sadness flashed across her face. Her lips pulled down, her chin
went back, and her eyebrows pinched together. She kept going.

"Wait!" I said, going back. "What do you think about this
one?"

"I dunno, nothing special." She tried to keep going, but I
knew I saw the sadness on her face. I'm a big believer in transparency and will often tell clients or people I am working with
what I see, so they can identify the emotion with me as opposed
to me working in secret.

"I don't know if your mom told you, but I read faces. It's not
a perfect science, but you flashed deep sadness when you looked
at that picture and I want to know why. Did you realize you
felt sad?"

She looked down at the picture again. "That's crazy you can do
that. I wish I could do that. Umm . . ." She paused and I waited for
her explanation. I assumed it was perhaps a garment she wanted, or
maybe a designer she didn't like on some personal level.

"Do you think I'm fatter than her?"

"What?" I was astonished. Natalie was a waif of a girl, very
much like a model, tall and thin. "Natalie, you want to learn
how to read faces? I can teach you. Let's start with this one.
Look at my face. You will see genuine surprise. My eyes are
wide, my eyebrows are up and curved—not up and straight, that

is fear. And my mouth is slightly open. That's surprise. So believe me when I say I'm surprised you could even think that you are fat."

"Ugh, I think about it all the time. My thighs are just so huge." She reached down and pinched at her inner thighs and disgust flashed across her face. I could literally see how disgusted she was with herself. I knew from experience that trying to convince her she wasn't fat would result in nothing, so I tried a different line of thinking that was closer to where I was hoping to get with her anyway.

"I can see you literally feel disgusted with yourself. But is there ever a time, even for a minute, when you feel thin? Or happy with your body?"

Natalie closed the magazine and tossed it on the desk. "I guess, when I'm with guys and they tell me I'm beautiful and want to hook up with me. It feels good to be wanted."

I kept my face neutral so as not to show her my sadness at this statement. "Do you do that often?"

She thought for a moment. "I have these guys in my group and I'm, like, in an open relationship with them. Well, one, Colby, is just a friend with benefits, but I guess we hook up occasionally."

"So you feel thin when this happens. Do you feel happy? Good about yourself? What goes through your mind?"

For a split second her chin jutted out in anger before she was able to recover and answer. "I mean, it's no big deal. I don't even know how I feel. Usually it is really casual. Like, we will"—she glanced at her closed bedroom door and dropped her voice— "you know, we will, like, smoke or whatever beforehand to take the awkwardness out of it. It's like taking an Ambien before watching a movie you have seen a hundred times. It just makes it better."

I put my hands up to show I meant no attack, I just wanted to get clarification. "Forgive me, but you showed anger before you said that. I know that a lot of people smoke and take pills to make an experience more fun or less awkward, but I don't know if *you* believe it does that for *you*. Your face didn't agree with your words that time."

I was a bit worried she would backtrack or get offended at me calling her out on the asynchronicity—the word we use when verbal content and facial expressions or body language do not match. But she just sighed. "I mean, sometimes it's cool. But then I wonder if I should be doing it. Like, am I a slut for hooking up with two guys? The guys are always telling me I'm an awesome chick for being so 'down.' But they also make fun of other girls at my school who hook up with multiple people. Does that apply to me? I also feel like I owe them for always sticking up for me and getting me free pot and Adderall before tests. It's, like, so confusing. So, I just don't know."

Her "not knowing" was answer enough for me, but I wanted to ask her about the drug use. "Do you like smoking, then? Since you hook up with them partially as a thank-you for the pot and Adderall, is it worth it?"

"I mean, I guess I like it. I like that it is a good excuse for whatever you want to do. If anyone were to call me a slut, I would just say I was too high to figure it out. I do it because they do it. I know that sounds bad, but it's true. If I didn't do it, they would think I was boring and wouldn't hang out with me. Also, it's not like there is anything better to do." This time I let sadness creep into my expression. I knew it wouldn't upset her because it matched the sadness on her face.

Before I share the rest of my discussion with Natalie at the end of the chapter, I want to review why many teens, including Natalie, engage in these kinds of risky behaviors. Then I will address what parents can do to prevent them.

The Centers for Disease Control and Prevention conducted

its 2009 Youth Risk Behavior Survey to see exactly how many teens were engaging in risky behaviors, and what kinds. They anonymously polled a sample of sixteen thousand high school students and found that during the thirty days before the survey, 28.3 percent of them had ridden in a car driven by a person who had been consuming alcohol, 17.5 percent had carried a weapon, 41.8 percent had drunk alcohol, and 20.8 percent had used marijuana. They also found that 34.2 percent of the students were currently sexually active and 38.9 percent of those sexually active students had not used a condom during their latrdy sexual intercourse. After I saw these shocking results, I wanted to know *why*. Why do teens like Natalie engage in these risky behaviors?

At Radical Parenting, we followed up on the study and found that there are two major causes of risky behavior. We did a survey with one hundred of our teen readers from all over the world. The survey was completely anonymous and the respondents agreed to answer the questions knowing we were researching why dangerous behavior is appealing to teens. This allowed us to get a high sample of kids who engaged in risky behaviors and were willing to talk about it, because they did not fear being caught or embarrassed. At the beginning of the survey we asked them to rank their risky behavior by checking off which dangerous activities they'd participated in, how often they did so, and why. The questions were created by our teen interns so all of the answer options were relevant. Here are some examples:

Have you smoked marijuana?

If so, how often?
        __Once __2–5 times __More than 10 times __More times than I can count __Only at parties __Once per week

If so, why do you smoke?
> __I like the feeling __Bored __My friends are doing it __It is the only thing there is to do __It's cool __Peer pressure __To fit in __It makes me feel grown up __To make adults in my life angry

If not, or not often, why not?
> __Bad for my health __Afraid of drug tests __Afraid of getting caught __It is illegal __I don't like the way it feels __I don't like the way it smells/tastes __I'm scared of it __Never have the opportunity __It's too expensive

·········

The survey, which covered marijuana, alcohol, breaking curfew, promiscuity, bullying, lying, and hazing, answered two questions for us: What kinds of risky behavior are teens engaging in? And, why do teens engage in risky behavior? In regard to the first question, we learned that the most popular types of risky behavior—all of the ones we cover in this book—included sexual promiscuity, marijuana use, abuse of prescription medication, alcohol consumption, bullying, and lying to parents. However, many of the most media-hyped dangerous activities ranked very low on the scale. For example, take a look at the following activities that we asked teens about that are often talked about in the media:

Rainbow Parties (A party where girls wear different colors of lipstick and perform oral sex on male attendees)
> __I participate in this activity regularly __I have participated in this activity less than 5 times __I know other people who participate in this activity __I only heard about this activity, never knew anyone who did it __I do not know what this is

The Choking Game (A game where players compete by hanging themselves with a rope or scarf to see who can go without air the longest and achieve a high from lack of oxygen to the brain)

> __I participate in this activity regularly __I have participated in this activity less than 5 times __I know other people who participate in this activity __I only heard about this activity, never knew anyone who did it __I do not know what this is

Cutting or Self-Harm

> __I participate in this activity regularly __I have participated in this activity less than 5 times __I know other people who participate in this activity __I only heard about this activity, never knew anyone who did it __I do not know what this is

Suicide Attempts

> __I participate in this activity regularly __I have participated in this activity less than 5 times __I know other people who participate in this activity __I only heard about this activity, never knew anyone who did it __I do not know what this is

·········

Of these activities, more than 92 percent of the time they were ranked with either the answer "I only heard about this activity, never knew anyone who did it" or "I do not know what this is."

It is important for parents to realize that many of the hyped teen activities are either extremely local—only performed in certain areas—or urban myths: teens have heard of the activities, but never knew anyone who actually engaged in them.

Once we knew which risky behaviors were most prevalent, we wanted to figure out why teens engage in them. What we were surprised to learn was that the majority of the answers fell into two categories: boredom and bad friends. These are two of the reasons that Natalie listed when I asked her why she smoked pot. Let's first talk about boredom. Many of the teenagers said that they drink alcohol and smoke marijuana because there is simply "nothing else to do" or because being intoxicated makes whatever they normally do on a Saturday night—movies, TV, video games—more exciting. Natalie also alluded to this when she claimed that smoking pot makes hooking up more comfortable and taking Ambien before an old movie makes it more interesting. Leisure studies researchers led by Linda Caldwell corroborated this theory and Natalie's behavior. Their work shows that many adolescents turn to risky behavior because they are bored and feel they have nothing else to do with their time. Researchers from these studies even created an in-school program called TimeWise to teach students how not to be bored, as a strategy for drug use prevention. Unfortunately, while the workshop worked in the short term, it did not have lasting effects.

Many of our teenagers also told us they constantly need more to feel stimulated or excited. What was exciting last week is no longer interesting today.

> "There is a whole crew of adrenaline junkies like me. We do things just because they are exciting, like riding roller coasters without our seat belts or snorting wasabi. The only problem is we have to keep going bigger and more dangerous because once you do it once, it's boring."
>
> —Dinah, 16

Dinah's quote is scary for parents because it puts more value on antiboredom than on personal safety. Many teens actually express a greater fear of boredom than of getting hurt. Take for example this conversation I had with a potential teen intern:

Teen: I love to do things that are kind of risky. That's a hobby.

Me: Like what?

Teen: Small stuff like snorting wasabi. And bigger stuff like driving down the street blindfolded to see if I can make it to my driveway, or taking vodka eye shots.

Me: But all of those things could have long-term damage, like burning your sinuses, crashing your car, or damaging your vision. Doesn't it hurt?

Teen: Yeah, it hurts—but it's better than being bored.

Me: Wait, do you really think that potentially losing your vision by pouring vodka in your eye is better than being bored at a party one night?

Teen: You don't understand. Being bored is, like, the worst. It means you are lame, it means you are left with yourself, it means you are lonely. I would do anything not to be bored.

This conversation was enlightening for me because it pinpointed the underlying emotions behind "boredom." Many teenagers equate being bored with being uncool. Most important, being bored means they might be boring, which to them means they will not have friends and are, consequently, alone. Therefore, antiboredom behavior ties right into the second reason teens are attracted to risky behavior: bad friends. Natalie also mentioned this in our discussion when she claimed that she was afraid that if she didn't smoke pot, people would think she was boring and she would therefore lose her friends. One of our seventeen-year-old interns, Alexandra, wrote an article titled "Why Do We Keep Bad Friends Around?" Below is an excerpt from her story:

> I had this one friend I met in the beginning of 9th grade. One certain instance I can recall so clearly, is one where I was forced to call my mom at 6:00 in the morning, from a motel that I ended up at. With K, I was very easygoing because she was so high-strung, which is usually how I am. That night, K, 2 other friends, and I got picked up by a couple of K's guy friends, that I knew from school. The girls I was with were drinking, except for myself. Being as vulnerable as they were, they agreed to go to a hotel for the night, even though I was literally screaming my head off and on the verge of crying when they agreed to this, but none of them could care an inch about me at that point. We get there, and I am texting my mom, normally, debating on whether I should tell her, and if so, what I should tell her. We get in the room and immediately one of the girls started getting sick (a friend of K's who also was not fond of this motel idea), so I stayed with her in the bathroom. While in there, I find out K and the other friend are sleeping with the two guys who brought us there. I am freaking out because I left my phone on the bed where one of the couples is hooking up. It is dark, I am crying because I wanted to go home, and the poor girl in the bathroom is sick as a dog. She ended up having alcohol poisoning, and if it weren't for me watching her and tending to her, God knows what would have happened? Eventually I found my phone, at 5:30 a.m., and went outside to call my mom, crying. She was completely understanding, but I was no longer allowed to hang out with K. But I just didn't have the heart for it, so I just continued to be friends with her.

Like many of the parents reading this story, I see this kind of behavior over and over again. Even if teenagers know that their friends are a bad influence, often treating them poorly and geting them into trouble, many continue to hang out with them. Natalie was only barely aware of the fact that she did not really like smoking pot and only did it to fit in. She also was not conscious of the fact that she was hooking up with these boys because *they* thought it was cool, even though it wasn't good or enjoyable for her.

. . . .

The type of peer pressure Natalie and many teens experience is very real. Emory University professor of neuroeconomics Gregory S. Berns and his fellow researchers wanted to understand how the neural and behavioral mechanics of social influence affect teens' decisions. They took a group of twelve- to seventeen-year-olds and had them listen to a short clip of a popular song. After they listened to the song, the participants marked how familiar they were with the song and how much they enjoyed it, on a five-point scale. The clip was then played again, but this time two-thirds of the participants saw how the others had rated it. When the popularity of the song was not shown, teens only changed their own ratings 12 percent of the time. But when they were shown how popular the song was, teens changed their ratings 22 percent of the time! Not surprisingly, 79 percent of the 22 percent who changed their rating did so to better match the other participants' ratings.

Following these findings, researchers wondered: Did participants actually like the song better because it was more popular? Or were they simply changing the ratings to fit in with what was more popular? To find out, they observed the brain behavior in each of the teen participants as they listened to the clips, voted, and saw (or did not see) the popularity ratings. They found that according to the brain activity, when teens adjusted their ratings to fit the song's popularity, it had nothing to do with their increased enjoyment of the music. Rather, the areas of the brain associated with anxiety and pain showed increased activity when participants realized the popularity rating did not correlate with their own. This shows that it is literally painful to not fit in with one's peer group. Our body and our mind will often do anything to fit in and avoid the "pain" of being left out. Taking this study into consideration, we see that if boredom can also potentially make you seem boring to your friends, and therefore not a part of your peer group, the brain sees this as painful and will do anything it can to avoid it—which, in real life, often means engaging in risky behaviors.

Before we review how parents can address boredom and negative peer influence, I want to briefly highlight some of the different areas of teens' risky behavior. Sexuality, self-esteem, dating, and substance abuse seem to top the list of both parent and teen concerns. First, sexual promiscuity is an issue that comes up over and over again for teens and their parents. Interestingly, the concerns surrounding sexuality are very similar for parents of both boys and girls. When we asked parents of boys and girls, "What are your biggest concerns regarding your son or daughter and sexuality?", the top three responses were that they worried their teens would not practice safe sex, that they would engage in sexual activities too early, and that sex was treated with less respect as oral sex, porn, and vulgar rap videos were becoming more acceptable and even "cool" to teenagers. This was a major concern for Natalie's parents, especially her father, who worried she was not respecting her body and was therefore engaging in mature sexual acts before she was ready. We presented these top three concerns to a group of fourteen- to sixteen-year-olds in a teen workshop on sexuality, and teens agreed that these are the issues that are also concerns for them! Here are a few anecdotes from this discussion:

"I think my parents would agree with these. The scary thing is they are right to be worried about it. When I think about sex, I also worry about having sex with my boyfriend too soon or whether or not I should use a condom if he doesn't like it. But I can't talk to them about it because they would just freak out."

—15-year-old female

"Oral sex is not a big deal. Parents can worry about it, but they need to know my friends and I think of oral sex more casually than they do. It's kind of expected of girls when you are hooking up with them."

—16-year-old male

Interestingly, the comment made by the sixteen-year-old male incited many angry remarks from females in the room. The girls argued that the expectation of oral sex was unfair, but still true. I challenged them on this, asking the girls, "If you think it is so unfair, why don't you say no?" Sadly, the answer was "I don't want to say no because then he might not like me." I will address how parents can talk to their teenagers about practicing safe and respectful sex at an appropriate age, but I also want to look at how this answer leads into our second major issue in risky behavior: self-esteem.

Sexuality and its ties to self-esteem are very confusing and dangerous for many adolescents. Women of all ages teeter on the edge of owning their sexuality, hooking up with guys when they feel empowered, but at the same time feeling ashamed or slutty. Natalie is a perfect example of this. She was extremely confused about how she was supposed to act and feel. She wondered out loud, "Am I a slut for hooking up with two guys? They are always telling me I'm an awesome chick for being so 'down.' But they also make fun of other girls at my school who hook up with multiple people. Does that apply to me? . . . It's, like, so confusing. So, I just don't know." Also look at the following contradictory anecdotes from both female and male teens from our articles and forums:

> *"I just fired my girlfriend."*
>
> —16-year-old male
>
> *"We play the grabbing butts game at school to see how many we can grab during recess. It's just fun, nothing serious."*
>
> —14-year-old female
>
> *"I never know if I should play hot and sexy or unreachable and an angelic virgin. Which do guys like better?"*
>
> —15-year-old female

It has been reported over and over again that the cause of youth's confused sexuality is due to the overt display of sexuality in the media because it sends mixed signals, causes desensitization, and, in some cases, glamorizes promiscuity. Yet a new influence on teens and their sexual identity is celebrity intimacy. Celebrities used to be faraway ideal figures, hard to reach and only visible in magazines. With the rise of movie stars tweeting about their lunch and posting personal pictures on their Facebook pages, and a slew of reality TV shows featuring "real lives" of famous people, celebrities seem much more relatable to teenagers. This greatly affects teenagers' self-esteem, body image, and sexuality. I hear tweens talk about celebrities like they are the newest small-town gossip. Because celebrities seem much more real, relatable, and easy to reach on Twitter and Facebook, adolescents are beginning to use them as points of comparison. *If Pink can't keep it together with all of her money, then I guess I'm okay. Paris is gorgeous and even she got breast implants—her sex video made her more popular!* Celebrities, whether they are actually engaging in or just pretending to be partaking in drunk driving, sex tapes, and other forms of risky behavior, seem normal to teenagers. Reality shows and racy dramas also portray seemingly average teenagers throwing lavish parties, getting arrested, and acting like overindulged, nearly criminal twenty-five-year-olds.

As teenagers experiment with their sexuality and celebrity behavior becomes the norm, the terms for dating and intimacy get even more complicated and diverse. One of our seventeen-year-old interns, Rachel, wrote an article about four of the different kinds of teen romantic relationships.

> From long distance to too much PDA, the fear of breaking up to flings, teens can be really confusing when it comes to why they date, who they date, and most importantly HOW they date. I will narrow it down to the most common relationships and explain the who, the how, the why, and what we really think.

1. Friend with Benefits

Who: Most likely your teen's close friend or an ex.

How: The two teens in question are "just friends" but do a little bit more than what friends would do, such as kissing.

Why: This is the awkward phase where you think you like your friend but they only think of you as a friend. Or your feelings for your ex still haven't gone away.

What we think: If your teen is in this type of relationship, they're probably either confused, or really hope that no one else finds out.

2. The "Tech" Relationship

Who: Someone your teen recently met through technology.

How: Their whole relationship consists of IMing and texting each other. It's difficult for them to talk in person with each other, but they talk nonstop when messaging.

Why: Technology gives teens a certain degree of confidence, so when you are face-to-face with someone, it feels awkward without that boost of confidence.

What we think: This form of "dating" is really unstable. Since there is only one form of communication between the two teens, when they actually go on a "real" date, there will be many, and I say MANY awkward silences. Respectfully yet casually mention to your teen that you don't think this kind of relationship is healthy. However, please try not to confuse a "tech" relationship with a regular relationship that texts each other a lot. In a regular relationship, though they text and instant message each other a lot, they still would rather talk to each other in person or call.

3. The "Wedding" Relationship

Who: A person who your teen has been dating for a while (as a teen, anything more than 8 months could be considered as "a while").

How: The two are joined at the hip, only going to certain outings with friends if the "other" is there.

Why: They want to be completely focused on their boyfriend/girlfriend, which may lead them to exclude their other friends.

What we think: It's not really healthy to have your life completely revolving around ONE person, especially if the relationship started not too "long" ago. These relationships can cause your teen the most heartache if or when it breaks up. Explain to your teen casually that you think he doesn't have to do everything with JUST his girlfriend and that you miss seeing _____ (insert best buddy's name here) around, though you like _____ (insert special other's name here) very much. This may not immediately change the situation, but at least, your teen will be thinking about what is absent in their life.

4. The Open Relationship

Who: A person your teen may or may not have been dating on-again, off-again.

How: They would say that they're dating each other, but they're okay if the other dates someone else on the side.

Why: Some teens are afraid of commitment or really just don't want to be "stuck" with someone else. They might use the buffet analogy (how they want to sample a little of everything before "sitting down" with one plate).

What we think: Just for the record, parents? Not ALL teens like this. Some of my friends are completely devoted to their one person. However, I do regret that some teens do believe in open relationships. They may be emotionally immature or (dare I say it?) indecisive. If your teen is in an open relationship and you're not okay with it, say something! This type of relationship is hard to point out (by the parent) without your child getting defensive. Just remember to keep an ear open to why, as it helps a lot during these types of conversations.

This is only a small review of the multitude of intricacies in teen dating life. Unfortunately, open relationships and friends with benefits are almost always lopsided, with one teen being more in "love" or "lust" than the other. Oftentimes the girl is the one left feeling unwanted or not good enough, which greatly affects her self-esteem. As we saw with Natalie, she said that she had one "friend with benefits" and one "open relationship." This made her question her own self-worth and value. To numb her "awkwardness," or her lack of desire to hook up with these boys, she turned to substance abuse—either marijuana or drinking. According to the Partnership Attitude Tracking Study (PATS), teen girls are at much higher risk and much more likely to identify "self-medicating" benefits with drinking and getting high. When teen girls were presented with the statement "using drugs helps kids deal with problems at home," 68 percent agreed. This is an 11 percent increase since 2008. In addition, 53 percent claimed that taking drugs helps them forget their problems.

Not only are teens using drugs to deal with—or not deal with—their problems, substance use has become a social unifier. We saw this in our survey as well as in Natalie's explanation of why she does drugs. Whether it is "pharma parties"—parties where teens get together and raid their parents' medicine cabinets—sharing bongs, or taking tequila shots, hundreds of teens have reported to us that using substances is the only way "nerdy" kids feel they can hang out with "cool" kids. The social camaraderie that comes with obtaining illegal substances, consuming them, and then hiding the evidence is, horrifyingly, a main way teens bond.

Can parents even begin to compete with all of these influences and motivations that cause teens to engage in risky behavior? Yes! Below I review a wide variety of tips that actual teens have shared with us to counteract the allure of dangerous activities.

1. Encouraging the Right Kind of Risk Taking

I believe the best way to discourage dangerous risk taking is to encourage positive risk taking. This is a technique I have had great success with because it both addresses the negative effects of boredom and scratches the adrenaline-junkie part of a teen's brain that itches. Positive risk taking can be supported in three ways, depending on your child's needs: family adventures, friend adventures, and personal adventures. Family risk taking is great when parents want to get to know their teens better or find more agreeable family-time activities. Family adventure ideas include:

- Roller coaster parks
- River rafting trips
- Camping
- Adventure vacations
- Ropes courses
- Geocaching scavenger hunts in your area

If your child has a proclivity for risk, but bad friends are not an issue, you can also encourage group activities for your teen and his or her peer group. Friend adventure ideas include:

- Skateboarding parks
- Surfing lessons
- Roller coaster parks
- Skiing and snowboarding
- Rock climbing
- Paragliding, hang gliding, skydiving, or parasailing

You can also encourage solo activities to help your teen not only get the advantages of positive risk taking, like feeling independent and self-confident, but also get in shape and spend time learning new things. Examples:

- High school sports teams
- Entering a competition (scholarships, marathons, poetry, writing, teen entrepreneur contests . . .)
- Running for student council
- Going into politics, working to change a law, or starting a blog
- Rock climbing or other classes for extreme sports

Taking risks is not only good for your kids to get the adrenaline healthily out of their system, but also helps them mature and learn their limits by taking educated risks.

2. Finding Passion

Another antiboredom strategy is encouraging your kids to find and follow what makes them passionate. This also works to boost their self-esteem because they can feel accomplished and proud of what they are doing. I used this strategy when I worked with the Curtin family on the show *The Real Housewives of Orange County*. Raquel Curtin was a self-proclaimed wild child. In our first meeting she explained that she felt lost and unmotivated as she approached her nineteenth birthday. I began by asking her what she loved to do, what made her feel excited and made time pass quickly. After a few false starts, she brought up her artwork. Although it had been years since she regularly practiced, and she admitted she didn't even have any supplies in the house anymore, I could see that it was something she really cared about. Before addressing some of the other issues, I wanted her to focus on this. Her assignments were to buy art supplies and start a few charcoal pieces on her own. In the few weeks before our next meeting, she had gotten supplies and completed a few oil paintings for the family's new house and made plans for a number of pieces she wanted to give away as gifts. The change was immediate. She said she felt happier, her relationships with her parents got better, and she was better able to articulate other areas in her life. Parents can help their teens to identify their passions and cultivate them to increase their child's self-esteem and self-worth. We include a series of questions in the Challenges section at the end of the chapter to help you identify and cultivate your teen's passions.

3. Embracing Change

Encouraging change can put distance between bad friends and your teen, and it can ward off boredom. I believe that change is one of the most important aspects of being human. Yet it has become something that people dread, avoid, and fear. Change can bring growth and new opportunities to challenge our habits and behaviors. Even though it can be scary, when we are taken out of our comfort zone, we are able to look at ourselves, our lives, and our habits from a new place and reevaluate. This can be empowering for teens as well as parents. There are three ways parents can use change as a tool for discouraging risky behavior.

First, changing friends can be a great way to eliminate negative peer influence. Of course, this is easier said than done. When friends are the problem, I encourage parents to attempt to bring new friends into their kids' lives by selecting camps or programs outside their hometown for the vacation breaks. This can help their children get distance from their peer group and see that there are alternative types of friends. Parents can also encourage their kids to join some activities outside of school that would not include the negative peer group. This can be sports teams, volunteer organizations, or religious groups. Parents can then ask after new friends that are not part of the peer group and invite them over for sleepovers, family outings, or other get-togethers. This way parents are not saying anything negative against their children's "bad" friends—this often alienates teens—but merely encouraging alternative positive friends and activities.

Another kind of change that can help prevent risky behavior is the introduction of a role model. I have asked many of the families I work with if they have a young role model we can introduce into the life of their teen. This can be a cousin, aunt, uncle, coach, teacher, or even an old babysitter. Same sex is preferable so they have someone to look up to. This person will be able to not only talk to your teen about goals, behavior, and friends, but also take them out to do alternative types of activities. This helps with boredom and gives teens a break from their friends. Most important, these changes will allow teens and parents to reset after vacations or role models are introduced. In this way, each person can reevaluate priorities, behavior, and emotions.

4. Choosing Battles and Gaining Perspective on What Is "Normal"

I am always surprised to find in the families I work with that either the teenagers do not exactly know what the house rules are, or they are trying to abide by what I call "swinging rules." Swinging rules are rules that change depending on the situation, mood of the parents, and what has happened that week. This sounds something like "Well, he usually has to be home by 11:00 p.m., unless it is a party we do not like, and then he needs to be home by 10:00 p.m. If it is a movie or something like that, we might push it back to 12:00 a.m." This kind of swinging rule is almost worse than having no rule at all, because it ensures there will be either an argument or a "misunderstanding" of the rule every time the teen wants to go out! It is very important to get clear on house rules and curfews and eliminate anything that could be open to interpretation. I understand that parents want to be flexible with teens and that is how these swinging rules get implemented. But you can still have "defined flexibility." A defined flexible version of the rule above would be "There is an 11:00 p.m. curfew on weekend nights. If we are not able to call and talk to the parents of the house he is spending time at, he must be home by 10:00 p.m. Movies with Brian, Josh, or David can push the curfew to 12:00 a.m. because we know those boys well." These kinds of rules make it very clear to teens what their limitations are and cut down on arguments and miscommunications.

I also recommend that parents put systems in place for checking in. We created a ninety-nine-cent iPhone application called iCurfew that parents and teens can use for exactly this purpose. Teenagers simply open the application whenever they get to their location and hit "check-in" on the application page. This sends an uneditable link to their parents' e-mail addresses. This way, parents can know exactly where their teenager is, which helps with safety but also with pickup locations later. If parents have had a problem in the past with their teen not being where he says he will be, this application can be an addition to a rule. For example, parents can say, "We will allow your curfew to be 12:00 a.m. tonight, but we want you to send an iCurfew check-in when you get to the party at 9:00 p.m., and at 11:00 p.m. so we know you are safe and where you are." This way teens get what they want—to stay out later—and parents can get what they want: knowing where their child is the whole night.

When setting up house rules, choose your battles wisely. Decide what the priorities are for you. A comic once joked, "Will Eminem's daughter rebel by listening to Christian music?" Every parent has different perspectives on what makes them uncomfortable or what they think is inappropriate for their teen. It is important to get clear on this. When making rules, think about the whole picture. If kids are getting good grades and doing well in extracurriculars, perhaps a later curfew is a good reward. On the flip side, if they are being rude at home, not doing chores, or not saying thank you, having an at-home weekend might not be a bad idea.

I also encourage parents to accept that some experimentation is normal. In fact, when talking about risky behavior, parents often ask me, "How do I know if my teen's acting out is worse than just normal teen experimentation?" The answer is unique for every family, but I always encourage parents to ask themselves two questions about their teen's behavior:

- Do I feel that I am being disrespected?
- Is my teen's safety or future endangered by these actions?

If the answer is no to these questions, then, as irritating as your teen's behavior might be, his or her actions fall in the realm of "normal" experimentation. If you answer yes to either of these questions, it is important to get very clear on which areas you and your teen need to set some boundaries on. As difficult as that is, being too strict or trying to limit teens in every area of their lives might encourage them to rebel more or even embrace risky behavior when they finally get into college or move out of the house. It is important for parents to realize that it is completely normal for teens to experiment with their boundaries and limits, as long as their personal safety is not in jeopardy and parents are not being disrespected.

5. The Power of Scapegoats

When teens are engaging in risky behaviors, I like to suggest the use of the "scapegoat" to parents and teens as well. A scapegoat is a person who is blamed for the wrongdoings, mistakes, or faults of others. I think that it is extremely important for teens to learn how to say no to peer pressure, but there are times when it is easier to use parents as a scapegoat. This is especially true when hazing takes place on sports teams or at after-school parties. On one of our teen forums, a teen posted the following question for fellow adolescents:

> "Situation: Your friends want you to go to a drinking party but you don't want to disappoint them or give them a chance of trying to convince you to go when you know you really don't want to. . . .
>
> "Is it okay to use your parents as an excuse by saying something like:
>
> —My mom wants me home tonight, sorry.
> —I've gotta check in at my house first and my parents might not let me leave again.

—My dad and I have plans tomorrow and I've gotta wake up early.

"Do you think we should use our parents as an excuse?"

Most of the teen responders said that teens should have good enough friends that they would be able to tell them the truth, but if not, then parents are a great excuse:

"There are some teens who aren't good with peer pressure. That has to be taken into consideration. I think using your parents as an excuse is a smart approach for certain situations. Not a lot of questions will be asked and it's an easy way out. Most parents never mind being used as an excuse."

Drinking and hazing are big issues for teens. I recommend first that teens say no and perhaps give an honest reason, but sometimes this doesn't cut it. Parents might want to have a discussion with their teens, letting them know that they can take the blame and teens have the option of saying, "My mom is waiting; she will smell it on me," or if it is another substance, "My parents randomly drug-test." This way if teens are ever being pressured to engage in risky behaviors or get hazed and are scared to say no (or no is not accepted as an answer), they have a last-resort escape.

6. Proper Discipline and Punishments

Unfortunately, even if you have nonswinging rules and agreed-upon systems, teens sometimes break them. Discipline not only serves as a consequence for the behavior, but also can encourage them to not break the rules next time. First, when possible, parents should try to fit the punishment to the crime. This helps reinforce the lesson. If your kid takes the car out without permission, make her wash the car every weekend for a month (without the keys). This helps them learn about cars and responsibility, which is what was missing when they took the car the first time around. Second, ask teens to come up with their own punishment. Often this helps them to be less angry at you and to own the consequences. Making them think about an appropriate punishment for the crime they committed means they have to think about the crime and its implications. Third, make sure the punishment does not also punish you. I have parents who take away the cell phone and then have no way to communicate with their kids when they need to pick them up from practice or school. If you make a punishment, stick to it, and if you say no, don't mean "maybe." Making a punishment and then not holding to it is worse than no punishment at all, because it teaches teens that you do not stay true to your word and if they wait long enough, you might forget. It also lessens the value of your "no."

7. Talking About Sex, Intimacy, and Dating

The proliferation of teen moms and underage sexuality on TV may be both a cause and a cure for promiscuity. Shows like *Teen Mom* and *16 and Pregnant*, as well as characters on popular teen shows, like Quinn in *Glee* or Amy in *The Secret Life of the American Teenager*, all bring teen sexuality to the surface. Although some of these shows glamorize teen sexuality, this is how parents can bring up the issues that their teens are dealing with. I highly recommend that parents, in addition to having the nuts-and-bolts sex talk, have an ongoing conversation about sexuality with their teenagers. The questions that a fifth grader might have are very different from the issues that come up for a tenth grader. Using media as a conversation starter not only brings up issues of safe sex, intimacy, and dating in a more casual and less threatening way, but also neutralizes the negative effect that shows can have—whether they are making teen moms famous or making teen motherhood look easy. This is also a great way for parents to talk to boys about respect, expectations from girls, and boundaries with the opposite sex, as all of these issues come up on shows. Here are some TV shows, books, and videos that either tackle or glamorize sexuality and serve as great conversation starters for parents:

16 and Pregnant, or *Teen Mom*

"What would it be like if you or your girlfriend got pregnant now?"

"Do you think these girls knew about safe sex and ignored what they had been taught, or do you think they did not know about practicing safe sex?"

Glee

"Some of the friends use each other for sex or practice bisexuality because they are 'bored.' What do you think of that?"

"Quinn gets pregnant when she cheats with Puck. Does cheating happen at your school? Do you think most people get pregnant their first time having sex with someone?"

"Quinn recovers from her pregnancy quickly. Do you think that is realistic?"

Twilight book or movie series by Stephenie Meyer

"Bella and Edward talk about being intimate quite a bit. What do they disagree on? Who do you agree with?"

Top rap videos on YouTube

"Do you think that these videos are a realistic portrayal of
    women?"
"Would you be proud to be in this video?"

Use these questions to discuss their ideas about sexuality
rather than challenge them. Parents can help teenagers think
through the messages that are being sent to them through media
and then about how they would act in their own life if such issues came up. In this way, parents can help teach about appropriate sexuality and intimacy, while still teaching them that their
sexual feelings are normal.

8. Dealing with Liars

Unfortunately, dealing with teens and lying could be an entire
book on its own. I know many teenagers lie to their parents
about their risky behavior and parents are desperately trying to
unmask, detect, and decipher what is truth and what is fiction. I
have worked with thousands of teens, many of whom have lied to
me. Some of the lies I have caught and some of the lies I missed,
but I have slowly integrated researcher Paul Ekman's studies on
lie detection into my work with teens. You may recall that we
discussed Paul Ekman's work in chapter 1 when we talked about
facial microexpressions.

Lie detection is more of an art than a science, but I have found
that when I follow a few rules, I can almost always decipher when
teens are lying to me or their parents. An example I will use to
demonstrate the following tips is when I was working with a teen
boy named Clayton and his parents. Clayton had broken curfew
the night before we met and had a large bruise on his face. His
parents also told me that he had smelled like alcohol when he stum-

bled home. His parents could not get anything out of him, but had heard through the grapevine that a party across town had gotten broken up by the cops. Pictures from a partier's camera were confiscated and turned in to the school by a parent. The school was preparing to take action against all of the kids at the party because marijuana was found. The school announced that they would be lenient with kids who came forward before being called in. Clayton's parents, believing Clayton to have been at the party—breaking both their rules and the school's rules on curfews and drug use—wanted Clayton to admit what happened and go directly to the school. Clayton insisted he had not been at the party—"and even if I was," he told them, "I wouldn't be dumb enough to be in any pictures with pot, so why should I turn myself in for no reason?" The parents called me in to verify or falsify his story and help encourage him to go in to the school. I look for four signals of lying when I am trying to figure out if a teen is telling the truth. Using Clayton as an example, I'll explain the four indicators:

- **If a teenager is talking and the facial expressions do not match the verbal content, he or she is usually lying or covering up an emotion.** When people are lying, they are focusing very hard on what they are saying and how the person they are speaking with is reacting to the lie. Therefore, they often forget that their own face needs to follow the lie as well. When I first sat down with Clayton, I asked him how he got the bruise on his face. He responded that he was just roughhousing with some friends and it was all fun and games. Even though his words made it sound like it was fun and "no big deal," his facial expression was pure fear and anger. His eyes were wide, his eyebrows were pulled together, and his mouth was taut. If he really had just been roughhousing, this answer would have been a breeze and his face would have been relaxed.

- **The sequence of events is an easy place to detect a lie.** A very easy way to tell if teenagers are lying about their detailed story or set of events is to ask them to tell the sequence to you backward. People who are telling the truth can effortlessly start with the end of the night and work their way backward—because it is the truth. Liars, on the other hand, have rehearsed the story they'll tell you only one way, so when you ask them to tell it backward they have a lot of trouble recalling details and the correct backward order. This is exactly what happened with Clayton. I asked him to describe what happened the night before. He easily said, "Met up with my friends at Tyron's place. We drove in his car to McDonald's for dinner. We stopped at 7-Eleven for sodas. Then we went to Stephen's house and chilled there. Played Wii. Then walked over to Tyron's again and roughhoused in the backyard. We watched a movie and it got late; I didn't realize I missed curfew. That's all." I replied that sounded simple enough. Then I asked him to tell me the events backward. After a few hesitations—"Do what? . . . Um . . . Well, let's see . . ."—I knew he couldn't tell me it backward because it was fabricated. He even mixed up the order of events by saying, "We watched the movie late, like I said. And then, uh, before that we played Wii and got drinks at 7-Eleven." I stopped him before he could even finish because the events did not match up.

- **Always pay extra attention to specific responses.** When people tell the truth, they are usually happy to answer your questions directly. Liars will often respond with general beliefs instead of specific responses. For example, I asked Clayton if he had drunk alcohol the night before and he responded, "I don't think it is good for people who are underage to drink." This is a subconscious way to avoid lying. Liars may also repeat the question back to you in order to buy time to think about their answer.

- **Watch their body language at the end of the discussion.** When someone is anxious or nervous about a topic—which can often indicate lying or at least covering up the truth—they'll be happy when you're done talking about it. If you change the subject, a phone rings, or you get off topic, and your teen shows relief—either in the face, by exhaling large amounts of air, or by relaxing the body—he or she is very happy to be off the topic you were just talking about. Now, if you are grilling your teen about a new boyfriend or girlfriend, this kind of behavior is expected; of course teens are anxious talking to you about that! But if your teen shows relief after a seemingly innocuous subject is changed, I encourage you to go back and figure out what he or she was so anxious about.

Deciphering lies is tricky because you always want to give your child the benefit of the doubt. Ekman also says that it is much harder to catch close friends and family members in lies because we know them too well. If you catch your child in a lie, you want to make sure that you emphasize the lie just as much as the crime. This reinforces the fact that as a parent, you would rather hear the truth about something bad than be lied to. I think it is also important to explain to kids that even if they do not get caught, there is a definite mental effect from telling lies. Often our own guilt can be the worst punishment of all. I encourage parents to reward honesty in their household and talk about previous mistakes and lies and how you have grown from those experiences. Unfortunately, lying is a natural part of being human, but we can teach our kids that it is not right. When I ended the discussion with Clayton and asked him about his schedule the next day at school, he showed instant relief—signifying to me that he couldn't wait to get off the subject of the party. Before bringing in his parents, I told him about the clues I had picked up on and that I was pretty sure he was lying. I gave him a choice, asking him if he wanted to tell his parents the truth or if he wanted me to tell them he was lying. Fortunately, he was willing to admit that he had been at the party and we made a deal with his parents that Clayton would go to the school administrator, but turn only himself in, as he did not want to be seen as a snitch. Most important, I wanted Clayton to see that by telling the truth, he actually gained his parents' respect and prevented more trouble later on, as the school did have pictures from the party . . . and he was in a few of them.

. . . .

I also want to address families that have moved past risky behavior into serious danger. Sometimes families need a little more help. When I am working with families, there is a check system I use to decide when we need to get help from a therapist or psychologist:

- The police have been involved more than once.
- The teen has talked about or hurting himself or herself with cutting, disordered eating, alcohol poisoning, or other behaviors that could cause self-harm.
- Family members or friends have been threatened or physically harmed by aggressive outbursts.
- The teen has had more than one failing grade on a report card.
- The teen has skipped school or cut class more than twice without the parents' knowledge.

These usually indicate deeper, more dangerous issues that need to be handled outside the home with a therapist. Many parents feel ashamed or mistrusting of therapeutic help. I work alongside many therapists with my clients who need a little bit of extra help, and I have seen tremendous improvement. It is okay to ask for outside intervention. In the resources section at the end of the book, we have listed some suggestions for finding extra help near you.

Often, though, what parents think is a really bad situation can be fixed by an in-depth, honest discussion. For instance, in the beginning of the chapter we left off talking to Natalie about how she hooks up with boys and does drugs because she thinks it makes her less boring to hang out with.

We both sat in silence for a moment. Natalie put her head in her hands. "It sounds really awful to say that out loud."

"Okay, really let yourself experience how awful it feels to admit that. But then also feel how good it is to get it off your chest. Talking about it is the first step to changing it." Natalie pursed her lips, a gesture that usually means the speaker is holding something back. "What is it?" I pushed.

"I do like hanging out and sometimes smoking is fun. But I really do hate hooking up with them. Colby is especially gross. The terrible part is even though I hate it, I cannot imagine changing it. There is just too much risk." Her voice raised a few notes and I could hear the panic.

"Whoa, whoa. No one is asking you to change this all at once. I know it is going to take courage and bravery and time. Remember how earlier I asked what made you feel thin?" She nodded. "What else makes you feel really good about your body and forget how much you hate your thighs?" I knew that Natalie did not experiment with risky behavior because she was a thrill seeker or adrenaline junkie, so I wanted to find a passion that could give her the confidence she needed to say no and accept change.

Natalie bit at her purple nails for a few moments. "I mean, it's been a while, but I guess I felt really awesome after I won a soccer game. I stopped playing in high school because I didn't think I would have enough time."

I smiled. "That is something we can definitely work with." I always ask my clients' permission before I challenge them to do some major change, because I want them to own it and feel I am respecting their space. "Look, Natalie, I think I can help you. I think that you can make your parents happy and your friends happy and, most important, make yourself happy. It's not going to be easy, but I'm willing to do it if you are. Do I have your permission to work with you on this?"

"Definitely," she said.

The rest of that session we worked on integrating soccer into her life. Her parents agreed that she could join a club team, outside of school, to get back into playing. I also wanted her to do something that would stimulate her intellectually. I thought a role model could be a great addition and change instigator in her life, but wanted to find someone who she could look up to and share her interests with. Knowing that she had a passion for fashion, I decided to validate her love of clothes by asking her to put together some drawings of her designs in a portfolio. Three weeks later, at our next meeting, Natalie had a few of her drawings done and had already attended two soccer practices.

Natalie cleared off her desk for us. "I actually forgot how much I like it. I mean, I'm so tired after practice, but it's going to whip me into shape and the girls are super nice."

My ears perked up at the mention of new friends. That was a side effect I had hoped Natalie would get from joining a soccer team, but I never want to push new friends on a teenager. "What are they like?"

"They are really cool. One girl goes to my school and the others go to school nearby, but they all hang out on the weekends and stuff and they invited me over on Saturday."

"That's awesome. Is there potential for friendship there?" Natalie's hand brushed against her forehead in a typical shame gesture. "Did something happen?"

She rolled her eyes at me. "Are you reading my face again? It's weird that it is both annoying and cool." We laughed. "I mean, yeah, I think there is potential there, but the girl from my school, Cierra, she said something to me about who I hang out with."

"What did she say?" I asked.

"I guess people think of me as a part of the stoner group, and she said that I could come Saturday, but I couldn't bring any pot or alcohol because the girls don't drink. I was so embarrassed."

I wanted to play devil's advocate. "Why? I mean, you do openly do those things, right?"

"I mean, yeah. But that doesn't mean I *have* to. I was ashamed that people think of me that way. I'm going to have to prove to them I'm not like that at all."

I smiled. "I think that would be a great thing to prove to them, and to yourself. I'm sure they hang out all the time, having fun, and don't get bored even if they don't have pot or pills or beer."

"I know, it's kind of a relief. I hope they don't find out about what I do with Colby and Aaron."

I nodded knowingly. "Are you ashamed of that, too?"

"It's not who I am. I wouldn't want them to know about it."

"Well, this is all about coming clean. You can have a fresh start. I told you, when you seek change, you can reset. This is all about starting fresh."

She beamed. "It's kinda exciting, you know? To have a new group of girls who I can start fresh with. I'm really psyched about it. Plus, I didn't realize how good soccer would be for my body and my college applications. Two bonuses." She giggled.

"Listen, I also wanted to talk to you about your portfolio. You have some amazing sketches and you are extremely knowledgeable about trends and brands. There is a fashion blogger I'm friends with. Her blog is S for Sasha, S for Style. Do you know her?"

"Oh, yeah, I think I do know her. She writes a really cute column."

"Well, anyway, she said that if you get your portfolio together, she would be happy to maybe go out to lunch, take you to a few sample sales to talk about clothes. She is very serious about fashion and would take you on as an intern if after a few weeks you prove you can be reliable and innovative."

"What? That would be so, so, so cool! I can totally do that. I would love that."

"Sasha is pretty awesome for only being twenty-three. I think you guys could work together well and she could be a great fashion role model for you."

"Yes! Thank you so much for asking her."

"No problem. Now, I'm happy to do that for you, but you have to do something, too."

"What? Anything," Natalie said, leaning forward in her chair.

"So, we have had two great sessions talking about the sneaking out and the pot and stuff. I told your parents I would keep your confidence, but I also want to make sure their rules are being respected. I thought we could all sit down and talk about curfew and rules and all of that. What do you think?"

"I'm okay with that. I know I have been difficult, but they have been cool about not bothering my time with you and letting us just talk and the soccer club team and all that."

Two weeks later we met for our follow-up family session. Clara and Bill had already reported to me that Natalie had been going out less and had not broken curfew, but I wanted to make sure we were very clear on what the rules were just in case there were any slipups.

I started the meeting. "Today should be pretty easy; everyone is in a good mood. I wanted to talk in detail about what the house rules are and the consequences if they are broken. Clara, Bill, I asked you both to come up with some rules for Natalie to hear."

Clara cleared her throat. "We love how easy things have been around here lately, but I know these things are up and down, so we wanted to see what you thought of the following rules." Clara then read from the following list:

1. Curfew 12:00 a.m. on weekends, 1:00 a.m. on dance nights as long as you remain at the official after-party.
2. You cannot sleep over at boys' houses. We can rediscuss when you are seventeen.
3. If you want to go to a party or a house where we do not know the parents, you have to iCurfew check in with your location when you get there so we know where you are.
4. We are happy to support club soccer and get you a sewing machine like you asked for as a reward if these rules are followed for two months.
5. We are not happy that you went on birth control without telling us and we are still unsure of your reasons. But at least you are being safe. We would like you to start seeing our family gynecologist to get birth control and talk to her about your sexual behavior since you do not feel comfortable talking to us about it. Then at least we know you are taking all the right precautions.
6. If these rules are broken, we will drug-test you.

I glanced at Natalie and could see she was calm and in agreement until the last rule was read. I put my hand on her arm.

"Natalie, think this through. Your parents were thinking about drug-testing you anyway. They want to respect you and trust you when you say you are not smoking anymore. The drug testing would only be if you broke a rule. It is *totally up to you* if you want to put yourself in that position."

"Okay," she said slowly.

"Also, your parents put in both rewards and consequences and they did not have to do that."

"What happens if the drug test is positive?" Natalie asked.

Bill cleared his throat. "Actually, we wanted to leave that up to you. Natalie, we do not want to get you in trouble. We want to keep you safe and healthy. What do you think is a fair punishment?" I was glad that Bill and Clara had decided not to come up with their own consequence, because I could see Natalie slowly get off the defensive.

Natalie sighed. "I don't plan on smoking anymore. So this might even help me say no anyway. I guess, if I fail, then I have 9:00 p.m. curfews on the weekends and can only go out one night per week, with approved friends?"

"Stricter than anything we could have come up with!" Clara exclaimed and we all laughed.

I added, "Also, I just want to mention something. You said that you hope that the consequence might help you say no. I talked to your parents and they said you are always welcome to put blame on them."

"What do you mean?" Natalie asked.

"If you ever feel like you can't say no or someone is pressuring you," Clara said, "you can tell them that we drug-test you once a week or will be waiting when you get home. Anything you need, if you feel like you can't say no. That is fine, no questions asked."

Although Natalie was a little uncomfortable with the potential drug test, she understood that it was a consequence of her actions and therefore her choice. It also made house rules for going out very clear, so there was less fighting. I met with Natalie once every two weeks after the first couple of months and watched her blossom into an amazing (and fashionable) soccer player. Although she never completely gave up her old group of friends, she began hanging out with them only during the day to avoid potentially pressured situations and got a lot better at saying "no, thanks."

Things to Remember

- Many adolescents engage in a variety of risky behaviors because they are bored and have negative peer influences.
- Studies have shown that peer pressure actually evokes fear and pain in a teen's brain. This reaction is enough to change a teen's behavior and preferences.
- Self-esteem and identity are very confusing for adolescents, especially teen girls, because of the mixed messages and influence of the media.
- Dating and adolescent romance have become increasingly complex and shallow. This negatively affects teens' self-confidence and can drive substance abuse.
- Many teenagers believe that substance use is a way to deal with personal problems, prevent boredom, and bond with each other.
- To curb dangerous behavior, boredom, and peer pressure, parents can encourage positive risk-taking behavior and cultivating personal passions.
- Change of friends, activities, and role models can help motivate and distract teenagers who need to reset their behavior.
- Parents should set up clear rules and systems to help their teens know their limits.

- Parents should consider talking to their kids about how to handle peer pressure by putting some of the "blame" on parents. This is not an answer for everyone, but may be a smart alternative way for kids to say no without losing face.
- Parents can have teenagers design their own punishments so that they fit the "crime" and do not also punish other family members in the process.
- Active listening, proper questioning, and follow-up can help parents detect lies and prevent them in the future.

Challenges You Can Do Right Now

Family Challenge: What is "risky"?

1. Sit down with your teens and ask them what they consider to be "risky" behavior.
2. Why do they think other teenagers engage in risky behavior? Do they agree or disagree with my assertion that boredom and bad peer influence are the main causes?

Personal Challenge: What are your limits?

1. What rules and systems are important for you to stick to in your household?
2. Do you think your children know about these rules?
3. Have you ever said yes when you really meant "maybe"?
4. Do you think your teen needs to find change? Do you know any possible role models for him or her?

Family Challenge: How can you prevent negative risk taking?

1. What are some positive risk-taking behaviors you can do together as a family? How about for your teens? How about for your teens and their friends?

2. What is each family member's personal passion? How can you help each other cultivate your passions?
3. What do you and your teens think about using parents as scapegoats? Is this a good or bad idea?

Personal Challenge: Review lying and past punishments.

1. Have you ever caught your teen in a lie? What happened?
2. Do you think your teen tells you the truth?
3. What are some previous punishments that have worked and why? Which ones haven't worked and why?

PART III

. . . .

Why You Don't Need to Worry . . . as Much

CHAPTER 7

Handling High School

Knowing that soon they will be entering a highly competitive college market and workforce, teens are feeling increasing academic pressure to succeed from schools, parents, and even fellow teens. This has forced many students to become either perfectionists or slackers and has even driven some to cheating. While school anxiety mounts, technology is both alleviating the stress and adding to it. However, parents can help students thrive in the changing academic environment whether they are overachievers or in danger of being left behind.

I was called in to work with a family that was having issues related to academics. The father explained that his son was struggling with all aspects of school—homework, grades, procrastination, burnout, teachers, and organization. This is typical, as these issues are all very closely tied. Unfortunately, his parents had started dealing with his behavior and lack of commitment to school a little too late, and they were now in crisis. The good news was that Jake, the sixteen-year-old client, was actually very open to seeing me. We gathered for our first meeting in the Loker family living room.

Jake sat calmly before me and relayed a long list of academic disappointments—upsetting for both him, his school, and his parents. "I have a 2.7 GPA, I have not been doing my college prep testing, I never get my homework done, and I really dread going to school. And . . ." He glanced up at his parents. "I just got caught for cheating."

His dad, Stan, added, "He is suspended for two weeks. A lot of other kids were also caught, so thank goodness Jake wasn't expelled. But, as he knows, it was the final straw. We need help. We have tried many other things, and sometimes he does super well for a few weeks and then he loses steam again."

Cheating is an incredibly tricky issue and I wanted to deal with it first. "What kind of cheating, Jake?"

Jake's shoulders tensed and I could see fear in his mother's face. Clearly this was something that Marissa had been nervous about. "Are there different kinds?" she asked me.

I raised my eyebrows at Jake, acknowledging that he should answer. "Yeah, there are lots of different kinds of cheating. It's practically a science." I nodded in agreement and his parents looked shocked. "Look, I'm not saying I'm proud of this, but there are a ton of different ways to cheat. Everyone at school has their thing. The way I cheated this time was by putting formulas and answers into my scientific calculator. I got caught when I texted one of my friends a formula during the exam. Really"—he turned to his parents—"that's not as devious as some of the other kids who *didn't* get caught. Some kids went on Facebook and shared answers the night before and, once in a while, kids cheat with essays on Google Documents."

"Doesn't it make you feel bad to cheat? You must know it's wrong," I said.

"Yeah, but everyone does it. And they give us so much work, I feel like people have to cheat to get by. Also, I swear, some of my teachers don't read our papers anyway."

I knew many kids felt justified in cheating because of the amount of work teachers gave them, but it was sad to hear it so blatantly expressed, although I did appreciate the honesty. I tried to gauge Jake's emotions. He had spoken truthfully, he did not feel proud of his cheating, but there was also no shame—a characteristic teens *should* have about cheating. He seemed calm, almost resigned to the fact that he was a failure at school. Luckily, I did not see pride—there are some students I have worked with who take pride in their academic or social deviance. I was not getting this from Jake. "Hey, Jake, I appreciate your honesty. But one thing that is bothering me is you don't seem too worried. Are you upset about it at all?"

I watched his face very closely for signs of deception—a shoulder shrug, heavy breathing, or a deep swallow. But I saw authenticity as he spoke. "I used to be upset. Really worried and disappointed in myself. But everything we try just doesn't seem to stick, so I have learned to just accept it. I mean, I still want to try with you, but I feel worn out."

Stan spoke up. "It just doesn't make any sense to me. Maggie, his sister, does amazing in school. She is always working away on the computer and she is all set to go to an Ivy next year."

Jake flashed anger for the first time all day. "Yeah, but we are both miserable. I'm miserable because I'm failing and she's miserable because she's succeeding. But we're both miserable."

"What do you mean?" I asked.

"Maggie succumbs to the pressure. I fight it. Sometimes I think about being like Maggie and doing what everyone wants me to do and getting good grades. But that also means having no life. Even though she gets perfect scores and grades, she still worries about college. So not only would I give up my life, but I'd still have to worry about my future. I would rather have a life and just worry about grades."

I shook my head and looked at Jake's weary face, his mother's puffy eyes, and his father's firm jaw—exhausted, sad, and angry. Not a great combination, but everyone seemed willing to try to fix what was happening. I knew that even though Jake was a good kid at home, had a nice group of friends, and did not engage in risky behavior, the poor performance at school was putting a cloud over everything else.

This family situation brought up a number of issues that teens deal with in their academic lives. On one side of the coin, you have Jake—a self-proclaimed slacker and disappointment who gets bad grades, cheats, fights with parents about homework, and dislikes school. On the other side, you have his sister Maggie—a typical overachiever and straight-A student who is constantly stressed, worried, and consumed by school. Both the parents and the teens in this family were struggling to balance the two major characteristics of current academic life: rising pressure and the introduction of technology.

Parents are overly familiar with the increase of pressure in high school in recent years. We hear about it over and over again on blogs, in the media, and from schools themselves. The majority of this stress comes from school. Before I review how parents can speak to their kids about dealing with academic stress and better handling school, I want to talk about some of the consequences of this pressure and how it is affecting the everyday life and attitude of teens. I have found that students are handling stress in three different ways. These are demonstrated in the Loker family.

The first way teens handle their growing stress levels is, like Jake, to become slackers. These students often become enveloped by school burnout. They also have early-onset "senioritis," where students want to do the least amount of work possible to get by and have zero to little motivation to do anything for school. This is now happening as early as ninth and tenth grade. Some of these students embrace their slacker status as the only way to handle their stress. I was giving a school presentation on study skills and time management and one boy approached me at the end of the session. He said, "I really liked your presentation, but there was one problem. It all works under the assumption that we want to do well. I used to want to do well, and then I realized that I wouldn't be able to cut it with the high expectations. So I stopped trying." This defeatist attitude was devastating to hear, but it made me want to investigate where he was coming from.

When teens do poorly in school, there is usually a combination of forces at work. First, overcoming laziness and learning to do activities that you may not like are two challenges young people still struggle to master. Second, as Jake explained, the extreme pressure kids are under has, in their minds, brought up a new choice for students: enjoy high school and do poorly, or get good grades at the sacrifice of happiness. The third cause of poor academic performance is that teens are often not taught how to be good at school. They are taught subjects and information, but they are rarely shown how to process and handle that information. So because they do not know how to handle stress, they succumb to it. But, of course, some kids do know how to study, memorize, or deal with large amounts of homework and assignments without feeling overwhelmed. This happens with the kids I call "sprinter" teens. If high school academics were like track and field, some teenagers today are operating as sprinters. They can go at maximum efficiency for very short periods. This is what happened to Jake. He could juggle and study well for a few weeks, but then lost momentum, got burned out, and ran out of steam. Oftentimes, poor students, slackers, or what adults call "lazy" students simply work at a different pace. Though these students can be extremely intelligent in short bursts, sprinters are more prone to dips and peaks in grades. In the tips section we will talk about how to teach balance, study and time management skills, and how academic sprinters can become more like "distance" students.

The second way that teens deal with the mounting pressure is to embrace perfectionism. Maggie, Jake's sister, gives us an example of how two siblings can deal with the stress of high school in totally different ways. Jake accuses his sister of making "the other choice," deciding to dive headfirst into school and sacrifice fun. I call these teens "unicorns" after a joke one of my parent clients made about her daughter. "My daughter is always anxious—fearful and nervous about her grades and her future. She wants everything to seem perfect—her notes, her backpack, and her transcript—even though she is barely holding it together on the inside. It's like a unicorn in a balloon factory." The "unicorn in the balloon factory" syndrome is a common way for teens to handle the stress of high school. Unicorns are just as burdened as slackers, but merely handle the stress in a different way. Like a unicorn who fears its horn will burst the balloons in the factory, teen unicorns also worry that they will be the cause of their own demise. Therefore, they are incredibly self-critical and full of self-doubt. Teens who deal with stress in this way tend to globalize their anxiety instead of localizing it. One of my unicorn teens got a bad grade in her history class, and suddenly every other class seemed just as bad. The bad quiz grade sent her into a tearful, overwhelmed state where she began to doubt her intelligence, her aptitude in all subjects, and even how liked she was by her teachers.

Unicorn teens not only have a tendency to lapse into complete breakdowns where everything seems terrible to them, but they can also be addicted to the illusion of efficiency. They believe efficiency makes them successful. Because unicorns are incredibly anxious about performance and rarely give themselves breaks, they are hypersensitive and fragile. They try to feel better about themselves or feel "productive" by keeping themselves busy. I call this the "busy paradox." Unicorn teens feel that the busier they are, the more successful they are. I see this in many adults as well. When I finally did meet Maggie, I noticed that she filled her schedules up with "things." This made her feel productive and efficient, which temporarily abated her anxiety and self-doubt. She explained, "When you are *accomplishing* things—whether they are necessary or not—you often feel *accomplished*." Unicorns, or perfectionists, therefore experience their own type of issues with school. They do have burnout like sprinting slackers, but unicorns tire themselves out from anxiety and the illusion of efficiency and perfection. Teachers also complain they have no passion in their work, that they beg for grades, and that they study to get by without a love for learning. It is also difficult for parents to distinguish between drive and passion with unicorns. They are usually incredibly driven, but passionless. Jake described his sister in this way. Both slackers and unicorns suffer from being passionless. Unicorns kick into overdrive, so that what they enjoy becomes irrelevant, and what they are good at moves to the forefront. Slackers don't feel passion and adopt patterns of avoidance or disinterest to trudge through the work that is making them stressed. Whether teens experience all of the characteristics or merely have tendencies toward unicorn or slacker, both kinds of student need to find balance.

The third way that teens deal with pressure is to cheat. Some students have made cheating an art form. When we asked students why they cheat, here are the answers we received:

> "School is so hard, the only way to get by is to cheat."
>
> —Allison, 13

"Everyone cheats. If you don't do it people think you are stuck up or, worse, a suck-up."

—Craig, 15

"Teachers don't notice because they don't even care. They barely read our papers. If they aren't going to take the time to assign interesting homework, then why should I do it?"

—Mikey, 17

"Why do teens cheat? There are many factors that lead to cheating. It may be a teen's own personal pressure to succeed that drives them to cheat, or mere peer pressure. But personally, I think that the most presiding factor is the parents who are pushing their kids to succeed. Of course kids want their parents, who are their role models and judges, to look upon them favorably. They want their parents to not be disappointed in them. So, they cheat. I know. I'm one of them."

—Karis, 16, Radical Parenting intern

Stress, bad assignments, peer pressure, and parents are all reasons teens feel almost justified in cheating. I believe students also turn to cheating because their fear of failure is greater than their fear of getting caught cheating. Before we review how parents can prevent cheating, perfectionist tendencies, and slacking, let's review the second major characteristic of how teen academic life has changed.

Administrators and teachers are trying desperately to find positive ways to use technology in school. According to a Pew Research Center study, 24 percent of teens attend a school that completely forbids cell phones. Yet the majority of teens, 62 percent, say that they can have a mobile phone at school but not in actual class. Only 12 percent of teens with cell phones say that they can have a cell phone at their school at all times. However, despite the rules, 77 percent of teens still do bring their phones to school.

As with most effects of technology, the integration of laptops and cell phones into classrooms can be both good and bad. For example, Dan Ackerman, vice principal at a Bronx high school, has integrated laptops into the school curriculum. His students use these for reports, research, homework, and classwork. The laptops have helped students stay up-to-date with modern technology and complete interesting assignments that were never possible before. Ackerman also uses the computers to "spy" on his students to see if they are working. Using special software, Ackerman can tap into any of the laptops' cameras and screens to see what students are doing. On the one hand, the spy software has been beneficial because Ackerman has been able to see what distracts students—chat clients, the mirror function of the camera, and games—and then block those sites and applications. He is also able to shut them down or alert the students that they are being watched so that they get back to work. The fear of this happening prevents many students from using the cameras or chats inappropriately. However, many parents and students have been outraged that this kind of access is infringing on students' privacy.

Privacy is only one downside of incorporating technology into academic life. Putting technology in the classroom adds another area where kids are constantly looking at screens instead of real people. Many parents think that school should be the area where kids get a break from technology and learn to do their activities offline, without the excitement that technology can bring to spruce up assignments.

Distraction has become a huge issue for both parents and schools that are attempting to integrate technology into assignments. When I work with college students, study skills are only one area I have to teach. Another skill that is now becoming essential for students is how to avoid distractions. One popular YouTube video, called "How to Write a College Term Paper," humorously demonstrates how technology can help and hinder a student needing to finish a paper. The video shows the computer desktop of a student who has to

"I'm upset that schools are integrating technology into every area of school life—homework, class time and teaching lessons. Shouldn't kids learn to read boring material without animation and chats running along in the background? Most workplaces and the SAT are not using that much technology. Kids have to be able to learn without it. Plus, putting screens in the classroom means my child is never getting a break. They go from school computers to cell phones to home computers. I think it is just more distraction."

—Parent e-mail to Radical Parenting

write a paper, "The Study of Ions," and turn it in the next morning. Yet each of the icons on the computer yells distractions at the student as he tries to research and write his paper. The Microsoft Word icon is the studious icon, encouraging the student to keep going as his ten-hour deadline slowly runs out. It competes with the Internet Explorer icon, who tempts the student to click on newly posted pictures of his crush on Facebook and check his e-mail. The chat and music icons beckon to him to make a "writing playlist" and chat with one of his friends from class who recently came online—ostensibly to talk about the paper and some other "class stuff."

Whenever I show this video to auditoriums full of students—even as young as third and fourth grade—all of the viewers break down in hysterics and agreement.

Privacy, distractions, and constant media interaction are some of the major reasons that some schools are working against technological integration and banning cell phones and computers at school entirely. Yet these schools are missing out on some of the positive aspects of technology. First, the Internet can provide extra help to students who might not have the means to obtain it otherwise. For ex-

> *"That's so true! When I have to do typed homework or research on my computer it is like the other programs are just beckoning to me. Come chat with me! Come play with me! Come look at Facebook with me! It's terrible. I love being able to type and look up stuff so easily, but the computer makes it so easy to get off track."*
>
> —Ashleigh, 12-year-old who had just watched the video

ample, I was volunteering in a poor school in downtown Los Angeles, and many students in these schools cannot afford textbooks, pencils, or paper. They are lucky if they come to school in shoes that fit them. If they fall behind in class, they are in deep trouble. With over forty students to a teacher, extra help is out of the question. Parents often do not speak English, or have barely finished high school themselves, so finding a tutor would be impossible.

One student, Diana, explained to me that she is grateful for the Internet because it "saved her grades" when she was having trouble in biology. She explained to me, "I want to get straight A's because I want to get a scholarship to college and be the first in my family. But I'm so, so, so bad at science. In biology I was so behind I would come home crying, but my mom couldn't help me. Finally I started using the computers at school to go on TeacherTube and biology help sites. They have free videos and demos and you can even submit questions to teachers they have on there! I would never have been able to get through without that help, and it was free and interactive. Actually, don't tell my school, but it was better than the teacher's lessons." More and more students are finding technology helpful as an alternative to classroom learning to supplement their education. Even third and fourth graders can play on educational game websites to practice what they have learned in class. This teaches students the best lesson: learning can be fun.

With the Amazon Kindle and Apple iPad, learning is taking on totally new dimensions and offering teachers a multitude of ways to engage students and teach a lesson. We have an entire section of our website dedicated to helping teachers integrate technology into the classroom in positive ways—everything from creating history wikis to Spanish study guides to virtual chats about the newest cell research in a distant lab. Technology is also helping integrate the different types of student learners.

Visual learners who have an audio teacher, one who only gives lectures, often cannot grasp lessons. They can use laptops to access additional video demonstrations. Audio learners who cannot use flashcards beneficially can now create virtual flashcards that read the terms and answers aloud to them from computer speakers. Some universities are actually adding Twitter to the class discussions to give shy students a chance to participate and help each other. These Twitter discussions actually happen during class. Students can text or tweet their comments and questions to a running log up on the screen next to the professor's PowerPoint. The professor can respond to questions verbally or let other students answer for him in the feed, post links, and make relevant comments. As one professor told me, "If they are going to text in class, I would rather have them texting about class."

Critics of Twitter in the classroom and technology integration worry that students need to learn not to text in class, not

"I like the idea of texting in the classroom in theory, but there is something very important about a teacher calling on a student, seeing his face and answering his question. That way when he comes to office hours or asks a question in the next class, the professor knows his name, his face and his history. And shouldn't we encourage shy students to be brave enough to raise their hands instead of diving into texting?"

—Teacher comment on RadicalParenting.com's virtual school section simply how to text about class. Naysayers also say that it is taking the face-to-face aspect out of learning.

Technology in the classroom does provide new ways of engagement, but it also lessens face time. These are extremely hard to balance, but it can be done.

How can teachers and parents provide balance between technology, academics, stress, and efficiency? Often parents feel at a loss when trying to help their stressed teenager. Adults tell me that it seems impossible to reach and help students when they are bogged down with difficult assignments, AP classes that did not exist even ten years ago, and a completely different academic environment. Here, I discuss tips that I created while working with teenagers in the throes of academic stress.

1. Embracing Study Skills: Creating Transition Time and Boundaries

One of the major causes of stress is that different areas of a teen's life are bleeding together. For example, with the increase in homework, school life takes over home life, and with the advent of cell phones and laptops, social life enters the classroom—even if it is forbidden. This puts a major strain on the average teenager because it forces them to be able to shift into very different gears quickly.

Teenagers often do homework on the computer while also checking Facebook or iChat. This has bad effects on all areas of their life. First, constantly being social and having to shift back to homework or studying makes school and home life seem even more boring and out of touch. Second, socializing can be positive for teens, but if they are trying to write a paper or listen to a lecture at the same time, they are not able to fully enjoy either the socializing or the interesting aspects of school. Therefore, there is a great benefit in parents bringing back transition time and the

> "Sometimes when I'm texting under my desk in class, it's like really funny and I kind of giggle. But then I look up and we are talking about Algebra and that is so boring. It's hard to switch back and forth."
>
> —Carrie, 15

lines between school life, home life, and social life. Parents can do this in a number of ways. I highly recommend having two separate computers in the home: one for academic work and one for play and socializing. If this is not an option, you can also use parental control software that allows computers to be in "academic" mode—no iChat or Facebook—or "social" mode. Setting up two different user accounts on the same computer can also do this. Encourage your teenager to understand the difference and the value of staying in one mode at a time. This can help them stay focused and get more enjoyment out of what they are doing, and it gives them time to reflect when they do ultimately transition into a different mode.

Transition times are another study skill parents can encourage to balance and lessen stress for teens. Once they learn to stay in one mode at a time, they can use transition time to reflect and switch mindsets. The best example of transition time is when kids go from school mode into home mode. Many of the examples I have used so far in this book talk about time periods that happen right after a teen gets home after school, sports practice, or extracurricular activities. This can be in the car, at the kitchen counter, or in their bedroom right after they have unloaded their stuff from the day. Parents often want to ask their children how the day was, tell them updates, and see if there is anything they need—whether it is a snack or homework help. The problem is, every teen reacts to this daily transition time differently—

and it is not always positive. Some teenagers are surly and cranky until they have their snack; others need to spew about everything that happened that day before they can relax into the home environment. Some teens can transition by unloading their bags and changing clothes; others need a bit of TV and a snack. It is important for parents to take note of their children's transition times and encourage them to take a pause between each area of their life. This will help them stay focused and have time to process their day, which leads to better sleep, less crankiness, and better communication.

Last, parents can implement specific study skills into their children's homework routine. I recommend that parents and teenagers focus on "chunking" and adopting subject-specific strategies. Chunking is when students break homework, projects, or assignments up into twenty-, thirty-, or forty-minute chunks. This is a great way for students to plan ahead because it forces them to look at the assignment, think about how much time each part will take, and then break up each section into digestible parts. It also helps prevent distractions. When students know they have a thirty-minute section of homework to do, they can turn off their phones and reward themselves afterward with a five- to ten-minute TV or phone break. This teaches students how to focus on studying, but also lets them practice an essential skill for real life: balancing work and play when there are many distractions. Adopting subject-specific strategies is a final study skill I like teens to implement; it requires them to think about how different subjects require different kinds of studying. It is extremely difficult to study for history in the same way one might study for math—yet students do this all the time because they do not know any better! I recommend that parents sit down with their student and review the studying techniques I list below. Make a list of which ones are best for each subject to study subject-efficiently.

- Flashcards: Word or phrase on one side of the ca nation on the other.
- Flip sheets: A single sheet of paper is folded in half. On one side are questions or terms, on the other are the answers.
- Practice tests: Having a teacher, parent, or tutor make sample questions in a mock test format, or the student can make them using chapter notes.
- Recorded terms: For audio learners, students can record stories, key terms, definitions, or dates into a recorder or iTunes and then play the recording back as they clean their room, lie on the bed, or eat a snack.
- Explain-away: Students can explain the process, problem, or story to a sibling or parent who knows nothing about the class. In this way, students have to include all the details and answer questions from the person they are explaining the issue to.
- Study groups: Sitting with other students, talking about sample questions and quizzing each other.

Some of these techniques can be used for multiple classes. For example, in history you might want to use a study group and a flip sheet. However, writing out a sample test might take more time than it is worth because history questions are so long and detailed. In math, students might use flashcards and a sample test, but would not want to record examples or questions into a recorder because equations and graphs need to be seen and drawn, not heard. Giving students these procedures and breaking them up by subject will help students feel less overwhelmed when memorizing or sitting down with a new subject.

2. Busting the Top Areas of Academic Stress

There are two different areas that our teens identified as being the most stressful in their academic lives: crunch time and classroom strain. Let's take a look at each area and then examine a few ways to alleviate the stress that they produce. First, "crunch time" is a term that I use to describe the inevitable times during the school year when a multitude of tests, quizzes, and assignments happen to fall on the same three or four days. Unlike midterms or finals, these areas often creep up on teens and their families. With finals, students know far in advance that they will need more time to study, parents book fewer appointments for them, and even teachers and friends are more lenient to allow extra sleep and cram time. In addition, everyone is going through finals, so social networking, texting, and parties are not occurring to distract or tempt students. Crunch time, however, usually creeps up after the first four weeks of school or midway through the semester, when all of the classes happen to have assessments at the same time.

This is usually the week when parents and teens fight most at

"It's always a random week in October where all of a sudden I have two essays, a science test, a lab, a math test, and a history oral report due in the same three days. Teachers don't care that we have a bunch of other stuff. All of a sudden you have tons of homework and sports practices and doctor's appointments. It's like finals, but nothing stops for you. That's when everyone gets sick and worn out . . . and when I start to hate school."

—A teen comment on our article called
"Crunch Week: Avoiding the Surprise of School Hell Week"

home. Teens are cranky, parents did not expect the onslaught of work, and usually—because of lack of sleep and extra stress—the following week everyone gets a cold. Luckily, there are a few easy ways parents can eliminate the stress that crunch week causes. At the beginning of a semester or quarter, parents should sit down with their teens to look at their syllabus from each class and enter assignments into a large planner. After doing this for a few classes, you will easily be able to identify crunch weeks. Parents should mark the calendar and be sure to avoid scheduling any appointments or weekend outings for the week before and after. Teenagers can also mark their calendar for the week before to begin to prepare early, get more sleep, and approach teachers with any overwhelming days—often schools will let students reschedule a test if there are more than three assessments in one day. During crunch week, parents can make sure that teens have more balanced meals, perhaps offer a temporary hiatus from chores that can wait, and be on alert for extra-long nights. If you have a procrastinator or slacker, which we address in the next section, parents can also limit texting, Internet, and TV time for the week before and during crunch time.

I also want to address what I call "classroom strain." This can be caused by boring subjects, especially tedious classes or difficult teachers.

> *"Teachers are defining the rest of my life."*
>
> —Abby, 17,
> Radical Parenting intern

Good teachers can change a student's life forever, but difficult teachers, as many parents know, can take over a teen's life. This is a major cause of academic stress because when students have a class that is bogging them down, they complain more, are cranky from homework and poor grades, and feel unfulfilled at school. This puts a strain on both teens and parents who are trying to help.

When your child experiences classroom strain, whether it is

"**W**hen my daughter, Lynette, had a hard math class this
year, it was like it put a shadow over her entire life. Even if
she got A's in other classes, no matter how hard she worked
for math she always got C's and the other grades didn't
matter. She came home every day in a bad mood—because
math class was last period—and then all we would do
was fight about how she could make it better. It was bad
enough that this class brought down her GPA, it was even
worse that it almost ruined our relationship for her entire
sophomore year!"

—E-mail from Lynette's mother

from a difficult subject or teacher, it is important for parents to
implement academic socialization. These are principles that will
also eventually make teens successful in the workplace. Academic socialization is being able to, first, address problem areas
calmly with superiors while focusing on solution-oriented outcomes and, second, use classmates to work together.

When helping your children approach and work with teachers, you want to give them language they can use and goals they
can address. If they are having trouble understanding the material
taught in class, encourage them to approach teachers, in a nonconfrontational manner, to ask for additional help. Parents should
also encourage feedback for teachers. I know most educators
greatly appreciate these kinds of positive and constructive comments. Even when a teacher or the material intimidates a teen,
there are a few neutral phrases parents can teach their teen to use:

"I wanted to thank you for going over that chapter again for me in class today. I still need a little more clarification, if that is okay with you. Do you think we could set up a time to talk about it?"

"I have not been doing as well as I would have liked on the previous assignments. I really want to do well, as this subject is one I like, but I think I'm doing something wrong. Could we maybe discuss some of the issues you think I should improve on?"

"I wanted to take a moment and tell you I'm sorry if I have been difficult in class. Sometimes I think I get stressed and then do not act the way I would like. Sorry about that. Can we start fresh?"

Teens can also start with e-mail versions of these approaches, which they can write together with you. Learning to deal with teachers, and seeing them as assets rather than enemies, is crucial for a teen's success and happiness in school and later in life.

Sometimes teens are fine with their teachers, but feel overwhelmed by a certain subject or the amount of work for a class. This can especially happen in advanced classes. I believe that parents can encourage peer-to-peer cooperation to lessen this stress and teach the lifelong importance of collaboration. Many teens are beginning to understand the value of study skills and time management, but do not know how to properly collaborate. Here are a few dos and don'ts parents can teach their kids when they want to work with fellow students:

Do

- Prepare ahead of time. Teens can plan for crunch week and set up study dates in advance with classmates. This teaches them time management.

- Share helpful tips during study sessions. Teens should work together on study sheets and review guides, making sure they are doing their own work, but cross-checking to make sure no details are missed. These types of study skills—*how* to study, not just *what* to study—are often missed in a school curriculum.
- Use virtual outlets like Google Documents, Skype video chatting, and IM to test each other and create practice questions.

Don't

- Plagiarize, even when you think no one would check. It is very easy to fall into the trap of copying and sharing work when studying is happening online. This not only can get teens in big trouble, but also cuts down on learning.
- Get distracted on virtual outlets. Video chat study sessions are great—if teens stick to studying and do not veer off topic or stay on too long. Parents can help by having teens set time limits.

Parents also need to be sure not to nag. Not only does nagging make teenagers mad at parents in addition to being stressed by the assignment pressure, it also does not teach them to be self-reliant. Encourage the dos and discourage the don'ts when they are feeling open to suggestion or asking for help.

Addressing each of the major areas of academic stress can help teens on a daily basis, but its value also lies in teaching them how to minimize similar pressures when they are on their own in college or the workplace.

3. Dealing with Slackers and Poor Grades

"Slackers" are students who are a bit slower to pick up subjects, have less motivation to work, and do not put a high value on grades. The slacker mentality can originate from three different attitudes. Jake Loker, from the story at the beginning of the chapter, exemplifies the first attitude: teens who feel that they have to choose between good grades and a happy life. The second type of slacker has very high intelligence and often had to work very little in elementary school for good grades. However, once they reach harder classes in high school, they are not used to having to work and do not like the feeling of being behind or having to work for grades. The third type of slacker—the hardest kind to inspire—simply does not see the value in school or grades. They have very little passion to learn, either because they find the work too hard or because activities outside of school appeal to them more than homework and classes.

Parents *can* help inspire all types of slackers to value school or, at the very least, learn the importance of getting respectable grades and meeting your requirements to receive privileges at home. Before we talk about the tools to help teens earn better grades and get more passionate about school, parents need to get very clear on what "respectable grades" means to them. Teenagers desperately need limits and consequences or else they will continue to simply "get by" semester after semester. What is the minimum acceptable GPA in your household? There are many different kinds of targets that parents can set: a minimum GPA, a minimum grade level in core classes, or a high grade for classes in the subject area their teen wants to major in. Once parents have set these limits, it is important to think about the nonnegotiable consequences for if they are not met. I recommend creating both limits and consequences with your teens so they have a part in the process. Often this helps them own the process and be less resentful of the new boundaries. Many of our interns actually identified themselves as being in the slacker category and then accepted the help that we offered during our procrastination study—including setting their own requirements and consequences! Here are the requirements and consequences our own resident slackers have come up with for themselves:

> **Requirement:** Minimum 3.0 GPA.
> **Consequence:** Pay for my own texting plan for the next semester out of my allowance or babysitting money.

> **Requirement:** Nothing lower than a B minus.
> **Consequence:** Wash the cars every weekend and take my little sister to practice on weekdays.

> **Requirement:** A's or A minuses in History, English and Spanish. C's or higher in other academic subjects. No more than one C.
> **Consequence:** No chatting online or Facebook on weekdays.

Once you have set limits and consequences, you can implement tools to help teens reach the goals. This way, teens do not feel that you made rules and are abandoning them to struggle to meet them. Rather, you are making clear boundaries to avoid fighting when the report card arrives or every night when homework should be getting done. First, ask them how you can help them. This sounds something like this: "I love you and want to help you if I can. How can I help you meet these goals?" Some teenagers might ask for homework reminders, a tutor, help studying, or some new notebooks to get organized. This is a great place to start. However, it is more likely that your teenager will be overwhelmed and out of ideas on how to begin to meet these new limits—after all, if they knew how to do better, they would have been doing it before having this conversation. Although, as you will see with the Loker family outcome later, many parents are surprised to learn that having specific goals and unappealing consequences can be a huge motivation in itself.

Second, parents should remove slacker roadblocks. Parents can sit down with teens to identify where in the process the study blockage happens. What I mean by "study blockage" is the point at which a teen tends to give up, get bored, or lose motivation in homework or studying. Common study blockage points to explore are subjects, times of day, and environmental distractions. Then parents and teens can work together to find ways to avoid them. Here are some of the study blockages and solutions our teen slackers identified in the procrastination forum:

> "My study blockage is when I get to my history homework. I find it so boring that it just makes me want to go to sleep or do something else. I can avoid this by doing my other homework first, so I do not have a lot left by the time I get to history. I also plan on doing history when I am not already hungry or tired or have a defined period of time. For example, doing it during my free period right after lunch. I am full and have 45 minutes to get it done."

> "My study blockage is when I do any kind of homework on the computer and then I leave open my chat and my Facebook. I get really inefficient and homework that should take fifteen minutes, takes hours. I think we are going to solve this by only using my dad's laptop to do homework. He does not have an IM client and he has Facebook blocked."

> "I think my study blockage is when I try to do my homework downstairs in front of the TV or around my siblings. I never get anything done and cannot focus and it takes hours to do anything. I'm going to

> set up a space for homework in the office with my
> supplies there and try to power through homework so
> I can have more free time."

Removing these roadblocks can really increase a student's productivity.

The third tip that parents of slackers can implement is to understand their child's pace. Slackers are often sprinters, not long-distance runners. This just means they work better in high bursts of energy, as opposed to slow and steady over many hours. Teens and parents should sit down together and think of times that they were successful in school—either getting good grades or feeling really good about an assignment. What went right? Did students break up the work into small chunks? Did they take frequent breaks? Did they study in a separate room or before dinner? These are important clues that many parents and teens do not think to look for. In fact, many so-called slackers simply have a different pace than the average student. Parents can help these types of students learn that this is totally okay, they just need to learn what their ideal pace and study timing are, so they can capitalize on them, instead of trying to fight them.

Finally, once parents set limits and consequences and then remove roadblocks and help set the pace, they need to back away. It is very hard to avoid the "superhero" parent tendency, where moms or dads swoop in to help and finish last-minute projects, keep a running test calendar on the fridge, and call teachers for their students. In the long run, this does not serve teens and puts a strain on your relationship. Backing off might mean letting kids fail or do poorly for a semester, but that is why there are the consequences in place. Teens need to learn to optimize their chances of doing well and then deal with any negative outcomes of their actions. Most important, they need to do this on their own, so when it comes to college or the workplace, they are ready.

4. Fostering Efficiency and Balance

To find balance, parents can help teens feel efficient and hone in on activities they are good at. This is the best way to alleviate school stress, motivate slackers, and cure school burnout. Helping teens feel efficient is actually a great way to boost productivity. It also is a way to help them balance restorative fun activities with tedious studying. When students sit down to start a large project, they often get overwhelmed and do not know where to begin. Many times the initial flame can be ignited if teens learn how to get themselves into an efficient and optimal mindset. I like to help teens figure out which subject they feel best at. They should often start homework with the subject they feel most proficient in and can complete most quickly. Many teens are advised to start with the hardest project first, but this is often daunting and exhausting. By beginning with a subject students feel confident in, they are able to carry that self-assurance into tougher assignments. This might not even be a school assignment. Sometimes I have students do a ten- to fifteen-minute activity as a primer. This can be whatever they feel productive doing and will put them into an efficient mindset. With one client, we learned that playing an old video game he felt really good at was actually a great primer. He felt confident and was working and thinking at high speeds and in a pleasant mood.

Another way teenagers can feel efficient and enjoy learning is by playing academic games online. I have listed a number of good educational websites in the resources section. Many teenagers have told us that these websites provide a nice break in schoolwork, but they still feel like they are doing something productive, thereby increasing their academic self-esteem. This is how parents can bring balance back into their teens' lives and show them that being productive does not just have to be with schoolwork.

5. Preparing for College

College admission is another huge source of stress for teenagers and parents, but with the right preparation it can be a smooth process. First I want to address the general paper clutter that accumulates on the path to college admission, as well as the organizational fights that can happen between parents and teens when an important document is lost. I recommend that families set up a portable plastic file box for college information. All office supply stores sell these, with a top drawer for pens, sticky notes, and paper clips. Stock the box with supplies and get color-coded folders for inside the box. You want to make the following folders:

- Testing
- Transcripts
- Financial aid
- College tour info
- Helpful articles or handouts on college admissions
- One folder for each school your student is interested in

Once this is set up, all papers should immediately be filed in the box. Students should also make a corresponding set of folders on their computer for digital documents.

Second, parents and teens should get very clear on their expectations. Look through the questions I include at the end of this chapter, in the Challenges section. Sometimes parents and teens have different ideas about the best type, cost, and location of schools. It is very important to get clear on these issues before a teen gets his or her heart set on an expensive private school on the California coast while the parent is thinking about them getting a scholarship at the home state's public university. When sitting down to talk through these questions, make sure both parent and teen are in a good mood, there are no siblings or phones to distract you, and you begin with an open mind. The point of having this discussion early, even as young as seventh or eighth grade, is not to put pressure on teens, but to take stress away. You do not need to arrive at answers during this talk—many teens have no idea exactly where they want to go to school, and this is totally okay! You want to have this talk merely to discuss options, clarify financial restrictions, and set the stage for a process where open and nonjudgmental communication is key. If you disagree on something that your teen wants, gather all of the information you can on this topic. The most popular complaint I get is when parents want their child close to home and teens want to go to the other side of the country. If this kind of disagreement happens, ask them why, how sure they are, and what made them feel this way. Before getting into an argument about the disparity in opinions, agree to hear each other's side and gather more information. This can include visiting schools in both areas, talking to a college counselor, or contacting alumni. This way teens feel that they can be honest with you about what they are thinking, and you can give them the opportunity to do more research. I have found that teenagers usually change their mind hundreds of time in this process, unless their parents have forbidden a school or idea. Vetoing a college, location, etc. typically only causes teens to become stubborn and scornful and—rationally or irrationally—to want whatever their parents have banned even more. Therefore, it is important to have discussions early, where both sides can make lists of what they want to know more about and get ideas about financial and geographic boundaries without making any binding decisions. This builds a solid foundation for the parent-teen relationship through the college admissions process and takes pressure off students, because they know they are not alone.

The preceding tips are the techniques I used to help both Maggie and Jake in the Loker household you read about in the beginning of the chapter. Let's take a look at how I implemented the different methods. During our first family meeting, each person was feeling drained and hopeless. I wanted to change this right away.

I glanced at all of the exasperated faces in the room. "I know that as parents"—I looked at Stan and Marissa—"you're not telling Jake to sacrifice happiness. You're only telling him that he has to get good grades."

"Absolutely," Marissa said. "We want you to be happy, honey." She took her son's hand. "And we know that for future happiness, that does mean good grades. There just has to be a balance."

"So, what does 'good' mean?" I asked. "Let's get really specific. What would be acceptable to you, so we know what we are working toward?"

Stan leaned in. "I think we would be happy with nothing lower than an eighty percent on anything more than ten points. I think that is reasonable."

I turned to Jake. "Is that okay with you? We are making a hard limit here. If you think it's fair, I would like you to set your own consequence for if you do not make it."

"That's fair." He thought for a few moments. "I guess take away my car for a week for any fun use, only to and from school and sports?"

Marissa's eyes widened. "You said it, not me."

We laughed. Jake shrugged. "I know it sounds really bad, but I think it will be the only thing that will make me want to meet the limit."

"Okay." I put my hands together. "Most of the work I will do with Jake alone, and hopefully we can work with Maggie, too, eventually, since she sounds miserable at school in a different kind of way. Most important, now we have the limit and consequence." I turned to Jake. "Unlike before, you need to know that your parents are not going to jump in and help on last-minute assignments like usual. No superhero parents, please." They smiled in understanding. "I will help them stay accountable to this. If there is an eighty percent or lower, there is no negotiation on the punishment, either. In exchange for your sticking to this, they will pay for you to work with me on getting your grades up. I will help you. You are not alone on this."

"I understand," Jake said, his face visibly relaxing. "To be honest, I'm just so relieved to get some help and know exactly what I need to do. I also am so tired of fighting about it. Even if I get bad grades, this simplifies the process."

"Absolutely," I said. We went up to Jake's desk and emptied out his backpack. I had him walk me through an average school day, after-school homework session, and nightly routine. We quickly identified his study blockages. His biggest hurdle was the most common one—a study blockage during typical transition time. Usually, he gets home from school and Marissa allows a snack before homework time because she wants him to finish before dinner.

Jake's chin jutted out in anger. "I think I just need more time. I like to get a snack and unwind a little from the day. Sometimes when she pushes me into homework I'm still tired from school."

I verbally noted the chin gesture to him. "And you are angry at her for not giving you space?"

His eyes widened in surprise, but he responded, "Yeah, I'm angry at her. When I'm angry, then nothing gets done because I want to work on my own time and can't focus." Jake crossed his arms defensively. I knew that to get him to compromise and not be self-protective, I needed him to see her side.

"I totally get that you need more unwind time and that you want to work at your own pace. You also need to be mindful that your mom is working from past experience. How many times did you stay up extra late doing homework and then ask your mom to help so it would get done?"

He shrugged, looking a little guilty. "More times than I can count."

"Right. So your mom is working from that past experience, trying to get your homework done early to save a fight later. She doesn't realize she is just making the fight earlier and not giving you time to settle before starting your homework. What kind of break do you think would be sufficient?"

"Maybe twenty or thirty minutes of something fun, like playing a game?"

I nodded in agreement. "Okay, we definitely want to keep it specific, to minimize fighting later—just like we made specific grade requirements and consequences. In the end, it helps you actually, because you have specific timing. Let's say thirty minutes. I will give you the benefit of the doubt and you can play ball outside or on the cool pinball machine I saw downstairs, but no TV watching. I think your parents will agree it should be something a little more engaging." I also knew that this could be a great primer for Jake in the future if it worked out the first few weeks.

"That's fair. You think my parents will agree?"

"Well, let's compromise. I can offer that they give you thirty minutes of transition time after school, but it has to be an engaging activity. And your mom cannot nag you during that time. In return you will set your own time limit and start homework on your own after thirty minutes." I had brought an egg timer with me for this purpose. "But if you exceed your limit or you watch TV instead, then we have to chop five minutes off each time it happens. And I'll be the one holding you accountable to this, not your parents."

He smiled, knowing that I could not be so easily duped with excuses. "That sounds fair. I will have to be really strict with myself."

"That's exactly it. You are going to be on your own in a few years and no one will be around to 'nag' you, so we have to work on you being your own best motivator. I think also you will find having that thirty-minute cushion is a great relaxing time for you. I think you will be way more motivated to do work because your needs are being met and people are respecting that." I did truly believe this would work and hoped it would be a great transition time for him. It also gave him high expectations to live up to. I wanted to plant the seed that this compromise would help him be both independent and motivated—two benefits he already craved.

I saw a genuine smile form. "That's true, I know I need to do it on my own. It will also probably make my mom less stressed to know we have a specific time set up with approved activities that help me study better. I think it will be awesome." I was glad to hear he saw these new rules as a way for him to be pumped up, not weighed down—a drag that many teenagers feel with new rules.

Jake and I also laid out his planner and assignment sheets with the home calendar and prepped for some of the upcoming crunch times. Marissa was kind enough to move a doctor's appointment and happily agreed to the after-school deal. I also looked at Jake's study habits and we quickly figured out he was a sprinter. He worked great in short bursts. I taught him how to "chunk," or break up work into twenty-minute segments, and set aside five- to ten-minute break activities and primers he could do that his parents would be okay with. It took a few weeks for him to get used to this method of studying, but more and more he found he could apply it and get his work done without getting burned out. Last, I encouraged him to visit with the teacher in his hardest class. These private meetings helped him with the material, and the teacher became more responsive to his needs in class because she knew where some of his weak points were.

After about six weeks there was one relapse a few days after a successful crunch week. "What happened?" I asked him after he brought back a D on a math project—typically a good subject for him. He was clearly worn out and demonstrating shame, so I wanted to make sure I was not beating him down, but just trying to figure out what went wrong so we could learn from it. "It's not bad; it happens. You made it six weeks and through a crunch week. This will only make you stronger. Your parents are okay because they know you are working on it."

"That's true, I guess. I did do well in crunch week, and then I was tired, so I slacked off on this project. I saved it til the last minute and then couldn't get it all done."

I knew he had asked his parents for a "sick" note and they had said no. "Sick note didn't work, huh?"

"Nope. I was pretty mad, but I guess I knew that would happen, and now I don't have the car for a week. It sucks." Many teens will go a few weeks after a change and let their behavior slip to test their parents and see if they will hold up the discipline end. The fact that Marissa and Stan held fast to their limits, but did not shame him or yell, was just as important as our initial goal-setting meeting.

"It does suck, but it's only a week and I can try to help you get your grade back up if you want. That was part of the deal. I know you are not happy about the grade, but there was a small success because you kept your end of the bargain on the consequence. Was it so bad, bringing home the bad grade?"

"You know, not as bad as it used to be. I brought it home, I was upset, and my parents were like, 'Okay, no car for a week.' And that was it. I just need to study harder and endure this week without a car. I used to bring home a bad grade and the house exploded—which was all the time. Now I know exactly what I need to do."

"And I'll help," I said. I learned with the Lokers and many

other families I have worked with that change is a process and happens slowly, over time and with strides and setbacks. But relapses and mistakes can reinforce the lessons if you stick to the deal and limits. Eventually, I was also able to work with Maggie. During our first meeting, she burst into tears because she thought her parents had called me in because she wasn't doing well *enough*. It took a few weeks, but I did convince her to start beading again—a hobby she found relaxing. She also finally came to terms with the fact that her school life *was* her life. We put in boundaries for homework time so she could get more sleep and find time to zone out and be creative for a little each day. Our concession was that finals time and crunch week were strictly all school. I was happy to make this deal with her because, as with all teens who want to make a change, it takes baby steps.

Things to Remember

- The two major shifts in the academic environment are the rising pressure and use of technology in school life.
- Students respond to stress in three ways: by becoming slackers, embracing perfectionism, or cheating.
- Poor academic performance happens because students have trouble doing activities they do not like (and school usually ranks high on this list); they feel they can never have balance, so they give up; or they do not know *how* to study, even if they like the material.
- "Unicorn" teens, or perfectionists, overanalyze, busy themselves to become numb, and are incredibly self-critical, often completely falling apart if and when they fail.
- Technology in academic life has both positive effects—including and engaging more students—and negative ones: endangering privacy and encouraging distractions in the classroom.

- Parents can help students succeed and manage stress by encouraging transition time and separation of home life, school life, and social life.
- Teaching students how to deal with crunch time and classroom strain will tackle the two major areas of stress in a teen's academic life.
- Parents can encourage "slackers" by setting limits for them, identifying and eliminating study blockages, and teaching time-management tools and study skills that work with their pace.
- Encouraging students to engage in activities they are passionate about and feel efficient in often spills over into helping relieve academic pressure.

Challenges You Can Do Right Now

Family Challenge: What kind of student are you?

1. Sit down with family members and talk about the different kinds of students. Did this chapter miss any? Do you know people in each category?
2. Which category does each family member most fit into? Is this good or bad?
3. What are the pros and cons of each type?

Family Challenge: How does technology fit with school?

1. Sit down with family members and talk about how technology has changed school.
2. Can your family use technology more to help with homework, studying, and comprehension? Can your family use technology less in order to help with focus and productivity and to guard against cheating?

Personal Challenge: Find the ideal pace and transition time.

1. What is each of your children's pace? Do they need transition time?
2. Approach them to see if they would like this built into their schedules.

Family Challenge: Cultivate time management and study skills.

1. Review each child's study blockages and each parent's grade requirements.
2. What areas can each student feel more passionate about? When do they feel the most efficient? How can you encourage these activities?
3. Go through the study skills list and talk about which would work in each subject.

Family Challenge: Begin your college discussion.

1. Have you thought about what area you want to go to school in?
2. Which is better: public or private universities?
3. Do you want to apply for scholarships? Do you think you would qualify?
4. How are we planning to pay for college?
5. Is national ranking important in your choice of school?
6. Does it matter to you where your friends want to go to college?
7. How are we going to organize our college materials?
8. Do we want a college counselor?

CHAPTER 8

The Greatest Generation?

Teenagers today are incredibly optimistic, creative, and entrepreneurial. However, many of these qualities have arisen because of the high pressure on young people to succeed and stand out. When I met one exceptional teen, I got great insight into the creative, adventurous, and brazen outlook he and his peers share. Patrick was a fantastic client. His parents had called me to work with him on my Teen Life 101 course. This is an eighteen-week program I created that deals with all aspects of teen life—study skills, self-esteem builders, budgeting, and even college preparation. Week six is all about personal passion projects and I sat down with Patrick to discuss the lesson.

"So, last week we talked about Internet safety and savvy, which you totally rocked. This week we're going to start working on your personal passion project. This is my absolute favorite lesson and we will continue it throughout the rest of the weeks," I said, pulling out my notebook.

"Awe-so-o-ome!" Patrick chimed. Energetic, optimistic, and silly, Patrick was willing to try almost every challenge I gave him and usually surprised me with his ideas and answers.

"Okay, a personal passion project is the biggest thing we will work on together. This is a project that ties together what you love to do, what you want to learn how to do better, and what we can use for your future, whether that is for your college applications or your career."

His face darkened. "College applications? I'm never going to get in anywhere," he groaned. At seventeen, Patrick was an extremely ambitious teenager. Despite his high grades, he was constantly worried about getting into college. During finals he often worked himself into a stupor from caffeine, Tylenol, and lack of sleep. Surprisingly, he also prided himself on being the class clown. As a thin, lanky, awkward boy who had to duck when walking through the doorway to his room, athletics were never his thing. He had once told me that he had to be funny so people wouldn't notice that he kept messing up the class curve when he got perfect scores on tests.

I rolled my eyes. "Don't be so hard on yourself. You're incredibly smart."

"I guess. But it's never going to be like what my teachers and parents"—here he put up his fingers in mock quotation marks—"expect of me." Last year Patrick had given up playing the saxophone because his college counselor said he needed to focus on scores and grades.

"They only expect you to be happy."

He put his feet up on the desk. "Right. I mean, I know I'll be rich and successful and happy one day, blah, blah, blah. But there is a ton of pressure to get there."

"Well, this project should be fun. You have no idea what you want to do when you get older, right?" He nodded, tossing a stress ball up and down. "When a client is unsure of the career direction he wants to go in—which is totally fine—it leaves lots of choices open to us. You have two options to choose from for your personal passion project. One, you can work on a novella. That is something you could include on your applications and we can use it to hone your writing and research skills. Two, you can put together your own business. We will write a business plan, and you can do research and possibly even do informational interviews with experts in the field you are thinking of working on."

He sat forward. "Oh, for sure I want to do the business one. You know I'm really into economics."

"Done. Here is the deal. I'll go over some basic business terms with you today. We're going to talk about budgets, overhead costs, profit, and revenue and go over what is in a basic business plan. Your homework this week is to come up with an idea to pitch to me at our next meeting in two weeks. Think of an idea for a business you would enjoy running and can make a profit from. You can also choose to pitch a nonprofit business. In that case you need to enjoy running the business and be able to break even helping a cause."

"Cool!" I could see his mind already whizzing away and had to stop him to go over the terms for starting a business.

"Okay, okay, focus. You'll have two weeks to work on it. Remember, the whole point of this project is to do something that makes you feel good and confident and gives us an opportunity to learn something." We finished the rest of the lesson and I left Patrick outlining and brainstorming ideas on his whiteboard. Two weeks later I came up the stairs and Patrick was waiting, hunched over, at his door.

"Vanessa! I have the best idea. You're going to love it." He leapt halfway across his room in one stride and skidded into his rolling desk chair.

I laughed at his Gumby-like features. "What did you think of?"

He held out his hands. "Come on, you know me. I didn't just think about it. I already put it into action."

"Wow," I said, impressed. "I can hardly wait. Explain it to me."

He gestured to his whiteboard. "So, this is a great business model because, like you said, it has very little overhead or start-up investment costs. I spent about thirty-five dollars for start-up supplies this week and it only takes about ten dollars per week to run as overhead. Revenue is projected to be about two hundred and fifty dollars per week, excluding holidays, of course."

I looked at the numbers in amazement. "Two hundred and fifty dollars per week? That's a lot of margin."

"Oh, that isn't even the best part. There is a complete possibility for franchising here. We could easily spread to other schools. I already talked to some of my buds. That could quadruple profits for passive income."

I couldn't help but chuckle. I had covered very basic business terms with Patrick, but he had clearly done his own research. "Franchising?" I said, marveling at how much time he had probably spent already teaching himself how to be a business owner. "What exactly *is* the business?"

"I thought you would never ask," he said with a wink. He spun around on his chair and crouched down underneath his bed. Soon he was pulling out a large cooler. "So, I found a market need—like we talked about"—he looked at me for affirmation and I nodded encouragement—"I found a market need for this product and realized I have an unlimited supply of it."

I looked at the cooler. *Cookies? Some kind of energy snack?* I wondered. "Go on," I said.

He popped open the lid and I peered inside. At first I was unsure of what I was looking at. Golden yellow jars stared back up at me. He continued, holding up a small cup. "I sell my own and my little brothers' clean urine to athletes at school. The athletes are in desperate need of urine that will pass drug tests. They can put in an order with me and I will deliver to them drug-free pee. I pay my brothers ten cents a piss—I mean every time they urinate," he clarified for me, "and then charge twenty dollars a pop. It's an amazingly successful business model based on all of the principles you taught me!"

I looked at Patrick's beaming face and sat with my mouth open, unsure of what to say next. Technically, he did follow the directions and came up with a very profitable business model. Yet I had not mentioned that the business needed to be *legal* and—dare I say—*ethical.* This experience with Patrick taught me how ingenious, unabashed, and imaginative teenagers can be, and how differently they respond to stress and pressure than adults do.

Patrick embodies his generation's top characteristics and future outlook because he is optimistic about a bright future ahead, and is extremely creative and out-of-the-box with his ideas, but constantly feels pressure and stress to stand out. Before I describe how I addressed Patrick's innovative yet illegal entrepreneurial endeavor, I want to talk about how these three characteristics are shaping our next generation of adults and their future. Despite Patrick's worry and anxiety about his future, he is absolutely sure that he will have a bright one. In fact, that assuredness itself is what causes him to feel the weight of his potential future on his shoulders every day. Teens today are incredibly optimistic about their futures. A Pew Research Center study conducted in May 2010 found that eighteen- to twenty-nine-year-olds have been the hardest hit by this recession. Yet this group is significantly more optimistic about the chance for improvement. In fact, eighteen- to twenty-nine-year-olds were the most likely to say that their financial circumstances would recover over the next year.

One of the reasons that young people are so optimistic about their futures is that they are much more creative than previous generations and see opportunities in new areas. They view their futures in a much less linear way. As the recession took many traditional job options away, many young people just created new ones. One of the reasons I work with clients on personal passion projects is to get them thinking outside the box. They need to stand out even more for college applications and job positions. Having them create alternative resumes and pursue volunteer opportunities and college application activities that they are actually passionate about is something I consider integral to my work with teens. Helping teens come up with these personal passion projects is surprisingly easy. I gave Patrick a thirty-minute tutorial on some basic entrepreneurial terms, and he was off and running with ideas. Unfortunately he went a little too out of the box. I have e-mailed with thousands of teenagers about business ideas, technology start-ups, and backyard entrepreneurial efforts. In fact, I run another website called LivingRadically.com, where my partner and I invest in small start-ups. Even though it is open to everyone, almost all of our applications for this program come from teens! Like many of his peers, Patrick was bursting at the opportunity to build a new and successful venture.

Although I do believe this generation is incredibly creative and adventurous, teens' increased entrepreneurial spirit is also caused by rising pressure. The stress of a dwindling job market, a hypercompetitive college application process, and an increasingly expensive lifestyle has given youth today one choice: join the rat race or fall behind. Stress comes from all of the areas of a teen's life we have discussed in previous chapters: school, friends, poor communication with parents, peer pressure, and technology. As my experience with Patrick demonstrates, expectations are another huge source of strain. Patrick felt he could never live up to the expectations his parents and teachers put upon him and therefore had to give up one of his hobbies—playing the saxophone—to have more time to study. One of our fourteen-year-old interns, Vivian, wrote an article about stress caused by expectations and how they cloud a teen's ability to form his or her identity. Here is an excerpt:

"This is the time to be able to find ourselves and define who we are by trying new things. When we try
new things and fail, the stress gets worse, and after a
while, we just give up and become emotionally depressed. Parents also cast inordinate amounts of pressure onto their kids, and eventually, the things
expected of them become impossible to achieve. For
example, my parents are always praising my brother
on how he was class valedictorian and all of his accomplishments. They also constantly say that I should
achieve as much as him, and sometimes, it is way too
much to handle. I'm afraid that when the time comes,
I will disappoint them and not live up to their
standards."

Vivian's comments speak directly to Patrick's situation. Patrick
loved playing the saxophone, but because he had not been playing it for very long, his counselor and parents decided he should
focus on schoolwork and activities he had been doing for many
years to show continuity on his applications. Patrick accepted
this limitation on his ability to experiment with his time and
hobbies because he was trying to achieve. This is a terrible cycle,
where everyone contributes. Patrick had told his parents and
counselor he wanted to go to a top-twenty school. In response,
his parents and the school counselor advised him to make certain personal sacrifices to strengthen his application and encouraged him to keep pushing through—which, of course,
added more stress. As Patrick began to feel the stress, he felt
more miserable but wanted to achieve even more because he felt
being successful would be the only escape from the pressure.

I believe the rat race has spread into the teen and tween years.
We also see this in the "busy paradox" I mentioned in relation to
unicorn students in the previous chapter. I personally stumbled
upon this concept when I realized that the only time I give my-

self to just think is when I lay my head down on the pillow at night to go to sleep. On one particular day, I had an early morning radio interview, answered 176 e-mails, ran at the gym, cooked a quick lunch, had a business meeting, wrote a blog post, saw a client, called my sister, grabbed a good-bye dinner with a friend, and then cleaned out TiVo with my boyfriend. I brushed my teeth and thought, "What a successful day." Yet when I got in bed, I realized I was exhausted—mentally and physically. My back was sore and I hadn't even registered it. I reviewed my meetings, thought about the call with my sister, and ruminated on all of the things that had happened to me that day . . . for the first time. Forty-five minutes later, no closer to sleep than I was when I first lay down, I couldn't help but wonder why *this* was the first time all day I was actually thinking.

Sure, I had been thinking all day. But I had not given myself a second to ponder, reflect, or *feel*. I was too busy to feel. I was just doing. This led me back to the thought I had while brushing my teeth: "What a successful day." What about it was so successful? I had some okay meetings and responded to normal e-mails, but nothing was particularly out of the ordinary. In fact, the day had been stressful. I had wolfed dinner and lunch, almost gotten a parking ticket, talked on the phone from place to place in the car to squeeze everything in, and had not done a single thing for the sake of enjoyment. Everything was work or obligatory. Even cleaning out the TiVo had become a task, not a time for relaxation. I think the reason I felt it was so successful was because I was busy. And somewhere along the line I have been trained to live by the mantra: *The busier you are, the more successful you are.*

·········

Yet when you are busy, you do not take breaks, you do not feel how your day is going—you just push through. Most important, you lose sight of what you enjoy, because all you want to do is get things done. I see the busy paradox in many of the parents and teens I work with. There are many who, like me, fill their days with being busy and almost never have a chance to take breaks. Many of the teen girls I work with who suffer from the busy paradox have trouble answering the question "What do you do for fun?" or "How do you like to relax?" This means that not only are teens incredibly busy and stressed, but they also have no idea how to decompress or, worst of all, they don't even know that they should!

·········

Teens also face extreme pressure to stand out. With each of my clients and teen interns, I ask them to pick three words to describe themselves. Patrick said, "smart, creative, and funny." These are some of the most popular words; "smart" or "intelligent" ranks second, "creative" or "imaginative" ranks third, and "funny" or "silly" ranks fifth. Can you guess which word ranks number one? "Unique." "Unique" is the most common answer from teenagers thirteen to nineteen. But what happens to a society where everyone thinks they are unique? Can "unique" still carry the same meaning if everyone describes themselves as embodying this trait? I believe that the self-described unique attitude of many teens today does indeed contribute to their adventurous, out-of-the-box imaginations, but it also puts pressure on them to constantly be special. And the pressure to feel special is a trap that can never be avoided. Patrick absolutely felt this pressure. He was constantly worried about his parents' expectations and his own need to be either the funniest in class or the head of the class.

In his outrageously popular book series *Diary of a Wimpy Kid*, Jeff Kinney offers us the perfect example of the need to be special at something—anything. The main character, Greg, tries desperately to get into the class favorites page of his year-book so he can be "known" for something. This resonates with many young readers. The pressure to be unique or special causes teens to constantly question whether they are good enough, cool enough, smart enough. I was sitting with a group of girls during one of my seventh-grade girl workshops and I overheard a group of teens in the corner arguing about something. When I walked over, I overheard, "But my leg hair *is* longer!" The girls looked up at me and giggled. "What are you guys talking about?" I asked. One girl looked sheepish but said, "We're competing to see who has the longest leg hair. We all are known for some-thing: mine is the curliest, Jen's is the darkest, Jackie's is—" "I got it," I interrupted.

The need to be the best or the worst or the most also ties into teenagers' obsession with categorizing themselves, which we talked about in chapter 1. However, categorizing ourselves lim-its our dreams, our ability to change, and our self-perspective. How can parents help their kids feel special without pressuring them with the need to be unique or fall into one limiting cate-gory? Additionally, how can adults encourage teens' creative, entrepreneurial, brazen spirit so that they can learn about them-selves and not worry about expectations? In the solutions below I address how parents can not only tackle stress and pressure, but also make their teens more well-rounded and happy for the future.

1. Remember It's Never Relative

Parents have trouble imagining that their teens could be stressed about anything serious. Parents often write to me that they can-not imagine what could be so stressful about their teenager's life. "After all," they tell me, "they don't pay bills, they have a great school and huge house! I give them all the latest gadgets and try

> "Some adults don't believe in 'teenage stress.'
> But, I am reassuring them, it's very possible.
> If the definition of stress is physical, mental,
> or emotional strain or tension, then teenagers
> definitely have it! Why do so many parents not
> realize their kids are stressed out? One of the
> huge mistakes being made today by parents is
> forgetting that their teens are still developing
> and need to learn how to do certain things,
> such as dealing with stress and pressure."
>
> —Hannah, 14,
> Radical Parenting intern

to keep them happy." Hannah, a fourteen-year-old intern, explains how teen stress is difficult for parents to comprehend.

Oftentimes, when teens come home and are stressed out about a friend, a test, a teacher, or some other issue, parents tell them "it's no big deal," or "well, that doesn't even compare to what I dealt with today," or "if your brother could do it, you can do it, too." These kinds of "relative" comments have three devastating effects. One, your child feels belittled and unimportant. Two, your child feels even more distant from you. Three, your child feels he or she should either completely shut down from talking to you because you "don't get it," or make an even bigger fuss until you understand how stressful it really is. Therefore, first and foremost, it is important for parents to address anxiety and worries with an open mind. Once you hear what the problem is, you can help your child identify the stress.

2. Localize the Anxiety and Identify the Stress

Teenagers have a tendency to globalize their anxiety. When people globalize their anxiety or stress, they take an isolated incident or stressor and inflate it so it infects their overall outlook, mood, and routine. Parents can help teenagers localize anxiety by identifying and isolating the cause. For example, I was working with a client named Will during his finals. I was teaching him how to prepare for each subject in different ways. We started with science and I easily taught him how to integrate key-word memorization into his lab findings and formulas. He was confident and feeling good until we moved on to Spanish. Spanish is his worst subject and immediately he started to tense up. As I began to teach Will to use mnemonic devices for hard vocabulary words, he began to experience globalized anxiety. His ability to absorb the technique dissipated and he began to overanalyze about other subjects. He would make comments like "If I can't do this, I'm going to flunk history," or "I'm going to fail finals." The worst was when he actually reworked how the previously easy subject had gone in his head: "And I didn't even really understand that science technique; I'm going to bomb that, too."

I'm sure many parents can think of times when their kids, spouse, friend, or they themselves went into globalized anxiety. Usually this is set off by a vulnerable topic or weak ability. For Will, Spanish was a trigger for him to go into panic mode and doubt his ability to perform in all of his other subjects. With teenagers who are in globalized anxiety mode, it is important to work two angles. The first is reminding them of what they are good at, and the second is getting them to focus on the local anxiety. With Will, it sounded something like this:

"Okay, let's pause for a second. Put Spanish out of your mind. When I taught you that technique with the formula for air pressure, how quickly did you memorize it?"

Will reluctantly thought back. "Right away, I guess."

"Right," I said. "Because you rock at science and you nailed those techniques. Remember that?"

"Yes. But Spanish is different, and I know I'm going to—"

"Whoa," I interrupted him. "You're right that you rocked science, but Spanish triggered your nerves, right?"

"Yeah. I'm not good at Spanish," he said sullenly.

"Well, you haven't done as well as you would have wanted in the past. But you didn't have these techniques in the past. Nor did you have all of the previous tests to learn from. I want you to be really clear for me on something."

"Okay, what is it?" he asked.

I motioned with my hands on one side. "Science is over here. You feel great about that, right? Own that feeling you had when you memorized a really hard formula in less than twenty seconds."

"Yes."

I moved my hands over. "Spanish is over here. Maybe a little bit tougher, but we are going to work it out. I need you to realize you let Spanish expand all the way into your other areas and cloud your awesome feeling you had with science. We have to keep it over here."

From that point on, whenever Will began to stress about something not related to the task at hand, I asked him where he was worrying, reminding him of how the Spanish "cloud" permeated the rest of his confidence. This works with all areas: school stress, friend stress, and family stress. Parents can teach teenagers to identify the stressor in their life and make sure it does not turn into overall panic and doubt.

Do a stress test together one night as a table topic over dinner. Answer the stress test questions I included at the end of the chapter and then see who gets closest to the right answers. Parents can use the answers to get to know each other and address their biggest worries and stresses. It is also a great way for parents to learn what makes their child feel confident and strong so that, in times of globalized anxiety, they can remind them of what they are good at.

3. Embrace the Idea of Whole Children

I hear many college counselors and parents say that they wish their student had "a thing"—something that admissions officers, employers, or family friends can identify as the child's specialty. This is great to have, but only if it is not forced. I like to encourage parents to embrace the concept of whole children. This means allowing teens to experiment with many hobbies, experiences, and specialties. Often this gives teenagers space and time to carve out their own identity, pick what they are truly passionate about, and become more well-rounded. This can also mean considering alternative career and college paths.

Here are just a few unique ideas I have implemented with teens when working on their future paths:

- **Voluntourism gap years:** Voluntourism is a way for young people to travel and see the world while helping others. Teenagers can do this on summer breaks, spring breaks, or before (or instead of) college. Participants travel to other countries and help build schools, teach English, or help others in need, and often their room, board, and food costs are covered.

- **International Baccalaureate:** This organization offers three educational programs, in both public and private schools, for children aged three to nineteen. The programs offer a different type of education for students who want to be challenged with a more international mindset.

- **Studying abroad in high school:** More and more programs are being created for students to take semesters abroad during high school. These programs offer teens many different opportunities to learn about life outside their hometown and school.

- **Joining SCORE:** If you have an entrepreneurial spirit in your home, you might want to consider having that teenager join SCORE for free. SCORE is a nonprofit group, partnered with the Small Business Administration, that gives free resources and support to small businesses and entrepreneurs. It has an amazing mentorship program and many teens can use its free Web seminars ("webinars") and resources to start their own businesses.

- **Teen writers:** I wrote my first book when I was seventeen and love working with young writers. Many teens have their own stories to tell, fictional or real. Teens can write their own book during November (National Novel Writing Month), keep their own blog, or try their hand at poetry and then work on getting it published. Check out some of our websites for teen writers in the resources section.

4. Encourage Mental Hygiene

I use the term "mental hygiene" all the time with my clients. Just like teens have to take care of their body, clothes, hair, and schoolwork, they also need to manage their mental state. I often encourage parents to help teens view their own mind like they view a home office. If you don't do some mini cleanups, take breaks, and have places for your tools, the mess will prevent you from getting anything done. There are a few ways to teach mental hygiene.

First, it is important for students to learn how to take breaks. We often talk to them about getting things done and working, but not about how to let their mind unwind. Just like we need sleep to recover and function properly, our brain also needs some time to reboot and process during the day. Teach your teens how good mental breaks are restorative, not numbing. If they are spending lots of time on the computer, they should switch mediums and take some time outside. Watching TV is also not a great break because instead of allowing teens to process and giving their brain a break, it just stimulates them more. Activities like sudoku, creative writing, singing, meditating, and playing sports are all different ways of exercising your mind and are essential for allowing it to function at top speed. Taking proper breaks every few hours is also a great way to fight off the busy paradox. For overbooked and overscheduled students, a few choice breaks in between activities are essential to prevent feeling stressed or overwhelmed.

Another strategy I use to help teens who feel bored or overwhelmed by the amount of stress and pressure in their life is to do a "mental vomit." I know that's a gross title, but it is very demonstrative of this concept! Sometimes my clients have a lot of mental stress because they are overly burdened with ideas or nagging thoughts, so I have them do a mental purge. When your teen gets into the car or comes home from school and seems worried or is venting about all of the things she is trying to keep straight, have her do a mental vomit with you. Usually I have kids work in a journal or on a whiteboard. Sit down together and have them write what is worrying them. When the list is finished, break the issues down into different categories of stress and immediacy. There can be a school to-do list, a worry list, or a happy list. Often the act of getting the thoughts out of their head and then organizing them is enough for them to breathe and brings relief. I have found that this is also a great strategy with teens who are depressed or have mood swings or high anxiety. It also, of course, helps them take a breather if they are in the trap of the busy paradox. Many parents talk about "enjoying the moment" or taking more "mental pauses." Mental vomiting is a concrete way for teens to take more moments.

Third, it is important to teach teens how to distinguish between what they enjoy, what is busywork, and what is essential. Many teens believe being busy means they are more successful, or they simply have so many pressures and things to do that they do not stop to think about *what* they are doing. Talk to your teens about the different activities they do in a day. Which things do they do because they simply enjoy them? Is there anything that used to be enjoyable, but now is simply another item on the list? Make sure their hobbies, sports, and activities that are meant to be fun still are. Also ask them if they do any activities that are not essential and are simply busywork. I often find myself reorganizing notebooks just because I have a free second to do it. Usually I do this just to fill the time and feel busy. Do your teens fall into this trap? You can also make them aware of "time-sucks"—Facebook, TV, chatting on IM, or texting can fall into this category. Very rarely are teens aware of how much time they actually spend on time-sucks. Parents can specify limited time allowances for time-suck activities, and ways to prevent exceeding them, like setting timers. Once you have reviewed the activities that fill your teens' day, have them go through and sort what they have to do. Knowing how to organize their activities is a huge part of mental hygiene because it teaches teens to really enjoy their fun activities, save a lot of time for essential to-do list items, and avoid doing busywork.

5. Encourage Them to Be More Grateful

Teaching your teens to be grateful is another way to help them get out of the rat race and appreciate what makes them happy, to prevent stress. It is also an essential life skill. In fact, I believe that being grateful is one of the most important qualities and values to teach young people. Refer back to the gratitude exercises in chapter 5 on bullying. Those ideas and challenges will help teens embrace their already very optimistic attitudes and prevent the negative effects of stress and pressure.

·········

At the beginning of the chapter I talked about Patrick and his new business idea—creative and profitable, but very illegal. Patrick epitomizes many of the characteristics of his generation. He is incredibly imaginative, optimistic, and hardworking, but constantly feels the pressure to stand out and succeed—two of his greatest desires. I used many of the preceding tips with Patrick to encourage his natural abilities and lessen the stress he was feeling.

I looked at what I now realized were tiny cups of urine—the kind they give you at the doctor's office.

"Isn't it a great idea?" he enthused.

"Well, it's a pretty different idea. . . . You thought of a business that sure does have a lot of profit and little overhead, which is great. . . ." His eyes widened a bit and his mouth dropped in a tiny expression of fear. "You know what I'm going to say, right, Patrick?"

He looked down at the cups of urine on ice. "I thought, maybe, you could overlook the legality part?" he said in a questioning tone.

I gave him an incredulous stare. "Really? You thought I might overlook that?"

We both laughed. But his face sobered. "I don't want to stop doing this." I could see panic in his face and hear it in his voice.

"Because of the money, or what?"

He shut the lid of the cooler. "I mean, that's great, but it's not just that. I really stand out now, you know. Kids at school think it's cool and a good idea and they seek me out to come talk to me. Jocks are asking for me at lunch now."

"And is that because they like you, or because they want your goods?" I said. I knew it was a bit harsh, but I didn't want to beat around the bush with Patrick; he was too smart for that.

He ran his hand through his hair. "I guess they really just want my goods and they want to be friends with me so I'll offer them discounts." I waited for this to sink in, hoping he would come to his own conclusion. "It feels good to be popular and do something that is successful. You know I put time into it and thought it through, and it's working. That feels good." I thought about the power of accomplishment and how it is so potent that it can actually blur the legality of an idea for even the brightest of people. I could see how proud Patrick was that he had built something from scratch and succeeded with it. That feeling of skillfulness and competence overshadowed the fact that he knew the business idea was morally wrong.

"So, it feels good to be good at something. And it feels good to be liked, even if it might not be for the best reasons. It seems like this 'feeling good' is a new thing. Why do you think you have so little to feel good about?"

His lips pulled down into a grimace, a microexpression for sadness. "I just always wake up and feel like I have mountains of work and tons of activities I don't even like, and I worry I won't be successful. Like, finals are coming up next week and I'm so anxious about them. I don't know if I'm going to do well. This project was an escape from all of that stress and anxiety. I know it seems like my life should be easy and my stress is nothing compared to other kids', but it feels awful."

"First of all, no stress is relative. Never think that your stress is less than or not as important as someone else's. Second, I get that you feel overwhelmed about finals. In fact, I think that this project has been a great escape from that pressure. Third, just because this project isn't going to work out doesn't mean you can't do something else that's even more awesome. You just got your feet wet!" I paused to make sure he was on the same page as me.

"I know I shouldn't do this anymore. I guess . . ."

He still seemed unsure. "Patrick, I know it makes you money and quasi-friends, but does this project make you feel good about yourself? Do you like that you are indirectly supporting athletes who use drugs and then lie about it?"

He laughed wryly. "When you put it that way, no." He took in a deep breath. "No, it doesn't feel good. It's not me. I can do better."

"Duh. You're one of the most creative people I know. You probably had more amazing ideas on the scratch piece of paper you threw away!"

"Do I even have time with finals coming up?"

"Okay, the rest of today let's work on your stress around finals. First we can do a mental vomit on your whiteboard and figure out all the stuff you have to do. Then we can sort it and plan it, so you can see everything you have to do and that you *will* have enough time for it."

"Yeah, that's a good idea. I just do not know if I'll finish everything."

"Well, to make sure you have time, we can also look at some possible time-sucks." I gave him a knowing look. "Maybe we will cool it on Facebook for the week. I also think we should charge your phone downstairs when you get home from school since we know that if you do it upstairs, texting is a problem."

"Ugh, I guess that's true. I get, like, nothing done with my phone around."

"And I can talk to your mom about maybe saving chores or appointments for next week so you can focus on the essential studying."

Patrick took a deep breath. "You know, I think it won't be so bad. We will figure out time for everything and then I can work on a new passion project. I already have some awe-so-o-ome ideas."

THINGS TO REMEMBER

- Teenagers today are incredibly optimistic about their future.
- This generation is full of innovative, entrepreneurial, and creative young people who are excited about building up their own companies, ideas, and projects.
- Increased pressure is also forcing teens to think outside of the box and be more creative to stand out from their peers.
- The "busy paradox" plagues many young people who believe that being busy makes them successful.
- The desire to be unique adds even more pressure to teens who feel they need to be successful.
- To lessen teens' anxiety, parents should keep an open mind regarding their child's stressors and never compare them to others.
- Parents can reduce a teen's tendency to globalize anxiety and help him or her identify and localize the stress to deal with it more effectively.
- Adults can emphasize well-rounded children and alterna-

tive paths to help teenagers who need different options or lifestyles.

- Practicing mental hygiene is a skill many teenagers lack, but desperately need. This includes learning how to take breaks, implementing mental purges, and distinguishing between time-sucks and essentials.

- Gratitude is one of the most important values we can teach our children, so that they appreciate what they have instead of worrying about what they do not.

Challenges You Can Do Right Now

Family Challenge: Outlook

1. Sit down with your family and ask them how they view the world. Is the glass half full or half empty?
2. Discuss whether you think an outlook can change and how this would happen.
3. Ask each other whether it is better to be optimistic or pessimistic, a worrier or an idealist.

Personal Challenge: Pressure Gauge

1. What kinds of pressure do you put on your kids?
2. What kinds of pressure do they put on themselves?
3. Are there one or two areas that you wish you could help your teens be less stressed about?

Family Challenge: Stress Busting

1. Is anyone in your family a victim of the busy paradox? Is the busy paradox true?
2. Think of a few times when family members have global-

ized anxiety as opposed to localizing it. Was this justified? What can family members do to help each other next time this happens?

3. Do the stress test together:

Me

What is the best thing in my life?
What is the worst thing in my life?
What am I most stressed about?
What are the top five things I worry about?
What is my greatest strength?
What is my greatest weakness?

Mom/Dad/Siblings

What is the best thing in their lives?
What is the worst thing in their lives?
What are they most stressed about?
What are the top five things they worry about?
What is their greatest strength?
What is their greatest weakness?

Family Challenge: Happy-Making

1. How does each family member take mental breaks? What are some fun mental break activities?
2. Try some of the grateful exercises together: taking away a sense, the gratitude brush, and empathy notes.

Conclusion

In this book we have covered a huge variety of issues facing teenagers and parents today—bullying, drugs, low grades, and even lying. I began by reviewing the fundamental aspects of healthy communication: removing expectations and programming, avoiding lensing, and adopting the art of protoconversations. These skills help us employ authentic responses over automatic ones and in turn allows our teenagers to see that we are truly trying to connect with them. Of course, this is very difficult when in the throes of a disagreement. Shockingly, we have to remind ourselves that fighting—or open communication channels—actually lessens a teenager's need to lie. This is important for teens because they need to understand the difference between their more primal emotions and their logical secondary emotions. I also encouraged parents to review a mental checklist when triggers are set off in the home and to always try to address emotional intent to decipher miscommunications. In the resources section coming up, I also include a list of bonding activities for parents and teens, as well as some fun "get to know each other" icebreakers that parents can use during car rides, meals, and alone time with their kids.

Of course, teen communication techniques would not be complete without chapters on friends, technology, and bullying.

As teens' identities become more closely associated with the amount and quality of friends they have, social support structures become even more important and precarious. Parents need to make sure that their children are developing offline friends as well as online ones, and model healthy relationships with their own peer group. Although computers, texting, social networks, and gaming can make parents increasingly nervous in the digital age, there are both positives and negatives to having our teens grow up as digital natives. Parents can learn to avoid the pitfalls and capture the benefits by setting up clear rules and boundaries and encouraging good cybercitizenship. Teenagers' online world also encompasses new social stresses, such as the digital bully. Drama and media stereotypes have both enabled and normalized meanness among teens. Parents can bring perspective to their teens by teaching empathy and kindness.

Unfortunately, I had to include a chapter on risky behavior to review why teenagers engage in dangerous activities. Boredom and negative peer influence seem to be the greatest motivating factors in teen promiscuity, drug use, and other unsafe behavior. The fear of boredom and of not being accepted by peers plays directly into problems for today's teens, such as low self-esteem and the need for identity. Parents can prevent and deal with risky behavior by finding positive role models, embracing change, setting up clear rules, and talking to kids about parental scapegoats. I also include some extra resources for parents if they need to get further help.

The other major area of a teen's life is academics. The increasing stress on teenagers has caused many to go in two different directions: perfectionist "unicorns" and slackers. Both types of students can be motivated by cultivating their passions, integrating technology into academic life, and reviewing clear limits and studying techniques. In the resources section I include some of my favorite educational resources, online games, and academic websites.

Despite this generation's issues with identity and self-confidence, they are in general incredibly optimistic, adventurous, and creative. A positive effect of the increase in stress and pressure on teenagers is that they have to think outside of the box for their careers. Parents who keep an open mind can not only encourage alternative paths, but also lessen the societal pressure on them to stand out unnecessarily. Most important, teaching them to be grateful and incorporating this attitude ourselves will help us overcome any challenge we might encounter.

You do not have to tackle these issues and changes alone. In the resources section I include a step-by-step guide for parenting groups. I also tell you how to access some of our online resources from the website to help you facilitate a parenting support group. I find that this is an amazing way for parents to not only help each other, but also stay updated on what is going on in their community. Parents can also use the recommended resources section that lists my other favorite parenting books and websites to discuss in their parenting support groups.

I know sometimes parents can feel overwhelmed, alone, and scared of pushing their teens away. Remember, every single one of our teens told us that they wished their parents would talk and listen to them *more*, not less. The tips in this book, while a little unconventional, can have tremendous impact on your home life—whether you do one tip a month or address a few different areas at the same time. Do not be afraid to try some of the advice that seems a little out of your comfort zone; this is how we get our teens' attention and in turn make big changes. Also remember that progress happens in waves. In many of the families you read about here, nothing changed instantly. We implemented tips slowly, regressed a little, and then kept pushing forward. This is not only normal, it's the best way for you and

your teens to learn, because it mirrors the back-and-forth process of life. Most important, teens can often be more grown-up
than we give them credit for.

I am often astonished by the maturity of teenagers today.
One of the exercises I give my teen interns is to write a letter of
advice to their ten-year-old selves. I am always touched by the
heartfelt, insightful, and incredibly deep perspective they have.
One of my favorites is Gema's letter to herself:

Dear 10-year-old Gema,

I'm a firm believer in having no regrets. I think that our
mistakes and our reactions to them are what make up our
personalities.

   1. School: Luckily, you'll always be in the honor roll.
Keep your ambitions. Aim to pass all your exams and give
math a little more effort than any other subject. Sure, you'll
be two years ahead, but you're a writer; math is your natural nemesis, the Joker to your Batman. However, don't get
carried away. Tests like the FCAT (Florida's Comprehen-
sive Assessment Test) and SAT are not a measure of your
ability but that of your teachers. Don't take school too seriously. Even though you'll get into some of the best universities, it doesn't mean you'll be able to go. For all you know,
you might end up in a community college anyways. (Not
that it's a bad thing.) I'm not saying to not think of the future, but like any time traveler, remember that your home
is in the present. Enjoy yourself.

   2. Enjoy Yourself: You only have about seven years left of
fun and a year to stress about being an adult. You'll spend
most of those seven years learning about the world through
books and the stories your friends tell you. This isn't a good
thing. Put the books down and take a stroll in the park. Ac-

cept more party invitations. It's good to be safe, but there are some things that can't be taught by reading. Some joys you can't feel through a character. You just need to experience things yourself. Do that. Adulthood will come all too soon.

3. Boys: They aren't the eighth wonder of the world, and while you know a very limited amount that have an even more limited interest in you, the world has an abundance of all things male. There will come a time when they will come to their senses and give you attention, just make sure to know that you're not obligated to make them all happy. Weed out the jerks, then move forward.

4. Image: You are not as fat as you imagine. And sure, there'll be bumps on your cheeks and a huge zit on your upper lip for your sixth-grade yearbook picture, but everyone will be so obsessed with how bad they look that it will go unnoticed. This is how it will be from now on. There's no need to stress about buying the most expensive dress or shoes for the school dances. In the end, they are minor details compared to the importance of actually enjoying the experience. While you think you're the ugliest thing since the color pink, someone else wishes to be you. Remember that confidence is two-thirds of beauty.

I'm sure my ten-year-old self would listen attentively. But like most at that age, she'll nod, saying she'll understand, and just go right back to repeating my mistakes. Some things you just have to go through in order to learn.

Love,

You

I think Gema's letter should give all parents hope. Like any teenager, she still fights with her parents and makes mistakes, but her priorities are in the right place. Every teenager makes mistakes! As Gema encourages in her letter, sometimes we have to make mistakes to learn from them. I stress this because even if you follow all of the advice in this book, you will still have tough moments with your teens. You should never feel guilty for mistakes. Guilt helps no one and hurts everyone because when we act out of guilt, we are living in the past. The future is bright. One day you can look back at the tough teen years with your child and savor the good moments and chuckle at the bad.

> *"Refrain from looking back over the past, rather look ahead. Times are changing, people are changing and teens are in a very dynamic point of life, they are changing all the time. So instead of wondering how you could solve a problem, why not consider how you can improve a situation?"*
>
> —Shamima, 15, Radical Parenting intern

Acknowledgments

There are so many people I have to thank for making this book possible. First, thank you to my family—Vance, Stacy, Anita, Larry, Robert, Courtney, Haley, and Peanut and Moose for being so supportive and encouraging through the entire process. Second, thank you to my fabulous, amazing book agents Joel Gotler and Mel Parker. You have believed in my crazy ideas and I hope we have a long future together. I want to thank the entire team at Penguin, especially my editor Meghan Stevenson for putting up with my endless questions and making my blogger writing into author writing. Thank you to Irene Dreayer, Ken Gross, Ivo Fischer, Sean Perry, and Carla Laur for helping me reach teens and parents everywhere.

There are also many colleagues and mentors who have given me words of wisdom, advice, and link love as I did research and built up my blog audience for this book over the past few years. Thank you to Emily Vaughn, Laurie Brown, David Bickham, Marian Merritt, Michelle Cove, Pam Sellers, Jen Feldman, Michal Osteen, David Suissa, Greg Gallant, and Mary Hanlon Stone. I also want to thank all of the other authors and experts who offered to give quotes for this book.

I also want to thank all of my friends who put up with my constant Facebook status updates on parenting teens, watch my videos, and click on my links, even though they are not yet parents. Especially Linsey Schwartz, Lindsay Tachibe, Bari Turetzky, Margo Aaron, Jessica Feldman, Paul Ross, Jonathan Osteen, and the Edwards family. Of course, I also want to thank Scott Edwards for reading every single draft of this book, listening to me talk through every single draft of this book, and never once complaining.

Last, I would like to thank the Radical Parenting team. Thank you to Nina Harada, Alexis Boozer, and of course all of my fabulous teen interns! You are all the reason I write. Thank you for your time, your effort, and your willingness to talk to me about what goes on inside the minds of teens. Also thank you to all of our Radical Parenting readers and blogging friends; you are a part of our Radical Parenting family because your comments, advice, and links are so important to the validity and warmth of the site. Thank you.

Resources for Parents

The Online Step-by-Step Parenting Guide

Log on to Vanessa Van Petten's website at www.radicalparenting
.com.

Go to the books section and print out the Online Parenting
Guide. You can use it to facilitate:

- Parenting discussion groups
- Practicing protoconversation skills and social literacy,
  from my antibullying workshops
- Mom-daughter workshops
- Father-son workshops
- Grade-level parent meetings at your child's school
- Community parenting support groups
- Updates on teen trends, bullying laws, and resources

Parenting Group Guide

I always encourage parents to build a parental support community. Starting or joining a parenting support group is a great
way to connect and stay updated with parents in your neighbor-
hood and ask for advice or extra help, and they can be fun and
educational.

What is a parenting support group?

You can define it! It can be as informal as a couple of parents getting together for coffee once a month or as formal as an organized group of forty parents who meet weekly and hear speakers, read books, and do activities. All parenting groups should provide a forum and support for you and other parents who have similar values.

Why have a Radical Parenting support group?

- To find people whose parenting values are similar to yours.
- To stay up-to-date in the community about what is going on with your teens. I recommend doing lots of activities with your teen and creating more family time to stay informed about issues with drugs, sex, and the Internet. Yet knowing what is going on in your individual community is even more important, because this is what your kids are experiencing.
- So much interaction is online; this is a great way to have offline interactions.
- Groups are a way to become accountable for some of your family goals and progress as you support and update each other.
- Groups can be a neutral and safe place where parents can ask for support and help.
- This is a way to have a break from your own family and make close friends.
- Groups are great for learning and discussing new concepts by reading books, hearing from others, and sharing articles.

How do I start one?

Step 1: Write your parenting group mission

First, you want to think about your group's mission and goals. Here is a sample mission you can use or modify for your needs: *Our goal is to bring together open-minded and forward-thinking parents. We hope to support and push each other to make stronger foundations for our individual families and community.*

Step 2: Invite members

You have to think about what kind of group you want. There are essentially two kinds of groups: those made up of close friends and those open to the community. In an exclusive group you can pick a small number of people you know very well to support each other and challenge yourselves. Open community groups are a great way to meet new people and encourage community parenting. It is also important to know your kids' friends' parents. Being friends with these parents will help you get to know your own child through their peers.

Step 3: First meeting

I highly recommend getting a three-ring binder to keep track of papers and notes. You might want to have snacks and bring extra pens and paper for people to take notes. Name tags can be helpful if you are having an open community group. In the first meeting be sure to go over why you have started this group, your mission, and possible logistics of when and where future meetings should take place. Next, you can ask members what kinds of activities they want to do and whether people want to take turns hosting. You can also take suggestions on books and topics.

Step 4: Subsequent meetings

Ideally, every meeting should start with an update and then cover a topic or book for discussion. You can also bring in speakers. You might want to have members discuss and stay accountable to goals. You can also log each member's goals in the notebook as a great way to track progress. You can use our list of recommended resources to have discussions with your group. There are also many free resources at RadicalParenting.com that you can use.

Activities and Bonding Ideas

Conversation Starters for Parents and Teens

What is your idea of an ideal day?

What is a quality you wish you could have more of?

What is your favorite and least favorite part of our relationship?

Is there something I can do better that I am not doing now?

What scares you the most and why?

What is your biggest goal this year?

If you had to give every human being one universal quality, what would it be and why?

Do you have any recurring dreams? Describe them.

If you could be a famous athlete, actor, writer, or musician, which would you choose and why? (It is fun to guess what the other people in the group will say before divulging answers!)

How do you choose your friends?

What is the first thing you notice about a person?

BONDING AND ANTIBOREDOM ACTIVITY IDEAS

- **Family geocaching:** Geocaching is an activity like a scavenger hunt, but using GPS coordinates. For example, you can search for geocaching locations in your area and then travel to find the spot where a special geocaching box, or "treasure," is. There are over eight hundred thousand locations right now! Many are even in smaller towns. You can also make your own scavenger hunt for others.

- **Writing and completing high school bucket lists:** Have your teens write a high school bucket list with everything they hope to get done before they graduate high school, and then complete it together.

- **Burn CDs for family and friends:** Teens love music. In this down economy, this is a great, cheap, heartfelt gift. It can also be a great way to bond with your teens to have them show you the kinds of music they like.

- **Paintball, mini golf, and laser tag:** Teens usually love doing these kinds of activities; they can be coed, and it's not that much money for a few hours of amusement (and physical activity).

- **Plan a tournament:** For boys and/or girls, host a video game tournament at your house (which usually just involves lots of your patience and food) or, if you have the space or live near a park, have a sports day. For girls, I would also put spa party, sleepover, chocolate-making party, and craft or jewelry-making party under this category. Notice how I use the term "party" loosely; in my opinion, the more you can make it feel like everyone is showing up for something special and that it is being planned for them, the more fun it can be.

Recommended Resources

Educational Resources

Here are the resources I recommend for homework help, research, organization, study skills, and online academic games:

Susan Kruger, *SOAR Study Skills Book* (Grand Blanc, MI: Grand Lighthouse, 2006).

> This is one of the few study skills books I like. The website, www.soarstudyskills.com, also offers a workbook and many online educational resources.

MathPlayground.com

> Math Playground has hundreds of games, puzzles, and interactive word problems for elementary school students.

KidsDomain.com

> This website has games that can be downloaded by age and subject for the special needs of your kid.

Ology.com

> Ology, a website of the American Museum of Natural History, has a large collection of material on all subjects, including a ton of science activities in subjects like biology and astronomy.

Zeeks.com

> Zeeks has a lot of trivia-type questions, like interactive logic and reasoning games.

FreeRice.com

> This is a great website that donates rice to people who need it for every question you get right! You have English, math, languages, and even art history questions to choose from.

TeacherTube.com

> This website has some great educational videos by teachers on all subjects. This can be a great way for students to review or get a different perspective on a complicated lesson.

Therapeutic Resources for Extra Help

GoodTherapy.org

If you feel that you would like to see a therapist or counselor with your teenager, GoodTherapy offers a service to help you find a therapist in your area and get a free consultation.

TeenWildernessPrograms.org

Some families have found wilderness programs to be extremely helpful for their teens. This website offers an overview of many programs across the globe.

Alternative Career Websites and Resources

Voluntourism.org

Voluntourism is a way for young people to travel and see the world while helping others.

LivingRadically.com

Urban nomads specialize in city-hopping or traveling to different cities with jobs that are location-independent.

Ibo.org

The International Baccalaureate offers alternative educational programs with an international emphasis in a network of private and public schools.

HighSchoolProgramsAbroad.com

These programs offer teens many different opportunities to experience life elsewhere.

Score.org

SCORE is a nonprofit group, partnered with the Small Business Administration, that gives free resources and support to small businesses and entrepreneurs.

RadicalParenting.com

Teens can apply for internships to write for or learn online marketing with our website.

BrazenCareerist.com

This is a great website and blog for young entrepreneurs and businesspeople wanting advice, inspiration, and help with unique career paths.

Donna Fenn, *Upstarts! How GenY Entrepreneurs Are Rocking the World of Business and 8 Ways You Can Profit from Their Success* (New York: McGraw-Hill, 2009).

This book talks about how this generation of youth can and will think outside the box to build their careers and how parents can support and benefit from them.

FiveStarLeader.com

Bea Fields offers books, Web shows, and videos geared specifically toward young leaders.

Other Great Parenting Resources

There are hundreds of thousands of parenting books and websites. Here I have selected a few of my favorite parenting books and helpful resources on this generation of teens.

NetFamilyNews.org

Larry Magid and Anne Collier make it possible for parents to keep up with the constant onslaught of new laws and information regarding child safety online.

Kit Yarrow and Jayne O'Donnell, *Gen BuY: How Tweens, Teens and Twenty-Somethings Are Revolutionizing Retail* (San Francisco, CA: Jossey-Bass, 2009).

This fascinating book takes a look into how spending and the outlook of Gen Y has changed.

Sue Blaney, *Please Stop the Rollercoaster!* (Acton, MA: Change-Works, 2004).

Sue Blaney's books are funny and poignant and I highly recommend the workbook.

Betsy Brown Braun, *You're Not the Boss of Me: Brat-Proofing Your 4- to 12-Year-Old Child* (New York: HarperCollins, 2010).

Betsy Brown Braun has an amazing perspective on kids and families. Her books are incredibly useful for parents who need extra help with communication techniques.

Stacy Kaiser, *How to Be a Grown Up: The Ten Secret Skills Everyone Needs to Know* (New York: HarperOne, 2010).

This book is a great gift for teen and tween girls. Stacy Kaiser's advice is heartfelt and extremely useful for any young adult.

Annie Fox, *Be Confident in Who You Are: Middle School Confidential Series* (Minneapolis, MN: Free Spirit, 2008).

If you have middle schoolers who are going through a tough time socially, this series of books by Annie Fox has great insight and advice.

Ypulse.com

Run by Anastasia Goodstein, this is a great website following teen trends and news updates. Parents and adults interested in what is going on in the teen world and media should absolutely use this website as a resource.

Rafe Esquith, *Lighting Their Fires: How Parents and Teachers Can Raise Extraordinary Kids in a Mixed-Up, Muddled-Up, Shook-Up World* (New York: Penguin, 2010).

Rafe Esquith's book is a wonderful guide for parents and teachers trying to guide and educate children.

JenandBarbMomLife.com

Jen and Barb's Mom Life is a fabulous Web series with episodes featuring all aspects of motherhood—both funny and insightful.

ShapingYouth.org

Shaping Youth, headed by Amy Jussel, is a nonprofit consortium of media and marketing professionals concerned about messages that are harmful to children.

ChaosChronicles.com

Lian Dolan has a humorous and fun perspective on being a mom. Her show with her sisters and the blog are well worth a look.

LivinginDigitalTimes.com

The digital lifestyle is pervasive—that's why technology is addressed in almost every chapter of this book. Robin Raskin offers great advice on raising kids in a digital world.

Get Ready to Learn Mom podcast on iTunes

Stacey Kannenberg's show brings in amazing experts on all topics related to parenting. It is fun, upbeat, and informational.

iKeepSafe.org

If you are worried about online safety and how to keep kids safe with technology, Marsali Hancock's iKeepSafe is a great blog.

MommaSaid.net

Jen Singer runs a wonderful website for moms, with articles on everything parenting.

JustForMom.com

Tara Patterson, founder of the Mom's Choice Awards, writes this blog and touches on how parents can learn intuitive parenting skills.

Rachel Simmons, *The Curse of the Good Girl: Raising Authentic Girls with Courage and Confidence* (New York: Penguin, 2010). Rachel Simmons digs deep into the stereotypes and messages young girls are being sent about their sexuality.

Bibliography

On media mirroring real life

Linebarger, D. L., and S. E. Vaala. "Screen Media and Language Development in Infants and Toddlers: An Ecological Perspective." *Developmental Review* 30, no. 2 (2010): 176–202.

On maturity and our expectations

Bruner, J. Lucariello, and Katherine Nelson. *Narratives from the Crib*. Cambridge, MA: Harvard University Press, 1989.

On construction workers and lensing

Levin, Daniel T., and Daniel J. Simons. "Failure to Detect Changes to Attended Objects in Motion Pictures." *Psychonomic Bulletin & Review* 4, no. 4 (1997): 501–6.

On blood sugar and ability to make decisions

Gailliot, M. T., R. Baumeister, C. N. DeWall, J. K. Maner, E. A. Plant, D. M. Tice, L. E. Brewer, and B. J. Schmeichel. "Self-Control Relies on Glucose as a Limited Energy Source: Willpower Is More Than a Metaphor." *Journal of Personality and Social Psychology* 92 (2007): 325–36.

On the open-palm gesture

Kendon, Adam. *Gesture: Visible Action as Utterance*. Cambridge, Eng.: Cambridge University Press, 2008.

On teens fighting with and lying to parents

Darling, Nancy, Patricio Cumsille, Linda L. Caldwell, and Bonnie Dowdy. "Parenting Style, Legitimacy of Parental Authority, and Adolescents' Willingness to Share Information with Their Parents: Why Do Adolescents Lie?" Presented at the Meeting of the International Society for the Study of Personal Relationships, Saratoga, NY (1998).

Darling, Nancy, Katherine Hames, and Patricio Cumsille. "When Parents and Adolescents Disagree: Disclosure Strategies and Motivations." Presented at the Biennial Meeting of the Society for Research on Adolescence, Chicago (2000).

On mother-daughter fighting

Holmes, Tabitha R., Lynne A. Nond, and Ciara Byrne. "Mothers' Beliefs about Knowledge and Mother-Adolescent Conflict." *Journal of Social and Personal Relationships* 25, no. 4 (2008): 561–86.

On contagious emotions

Goleman, Daniel. *Social Intelligence*. New York: Bantam Dell, 2006.

Neumann, Roland, and Fritz Strack. "'Mood Contagion': The Automatic Transfer of Mood between Persons." *Journal of Personality and Social Psychology* 78, no. 2 (2000): 3022–3514.

On this generation's lack of empathy

Konrath, Sarah H. "Empathy Is Declining over Time in American College Students." Presented at the Association for Psychological Science Annual Convention, Boston (May 27–30, 2010).

On the importance of words versus tone versus body language

Mehrabian, Albert. *Silent Messages: Implicit Communication of Emotions and Attitudes*. Second edition. Belmont, CA: Wadsworth, 1981.

On Paul Ekman and microexpressions

Ekman, Paul. *Emotions Revealed: Recognizing Faces and Feelings to Improve Communication and Emotional Life*. New York: Henry Holt, 2003.

On self-control and picking your battles

Baba, Shiv, and Alexander Fedorikhin. "Heart and Mind in Conflict: The Interplay of Affect and Cognition in Consumer Decision Making." *Journal of Consumer Research* 26, no. 3 (December 1999): 278–92. http://www.jstor.org/stable/2489734.

On the lack of privacy on Facebook

Boyd, Danah, and Eszter Hargittai. "Facebook Privacy Settings: Who Cares?" *First Monday* 15, no. 8 (August 2, 2010).

West, Anne, Jane Lewis, and Peter Currie. "Students' Facebook 'Friends': Public and Private Spheres." *Social Policy: Journal of Youth Studies* (London School of Economics) 12–v1212, no. 6 (December 2009): 615–27.

On top teen searches

Norton Online Family Report. "Kids' Top 100 Searches of 2009." http://onlinefamilyinfo.norton.com/articles/kidsearches_2009.php. Accessed October 16, 2010.

On virtual worlds mirroring real life

Marsh, J. "Young Children's Play in Online Virtual Worlds." *Journal of Early Childhood Research* 8, no. 1 (2010): 23–39.

On depression and Internet addiction

Lam, Lawrence T., and Michael Gilbert. "Addictive Internet Use Tied to Depression in Teens." *Archives of Pediatrics & Adolescent Medicine* (August 2, 2010).

On bullying and cyberbullying frequency

Patchin, J. W., and S. Hinduja. "Traditional and Nontraditional Bullying among Youth: A Test of General Strain Theory." *Youth & Society* (May 7, 2010).

On cyberbullying

Hinduja, S., and J. W. Patchin. "Cyberbullying: Identification, Prevention, and Response." Cyberbullying Research Center (2010). http://www.cyberbullying.us/.

Fetchenhauer, Detlef, Frank D. Belschak, and Catarina Katzer. "Cyberbullying: Who Are the Victims? A Comparison of Victimization in Internet Chatrooms and Victimization in School." *Journal of Media Psychology* 21, no. 1 (2009): 25–36.

Gross, Elisheva F., and Jaana Juvonen. "Extending the School Grounds? Bullying Experiences in Cyberspace." *Journal of School Health* 78, no. 9 (2008): 496–505.

Patchin, J. W., and S. Hinduja. "Cyberbullying and Self-Esteem." *Journal of School Health* (forthcoming).

Hinduja, S., and J. W. Patchin. "Bullying, Cyberbullying, and Suicide." *Archives of Suicide Research* 14, no. 3 (2010): 206–21.

Patchin, J. W., and S. Hinduja. "Traditional and Nontraditional Bullying among Youth: A Test of General Strain Theory." *Youth & Society* (forthcoming).

On cyberbullying law

"Who's the Bully? FCC to Impose Anti-Bullying Mandates on Schools." Heritage.org. http://blog.heritage.org/?p=45958. Accessed November 3, 2010.

On sexting

Cox Communications. "Sexting." Teen Online & Wireless Safety Survey (2009). http://www.cox.com/takecharge/safe_teens_2009/media/2009_teen_survey_internet_and_wireless_safety.pdf. Accessed November 1, 2010.

On texting after bed

Kelly, Christina M. "Lights Out, Phones On: Many Teens Text All Night Long." Msnbc.com. http://www.msnbc.msn.com/id/39917869/ns/health-kids_and_parenting/. Accessed November 1, 2010.

On the importance of rules

Ariely, Dan. *Predictably Irrational: The Hidden Forces That Shape Our Decisions.* New York: HarperPerennial, 2010.

On having screen-time rules

Carlson, S. A., J. E. Fulton, S. M. Lee, J. T. Foley, C. Heitzler, and M. Huhman. "Influence of Limit-Setting and Participation in Physical Activity on Youth Screen Time." *Pediatrics* (June 14, 2010).

On parents' Internet use predicting children's use

Valckea, M., S. Bontea, B. De Wevera, and I. Rotsa. "Internet Parenting Styles and the Impact on Internet Use of Primary School." *Computers & Education* 55, no. 2 (2010): 454–64.

On teens thinking their parents are riskier online

Glassman, Neil. "Report: 50 Percent of Children Think They Are More Careful Online Than Their Parents." SocialTimes.com (June 16, 2010). http://www.socialtimes.com/2010/06/kids-s-online-norton-report/. Accessed October 16, 2010.

On how the value of privacy is underestimated

Acquisti, Alessandro, and Ralph Gross. "Imagined Communities: Awareness, Information Sharing, and Privacy on the Facebook." Proceedings of the Privacy Enhancing Technologies Workshop (PET), Lecture Notes in Computer Science 4258, Springer (2006): 36–58.

On kids who watch a lot of television

Ostrov, Jamie M., Douglas A. Gentile, and Nicki R. Crick. "Media Exposure, Aggression and Prosocial Behavior during Early Childhood: A Longitudinal Study." *Social Development* 15, no. 4 (2006): 612–27.

On textPlus reporting kids are not really friends with their Facebook friends

Nichols, Liz. "Tired of Social Networking: Do You Suffer from 'Facebook Fatigue'?" Fox 59 Indianapolis Indiana (July 13, 2010). http://www.fox59.com/news/wxin-facebook-fatigue-071310, 0,7404305.story.

On principals and technology

Smith, Catharine, and Bianca Bosker. "School Administrator Boasts about Spying on Students Using Laptop Webcams." Huffington Post (February 26, 2010). http://www.huffingtonpost.com/2010/02/26/dan-ackerman-school-sdmin_n_477935.html.

On texting in the classroom

Center on Media and Child Health. "Are Smartphone Apps in the Classroom a Good Thing?" (June 28, 2010). http://cmch.type pad.com/mediatrician/2010/06/smartphone-apps-in-the-classroom.html.

On teens and risky behavior

Centers for Disease Control and Prevention. "Youth Risk Behavior Surveillance—United States, 2009." *MMWR* 59, no. SS-5 (June 4, 2010): 1–142.

On boredom causing risky behavior

Caldwell, Linda L., and Edward A. Smith. "Leisure as a Context for Youth Development and Delinquency Prevention." *Austra-*

lian and New Zealand Journal of Criminology 39, no. 3 (2006): 398–418.

On social conformity

Berns, G. S., J. Chappelow, C. F. Zink, G. Pagnoni, M. E. Martin-Skurski, and J. Richards. "Neurobiological Correlates of Social Conformity and Independence during Mental Rotation." *Biological Psychiatry* 58 (2005): 245–53.

On girls, drugs, and self-esteem

Partnership for a Drug-Free America, and MetLife Foundation. "2009 PATS Teen Study." *National Survey on Drug Use and Health* (2009). http://www.drugfree.org/Portal/About/News Releases/New_Data.

On Paul Ekman's research on lying

Ekman, Paul. *Telling Lies: Clues to Deceit in the Marketplace, Politics, and Marriage.* New York: W. W. Norton, 2009.

On young and optimistic teens

Taylor, Paul, Rich Morin, and others. "How the Great Recession Has Changed Life in America." Pew Research Center (June 30, 2010). http://pewsocialtrends.org/files/2010/11/759-recession.pdf.

On the rise of entrepreneurs

Kourilsky, Marilyn L., and William B. Walstad, with Andrew Thomas. *The Entrepreneur in Youth: An Untapped Resource for Economic Growth, Social Entrepreneurship, and Education.* Northampton, MA: Edward Elgar, 2007.

Index